C BY DISSECTION

The Essentials of C Programming

By Al Kelley & Ira Pohl

D1506264

The Benjamin/Cummings Publishing Company, Inc.
Menlo Park, California ■ Reading, Massachusetts ■ Don Mills,
Ontario ■ Wokingham, U.K. ■ Amsterdam ■ Sydney ■ Singapore ■
Tokyo ■ Madrid ■ Bogota ■ Santiago ■ San Juan

Sponsoring Editor: *Alan Apt*
Cover Designer: *Brenn Lea Pearson*
Cover Photo: *David Powers*
Book Designer: *Brenn Lea Pearson*
Copy Editor: *Carol Dondrea*
Proofreader: *Nancy Riddiough*
Production: *Partners in Publishing/Pat Waldo*
Composition: *UNICOMP*

UNIX is a registered trademark of Bell Laboratories

Library of Congress Cataloging in Publication Data

Kelley, Al.
  C by dissection.

  (The Benjamin/Cummings series in structured
programming)
  Includes index.
  1. C (Computer program language) I. Pohl, Ira.
II. Title. III. Series.
QA76.73.C15K45 1987   005.13'3   86-17406
ISBN 0-8053-6861-2

BCDEFGHIJK-DO-8987

The Benjamin/Cummings Publishing Company, Inc.
2727 Sand Hill Road
Menlo Park, California 94025

The Benjamin/Cummings Series in Structured Programming

G.Booch
Software Engineering with Ada, Second Edition (1987)

F. Carrano
Assembly Language Programming Language for the IBM 370 (1987)

D. M. Etter
Structured FORTRAN 77 for Engineers and Scientists, Second Edition (1987)

D. M. Etter
Problem Solving with Structured FORTRAN 77 (1984)

D. M. Etter
WATFIV: Structured Program and Problem Solving (1984)

A. Kelley and I. Pohl
A Book on C (1984)

A. Kelley and I. Pohl
C by Dissection: The Essentials of C Programming (1987)

R. Lamb
Pascal: Structure and Style (1986)

W. Savitch
Pascal: An Introduction to the Art and Science of Programming, Second Edition (1987)

W. Savitch
An Introduction to the Art and Science of Programming: TURBO Pascal Edition (1986)

R. Sebesta
Structured Assembly Language Programming for the VAX II (1984)

R. Sebesta
Structured Assembly Language Programming for the PDP-11 (1985)

Titles of Related Interest:

M. Sobell
A Practical Guide to the UNIX System (1984)

M. Sobell
A Practical Guide to UNIX System V (1985)

TO OUR WIVES

PREFACE

C is the language of computer professionals and is rapidly becoming the language of choice for personal computer users and introductory programming courses. By carefully developing working C programs, using the method of **dissection**, this book presents a simple and thorough introduction to the programming process in C. Dissection is a tool, developed by the authors, to illuminate key features of working code.

This book assumes no programming background and can be used by students and first-time computer users. For student use, it is intended as a first course in programming. Each chapter presents a number of carefully explained programs, which lead the student in a holistic manner, to ever-improving programming skills. The student is introduced to complete programs right from the start. Many programs and functions are dissected. Dissection is a revolutionary technique for explaining new elements in a program that the student is seeing for the first time.

Each chapter has:

Programming Style. A consistent and proper coding style is adopted from the beginning with careful explanation as to its importance and rationale. The style standard used is one chosen by professionals in the working C community.

Common Programming Errors. Many typical programming bugs, along with techniques for avoiding them, are described. Much of the frustration of learning a language is in encountering obscure errors. Most books only discuss correct code and leave the reader to a trial-and-error process for finding out about bugs. This book explains how typical errors in C are made and corrected.

Operating System Considerations. While C is available on almost any computer and under most operating systems, there are occasional differences in behavior from system to system. C is always found in a UNIX environment. This section explains a number of UNIX tools as well as system-dependent language features.

Summary. A succinct list of points covered in the chapter are reiterated as helpful review.

Exercises. The exercises test the students' knowledge of the language. Many exercises are intended to be done interactively while reading the text. This encourages self-paced instruction by the reader. The exercises frequently extend the readers' knowledge to an advanced area of use.

While intended for the beginning programmer, *C by Dissection* is a friendly introduction to the entire language for the experienced programmer as well. Furthermore, in conjunction with *A Book on C* by Al Kelley and Ira Pohl (Menlo Park, California: Benjamin/Cummings, 1984), the computer professional will gain a comprehensive understanding of the language, including key points concerning its use under UNIX. As a package, the two books offer an integrated treatment of the C programming language and its use that is unavailable elsewhere.

This book can be used as a one-semester text for an introduction to programming. Chapters 1 through 10 cover the C programming language through the use of pointers, strings, and arrays. A second-semester course can be devoted to more advanced data types, file processing, and software methodology as covered in Chapters 11 through 15. The instructor can also use this text in conjunction with other computer science courses that require the student to know C.

Interactive Environment. This book is written with the modern interactive environment in mind. Experimentation is encouraged throughout. A keyboard and screen for input and output are assumed throughout. Thus this book is useful to users of personal computers and small business computers, as well as to users of large interactive systems. The text can be used with any C system, including those found under UNIX, MS-DOS, and CP/M operating systems.

Holistic Approach. Right from the start the student is introduced to full working programs. Excessive detail is avoided in explaining the larger elements of writing working code. The student is introduced to writing functions at an early point in the text, as a major feature of structured programming.

Dissections. Each chapter has several important example programs. Major elements of these programs are explained by the method of dissection. This unique explanatory tool was first developed by the authors in *A Book on C*. It is similar to a structured walk-through of the code. Its intention is to explain to the reader newly encountered programming elements and idioms.

Programming Methodology. Programming style and methodology is stressed throughout. Chapter 4 introduces the concept of **top-down design** and **structured programming**. Chapter 7 shows how the goto statement can be avoided with structured branching statements and nested flow of control. Chapter 8 carefully explains how call-by-reference can be implemented. Chapter 11 treats modularity and shows how to use the preprocessor to improve the portability and readability of code. Chapter 12 describes the importance of recursion. It develops the *divide and conquer* methodology for solving problems. Finally, Chapter 15 describes a number of UNIX utilities for developing correct code.

A Book on C. This text, *C by Dissection*, leads the reader into its companion volume, *A Book on C*. *A Book on C*, a more advanced text, is useful as a professional reference or as an introduction to advanced programming techniques. The pair of books allows an instructor a wide range of course material suitable for a thorough course sequence in programming and problem solving.

ACKNOWLEDGMENTS

Our special thanks go to Robert Field, University of California, Santa Cruz, who acted as the chief technical editor for this book. His careful reading of the working code often led to important improvements. He also provided many useful insights on programming practice and methodology. Others who provided helpful suggestions include:

John Berry   Foothill College, California
Dan Drew   Texas A & M
Arthur Geis   College of DuPage, Illinois
Michael Beeson   San Jose State University, California
Al Conrad   University of California, Santa Cruz
Susan Graham   University of California, Berkeley
John de Pillis   University of California, Riverside.

Al Conrad's use of an early draft of this book provided useful classroom experience. In addition we would like to thank our sponsoring editor Alan Apt for his encouragement and constant support.

Al Kelley   Ira Pohl
University of California, Santa Cruz

CONTENTS

CHAPTER 2
FUNDAMENTALS

CHAPTER 3
FLOW OF CONTROL

CHAPTER 4
FUNCTIONS AND STRUCTURED
PROGRAMMING   103

CHAPTER 5
CHARACTER PROCESSING   133

CHAPTER 6
THE ARITHMETIC DATA TYPES 161

CHAPTER 7
BRANCHING AND NESTED FLOW
OF CONTROL 193

CHAPTER 8
FUNCTIONS AND POINTERS:
CALL-BY-REFERENCE   227

CHAPTER 9
ARRAYS AND POINTERS   247

CHAPTER 10
STRINGS AND POINTERS   275

CHAPTER 11
THE PREPROCESSOR AND
SOFTWARE METHODOLOGY   301

CHAPTER 12
RECURSION 331

CHAPTER 13
STRUCTURES 357

CHAPTER 14
INPUT/OUTPUT AND FILES   397

CHAPTER 15
SOFTWARE METHODOLOGY
IN A UNIX ENVIRONMENT   427

C BY DISSECTION

The Essentials of C Programming

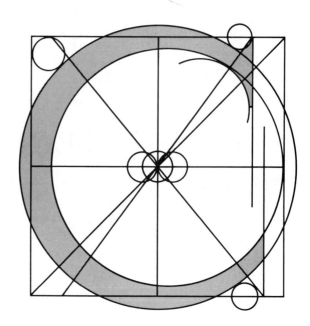

1

WRITING
AN ELEMENTARY
PROGRAM

This chapter introduces the reader to the C programming world. Some general ideas on programming are discussed, and a number of elementary programs are thoroughly explained. The basic ideas presented here become the foundation for more complete explanations that occur in later chapters. An emphasis is placed on the basic input/output functions of C. Getting information into and out of a machine is the first fundamental task to be mastered in any programming language. An interactive environment with keyboard and screen is assumed throughout. The ability to experiment interactively greatly accelerates the learning process.

C uses the functions `printf()` and `scanf()` extensively for output and input, respectively. The use of both of these functions is explained. Other topics discussed in this chapter include the use of variables to store values, and the use of expressions and assignment to change the value of a variable. The chapter also includes a discussion of the `while` statement. An example is presented to show how a `while` statement provides for repetitive action.

Throughout this chapter and throughout the text many examples are given. Included are many complete programs, and often they are dissected. This allows the reader to see in detail how each construct works. Topics that are introduced in this chapter are seen again in later chapters, with more detailed explanation where appropriate. This spiral approach to learning emphasizes ideas and techniques essential for the C programmer.

1.1 GETTING READY TO PROGRAM

Programs are written to instruct machines to carry out specific tasks, or to solve specific problems. A step-by-step procedure that will accomplish a desired task is called an *algorithm*. Thus programming is the activity of communicating algorithms to computers. We are all used to giving instructions to someone in English and having that person carry out the instructions. The programming process is analogous, except that machines have no tolerance for ambiguity and must have all steps specified in a precise language and in tedious detail.

The programming process

1 Specify the task.
2 Find an algorithm for its solution.
3 Code the algorithm in C.
4 Test the solution.

A computer is a digital electronic machine composed of three main components: processor, memory, and input/output peripherals. The processor carries out instructions that are stored in the memory. Along with the instructions, data is also stored in memory. The processor typically is instructed to manipulate the data in some desired fashion. Input/output devices take information from agents external to the machine and provide information to those agents. Input devices are typically terminal keyboards, disk drives, and tape drives. Output devices are typically terminal screens, printers, disk drives, and tape drives. The physical makeup of a machine can be quite complicated, but the user need not be concerned with the details. The operating system on a machine looks after the coordination of machine resources.

The *operating system* consists of a collection of special programs and has two main purposes. First, the operating system oversees and coordinates the resources of the machine as a whole. For example, when a file is created on a disk, the operating system takes care of the details of locating it in an appropriate place and keeping track of its name, size, and date of creation. Second, the operating system provides tools to users, many of which are useful to the C programmer. Two of these tools are of paramount importance: a text editor and the C compiler.

We assume that the reader is capable of using a text editor to create and modify files of C source code. After a file containing source code has been created, the C compiler is used to translate the source code and to create a file containing object code that can be executed by the machine. Thus part of the programming process consists of the cycle

$$Edit \longrightarrow Compile \longrightarrow Execute$$

There is nothing special about a compiler. It is itself just a program, although a rather large one. The compiler takes as its input text files containing C code. These files of C code created by programmers are also called source files, or source code. The output of the compiler is another file called an object file, or object code, that is suitable for execution by a machine. Object code, unlike source code, is not usually read by humans.

At the end of this chapter in Section 1.11, "Operating System Considerations," we present in more detail the steps necessary to compile and execute a program. The precise details vary from one machine to another.

1.2 A FIRST PROGRAM

The first task for anyone learning to program is to get the machine to print on the screen. Let us begin by writing a program that prints the phrase "she sells sea shells" on the screen. The complete program is

```
main()
{
    printf("she sells sea shells\n");
}
```

Using a text editor, the programmer types this into a file ending in
.c. The choice of a file name should be mnemonic. Let us suppose
that *sea.c* is the name of the file in which the program has been
written. When this program is compiled and executed, it prints on
the screen

```
she sells sea shells
```

■ DISSECTION OF THE *sea* PROGRAM

`main()`

- Every program has a function named `main` where execution
  begins. The parentheses following `main` indicate to the compiler
  that it is a function.

`{`

- A left brace begins the body of each function. A corresponding right brace must end the function. Our style will be to
  place these braces on separate lines in column 1. Braces are
  also used to group statements together.

`printf()`

- The C system contains a standard library of functions that can
  be used in programs. This is a function from the standard
  library that prints on the screen.

`"she sells sea shells\n"`

- A string constant in C is a series of characters surrounded by
  double quotes. This string is an argument to the function
  `printf()`, and it controls what is to be printed. The two characters \n at the end of the string (read "backslash n") represent a single character called *newline*. It is a nonprinting

character. Its effect is to advance the cursor on the screen to a new line.

```
printf("she sells sea shells\n");
```

■ This is the function `printf()` being called with a single argument, namely, the string

```
"she sells sea shells\n"
```

Even though a string may contain many characters, the string itself should be thought of as a single quantity. Notice that this line ends with a semicolon. All statements in C end with a semicolon.

```
}
```

■ This right brace matches the left brace above and ends the function `main()`.

The function `printf()` acts to continuously print across the screen. It moves to a new line when a newline character is read. The screen is a two-dimensional display that prints from left to right and top to bottom. To be readable, output must appear properly spaced on the screen.

Let us rewrite our program to make use of two `printf()` statements. Although the program looks different, its output is the same.

```
main()
{
    printf("she sells ");
    printf("sea shells\n");
}
```

Notice that the string used as an argument to the first printf() statement ends with a blank character. If the blank were not there, then the words sells and sea would have no space between them in the output.

As a final variation to this program let us add the phrase "by the seashore" and print on three lines.

```
main()
{
    printf("she sells\n");
    printf("sea shells\n");
    printf("by the seashore\n");
}
```

When we execute this program, the following appears on the screen:

```
she sells
sea shells
by the seashore
```

Notice that the three printf() statements in the body of main() could be replaced by the single statement

```
printf("she sells\nsea shells\nby the seashore\n");
```

The availability of useful functions such as printf() in the standard library is a powerful feature of C. Although technically the standard library is not part of the C language, it is part of the C system. Because the functions in the standard library are available wherever a C system is found, programmers routinely make use of them.

1.3 VARIABLES, EXPRESSIONS, AND ASSIGNMENT

Our first program illustrated the use of printf() for output. In our next program we want to make use of variables to manipulate integer values. Variables are used to store values. Since different kinds of variables are used to store different kinds of data, the type of each variable must be specified. To illustrate our ideas, we will write a program based on the wreck of the *Hesperus*, a calamity at sea made famous in a poem by Henry Wadsworth Longfellow. The wreck occurred off the reef of Norman's Woe near Gloucester, Massachusetts, in 1839. The waters off the reef are about 7 fathoms deep. In the program we will convert this depth to other units of measure.

```
main()
{
    int    inches, feet, fathoms;

    fathoms = 7;
    feet = 6 * fathoms;
    inches = 12 * feet;
    printf("Wreck of the Hesperus:\n");
    printf("Its depth at sea in different units:\n");
    printf("   %d fathoms\n", fathoms);
    printf("   %d feet\n", feet);
    printf("   %d inches\n", inches);
}
```

When we compile this program and run it, here is what appears on the screen:

```
Wreck of the Hesperus:
Its depth at sea in different units:
    7 fathoms
    42 feet
    504 inches
```

■ DISSECTION OF THE *depth_at_sea* PROGRAM

```
main()
{
    int    inches, feet, fathoms;
```

■ The first line within the body of the function main() is a declaration. The variables inches, feet, and fathoms are declared to be of type int, one of the fundamental types in C. A variable of type int can take on integer values. All variables in a program must be declared before they can be used. Declarations, as well as statements, end with a semicolon.

```
fathoms = 7;
```

■ This is an assignment statement. The equal sign = is the basic assignment operator in C. The value of the expression on the right side of the = symbol is assigned to the variable on the left side. Here, the expression on the right side is the constant expression 7. That value is assigned to the variable fathoms.

```
feet = 6 * fathoms;
inches = 12 * feet;
```

■ These are assignment statements. Since one fathom is equal to six feet, to convert a given number of fathoms to an equivalent number of feet, one must multiply by 6. The symbol * is the multiplication operator. The value of the expression 6 * fathoms is assigned to the variable feet. Since the current value of the variable fathoms is 7, the expression 6 * fathoms has the value 42, and this value is assigned to feet. To convert feet to inches, we must multiply by 12. The value of the expression 12 * feet is assigned to the variable inches.

```
printf("   %d fathoms\n", fathoms);
```

■ This printf() statement has two arguments

```
   "   %d fathoms\n"        and        fathoms
```

The first argument in a printf() function is always a string, called the *control string*. In this example the control string contains the conversion specification %d. A conversion specification is also called a format. The format %d causes the value of the expression in the second argument, in this case the variable fathoms, to be printed in the format of a decimal integer. Ordinary characters in a control string, that is, characters not comprising a format, are simply printed on the screen. Notice that the control string in this example begins with three blank spaces, causing the line being printed to be indented. The remaining printf() statements in the program are similar to this one.

In C all variables must be declared before they are used in expressions and statements. The general form of a simple program is

```
main()
{
    declarations
    statements
}
```

The declarations tell the compiler what kind of data can be stored in each of the variables. We have already seen the use of integer data. Shortly we will discuss character data and floating data. The compiler needs this information to be able to set aside the appropriate amount of memory to hold the data.

A variable name, also called an identifier, consists of a sequence of letters, digits, and underscores, but may not begin with a digit. Identifiers should be chosen to reflect their use in the program. In this way they serve as documentation, making the program more readable. After variables have been declared, they can be assigned values and used in expressions.

Certain reserved words, called keywords, cannot be used by the programmer as names of variables. For example, char, int, and float are keywords. In Chapter 2 a table of all the keywords is presented. Other names are known to the C system and normally would not be redefined by the programmer. The name printf is an example. Since printf is the name of a function in the standard library, it usually is not used as the name of a variable.

Expressions typically are found on the right side of assignment operators and as arguments to functions. The simplest expressions are just constants such as 6 and 12, which were both used in the previous program. The name of a variable alone can be considered an expression, and meaningful combinations of operators with variables and constants are also expressions.

Among the many operators in C are the binary arithmetic operators

```
+    -    *    /    %
```

used for addition, subtraction, multiplication, division, and modulus respectively. These are called *binary* operators because they act on two operands, as in the expression

```
a + b
```

Here, the operator + is acting on the two operands a and b. An expression such as this has a value that depends on the values of a and b. For example, if a has value 1 and b has value 2, then the expression a + b has value 3.

In C an integer expression divided by another integer expression yields an integer value. Any fractional part is discarded. Thus 1/2 has value 0, 7/2 has value 3, and -19/4 has value -4. Division by zero is not allowed.

Most beginning programmers are not familiar with the modulus operator %. As we shall see, it has many uses in programming. The expression a % b yields the remainder after a is divided by b. For example, since 5 divided by 3 is 1 with a remainder of 2, the expression 5 % 3 has value 2. In a similar fashion the expression 7 % 4 has value 3. In the expression a % b the value of b cannot be zero, since this would lead to division by zero. The modulus operator can act only on integer data, whereas all the other arithmetic operators can act on both integer and floating data.

The keyword char stands for character. Variables and constants of type char are used to manipulate characters. Constants of type char are written within single quotes as in 'A' and '1' and '+'. As a simple example consider the program

```
main()
{
    char   c;

    c = 'A';
    printf("%c\n", c);     /* the letter A is printed */
}
```

The output of this program is the letter A followed by a newline. First the variable c is declared to be of type char. Then c is assigned the value 'A'. Finally, the printf() statement causes printing to occur. Notice that the control string in the argument list for printf() contains the format %c. This causes the variable c in the second argument to be printed in the format of a character.

There are two floating types in C, float and double. They are used to manipulate real numbers, also called *floating* numbers or *floating point* numbers. Floating constants such as 1.069, 0.003, and 7.0 are all of type double; there are no constants of type float. Note carefully that the floating constant 7.0 and the int constant 7 are different. Although their conceptual values are the same, their types are different, causing them to be stored differently in a machine. The technical details concerning float and double will be discussed in Chapter 6.

Let us next give a simple illustration of the use of floating point constants and variables. Consider the program

```
main()
{
    float   x, y;

    x = 1.0;
    y = 2.0;
    printf("The sum of x and y is %f\n", x + y);
}
```

The output of this program is

```
The sum of x and y is 3.000000
```

First the variables x and y are declared to be of type float. Then x
and y are assigned the floating values 1.0 and 2.0, respectively.
Although the constants are of type double and the variables are of
type float, there is no difficulty. Floating types can be freely mixed
in expressions and assignments. The control string in the first argument to printf() contains the format %f. This causes the value of
the expression x + y in the second argument to be printed in the format of a floating number with six digits to the right of the decimal
point.

The division of floating values works as expected. For example,
the floating expression 7.0/2.0 has 3.5 for its value. In contrast to
this the int expression 7/2 has the value 3, since with integer division any remainder is discarded. Again, division by zero is never
allowed.

The modulus operator % works with integer expressions only. If x
and y are variables of type float or double, then an expression such
as x % y is not allowed.

Typically, an assignment statement is composed of a variable on
the left side followed by an = followed by an expression on the right
side. The expression can be simple or complicated, and can contain
function calls. Constants and ordinary expressions are not allowed
on the left side of an =. We can write

```
a = b + c;
```

but not

```
a + b = c;      /* assignment to this expression is not allowed */
2 = c;          /* assignment to a constant is not allowed */
```

1.4 INITIALIZATION

When variables are declared, they may also be initialized. As an
example of this, consider the declarations

```
char   c = 'A';
int    i = 1;
```

The variable c is declared to be of type char, and its value is initialized to 'A'. The variable i is declared to be of type int, and its value is initialized to 1. As another example of initialization, the *depth_at_sea* program can be rewritten as follows:

```
main()
{
    int    inches, feet, fathoms = 7;

    feet = 6 * fathoms;
    .  .  .  .  .
```

Whether a variable is initialized depends on its intended use in a program. Only constants or constant expressions can be used to initialize a variable. We could have written

```
    int    inches, feet, fathoms = 3 + 4;
```

but not

```
    int    inches, feet = 6 * fathoms, fathoms = 7;
```

In the exercises at the end of the chapter we will point out a situation where it makes sense to use a constant expression as an initializer.

1.5 THE USE OF #define

The C compiler has a preprocessor built into it. Just before compilation takes place, the preprocessor causes the source code being passed to the compiler to be modified. Specified character strings in the source code are changed into other specified strings. Those lines in a program that give commands to the preprocessor are called *control lines*. Some examples are

```
#define    LIMIT    100
#define    PI       3.14159
```

If these control lines occur in a file that is being compiled, the preprocessor first changes all occurrences of the identifier LIMIT to 100 and all occurrences of the identifier PI to 3.14159, except in quoted strings. A #define line can occur anywhere in a program, but it must start in column 1. Its effect is only on lines in the file that come after it. Normally, all #define lines are placed at the beginning of the file. By convention identifiers that are to be changed by the preprocessor are written in capital letters. The contents of quoted strings are never changed by the preprocessor. For example, in the statement

```
printf("PI = %f\n", PI);
```

only the second PI will be changed. Since the identifier PI will be replaced everywhere (except in quoted strings) by 3.14159, it is called a *symbolic constant*.

The use of symbolic constants in a program makes it more readable. More importantly, if a constant has been defined symbolically by the #define facility and then used throughout a program, it is easy to change it later, if necessary. For example, if we write

```
#define   LIMIT   100
```

and then use LIMIT throughout thousands of lines of code to symbolically represent the constant 100, it will be easy to change the code later. Suppose that we want to redefine the symbolic constant LIMIT from 100 to 10000. Then all we have to do is to change the control line to

```
#define   LIMIT   10000
```

This automatically updates all the code.

In the next section we will present a program that makes use of a symbolic constant.

1.6 THE USE OF printf() AND scanf()

The function printf() is used for printing formatted output. In an analogous fashion the function scanf() is used for reading formatted input. These functions are in the standard library and are available for use wherever a C system resides. Both printf() and scanf() are passed a list of arguments that can be thought of as

> *control_string*   and   *other_arguments*

where *control_string* is a string that may contain conversion specifications, or formats. A conversion specification begins with a % character and ends with a conversion character. For example, in the format %d the letter d is the conversion character.

THE USE OF printf()

As we have already seen, the format %d is used to print the value of an expression as a decimal integer. In a similar fashion %c is used to print the value of an expression as a character, %f is used to print the value of a floating expression, and %s is used to print a string. The formats in a control string are used to determine how the other arguments are to be printed. Formats that are appropriate for the arguments should be used. Consider

```
printf("Get set:  %s %d %f %c%c\n", "one", 2, 3.33, 'G', 'O');
```

In this example the arguments to printf() are

> "Get set: %s %d %f %c%c\n"   "one"   2   3.33   'G'   'O'

The first argument is the control string. The formats in the control string are matched with the other arguments. In this example the %s corresponds to "one", the %d corresponds to 2, the %f corresponds to 3.33, the first %c corresponds to 'G', and the second %c corresponds to 'O'. Each format in a control string specifies how the value of its corresponding argument is to be printed. When executed, the above printf() statement causes

```
Get set:  one 2 3.330000 GO
```

to be printed. Sometimes it is convenient to write a long `printf()` statement on more than one line. As an example consider

```
printf("%s%s\n",
   "This statement will print ",
   "just one very long line of text on the screen.");
```

The following table describes how the conversion characters in formats affect their corresponding arguments.

printf()	
Conversion character	**How the corresponding argument is printed**
c	as a character
d	as a decimal integer
e	as a floating point number in scientific notation
f	as a floating point number
g	in the e-format or f-format, whichever is shorter
s	as a string

When an argument is printed, the *place* where it is printed is called its *field* and the number of characters in its field is called its *field width*. The field width can be specified in a format as an integer occurring between the % and the conversion character. Thus the statement

```
printf("%c%3c%7c\n", 'A', 'B', 'C');
```

will print

```
A B      C
```

First the letter A is printed. Then the letter B is printed in a field of three characters. Since the letter B requires only one space, the other two spaces are blanks. Then the letter C is printed in a field of seven characters. Since the letter C requires only one space, the other six spaces are blanks.

For floating values, we can control the *precision*, as well as the field length. The precision is the number of decimal digits printed to the right of the decimal point. In a format of the form %*m.n*f the field length is specified by *m* and the precision is specified by *n*. With a format of the form %*m*f only the field length is specified. With a format of the form %.*n*f only the precision is specified. As an example of these ideas the statements

```
printf("Some numbers:  %.1f %.2f %.3f\n", 1.0, 2.0, 3.0);
printf("More numbers:%9.1f%9.2f%9.3f%9.4f\n", 4.0, 5.0, 6.0, 7.0);
```

cause the following two lines to be printed:

```
Some numbers:  1.0 2.00 3.000
More numbers:      4.0     5.00    6.000   7.0000
```

The function printf() gives the programmer the capability of printing neatly on the screen. Nonetheless, getting printout to "look right" can be a very tedious business.

THE USE OF scanf()

The function scanf() is analogous to the function printf(), but is used for input rather than output. Its first argument is a control string having formats corresponding to the various ways the characters in the input stream are to be interpreted. After the control string, the other arguments are *addresses*. The symbol & represents the address operator. In the example

```
scanf("%d", &x);
```

the format %d causes the input characters to be interpreted as a decimal integer, and causes the resulting value to be stored at the address of x.

When the keyboard is used to input values into a program, a sequence of characters is typed, and a sequence of characters is received by the program. This sequence is called the *input stream*. If 5773 is typed, the person typing it may think of it as a decimal integer, but the program receives it as a sequence of characters. The scanf() function can be used to convert strings of decimal digits, such as 5773, into integer values and store them in the appropriate place.

The following table describes the effects of the conversion characters in formats used with the function scanf().

scanf()	
Conversion character	**What characters in the input stream are converted to**
c	to a character
d	to a decimal integer
f	to a floating point number (float)
lf	to a floating point number (long float or double)
s	to a string

Let us write a program in which the user is prompted to input her initials followed by her age, and scanf() is used to read in what is typed.

```
main()
{
    char    first, middle, last;
    int     age;

    printf("Input your three initials and your age:  ");
    scanf("%c%c%c%d", &first, &middle, &last, &age);
    printf("\nGreetings %c.%c.%c.  %s %d.\n\n",
        first, middle, last,
        "Next year your age will be", age + 1);
}
```

Notice carefully that the arguments passed to scanf() are

```
"%c%c%c%d"        &first        &middle        &last        &age
```

The first argument is the control string. Each format in the control string corresponds to one of the remaining arguments. More explicitly, the first format is %c, which corresponds to &first, the first argument following the control string; the second format is %c, which corresponds to &middle, the second argument following the control string; and so forth. Except for the control string, all the arguments passed to scanf() must be addresses. To get the address of a variable, we apply the address operator &.

Suppose that we execute the above program and input CBD and 19 when prompted. Then the following appears on the screen:

```
Input your three initials and your age:  CBD  19

Greetings C.B.D.  Next year your age will be 20.
```

When reading in numbers, scanf() will skip white space (blanks, newlines, and tabs), but when reading in a character, white space is *not* skipped. Thus the program will not run correctly with the input CB D. Instead, the third character will be read in as a blank, a perfectly good character, and then scanf() will attempt to interpret the character D as a decimal integer. This will cause the program to misbehave.

Here is another program that makes use of scanf(). This program also illustrates the use of a #define line to create a symbolic constant, and illustrates the use of formats.

```
#define   PI   3.14159

main()
{
   float   radius;

   printf("\n%s\n\n%s",
      "This program computes the area of a circle.",
      "Input the radius: ");
   scanf("%f", &radius);
   printf("\n%s\n%s%.2f%s%.2f%s%.2f\n%s%.5f\n\n",
      "Area = PI * radius * radius",
      "     = ", PI, " * ", radius, " * ", radius,
      "     = ", PI * radius * radius);
}
```

Suppose that we execute this program and input 2.333 when prompted. Then the following appears on the screen:

```
This program computes the area of a circle.

Input the radius:  2.333

Area = PI * radius * radius
     = 3.14 * 2.33 * 2.33
     = 17.09932
```

One of the differences between printf() and scanf() involves the format %f. With printf() this format can be used to print the value of an argument of either type float or type double. In contrast, when scanf() is used to read in a real number and to store its value at the address of a variable, the format %f is used if the variable is of type float and the format %lf is used if the variable is of type double. The letter l in this context stands for "long," and long float is a synonym for double.

Another difference between printf() and scanf() is that printf() does not return a value, but scanf() does. It returns as an int the number of its successful conversions. We will illustrate in Section 1.8 how the value returned by scanf() can be used.

For complete details concerning printf() and scanf(), see Chapter 14.

1.7 THE while STATEMENT

Counting, adding, searching, sorting, and other tasks often involve doing something over and over. In this section we illustrate how a while statement can be used to perform a repetitive action. In so doing, we will also illustrate many of the other ideas already presented in this chapter.

The following program makes use of a while statement to add the consecutive integers from 1 to 10. In the dissection that follows we will explain how a while statement works.

```
main()
{
   int   i = 1, sum = 0;

   while (i <= 10) {
      sum = sum + i;
      i = i + 1;
   }
   printf("Sum = %d\n", sum);
}
```

■ DISSECTION OF THE *add_consecutive_integers*
PROGRAM

```
int   i = 1, sum = 0;
```

■ The variables i and sum are declared to be of type int and are initialized to 1 and 0, respectively.

```
while (i <= 10) {
   sum = sum + i;
   i = i + 1;
}
```

■ This whole construct is a while statement, or while loop. First the expression i <= 10 is evaluated. One reads this as "i is less than or equal to 10." Since the current value of i is 1, the expression is *true*, causing the statements between the braces { and } to be executed. The variable sum is assigned the old value of sum plus the value of i. Since the old value of sum is 0 and i is 1, sum is assigned the value 1. The variable i is assigned the old value of i plus 1. Since the old value of i is 1, i is assigned the value 2. At this point we have gone through the loop once. Now the program goes back and evaluates the expression i <= 10 again. Since i has the value 2, the expression is still *true*, causing the body of the loop to be executed again. At the end of the second time through the loop the value of sum is 1 + 2 and the value of i is 3. Since the expression i <= 10 is still *true*, the body of the loop is executed again. At the end of the third time through the loop the value of sum is 1 + 2 + 3 and the value of i is 4. This process continues until i has the value 11, which causes the expression i <= 10 to be *false*. When this happens, the body of the loop is skipped and the next statement after the while statement is executed.

```
printf("Sum = %d\n", sum);
```

■ This printf() statement causes the line

```
Sum = 55
```

to be printed.

A while loop has the general form

```
while (expression)
    statement
```

where *statement* can be a single statement or a group of statements enclosed between the braces { and }. A group of statements enclosed in braces is called a compound statement. In C a compound statement can go anywhere that a statement can go.

1.8 AN EXAMPLE: COMPUTING SUMS

As a final program in this chapter we want to illustrate how numbers that are typed in by the user can be added. Use is made of the value returned by scanf() to control the action of a while statement. We will explain the mechanisms that allow the user to type in an arbitrary amount of data.

```
/* Sums are computed. */

main()
{
   int     cnt = 0;
   float   sum = 0.0, x;

   printf("The sum of your numbers will be computed.\n\n");
   printf("Input some numbers: ");
   while (scanf("%f", &x) == 1) {
      sum = sum + x;
      cnt = cnt + 1;
   }
   printf("\n%s%5d\n%s%12f\n\n",
      "Count:", cnt,
      " Sum:", sum);
}
```

■ DISSECTION OF THE *compute_sum* PROGRAM

```
scanf("%f", &x) == 1
```

■ The symbols == represent the equals operator. An expression
such as a == b tests to see if the value of a is equal to the value
of b. If it is, then the expression is *true*; if not, then the
expression is *false*. For example, 1 == 1 is *true*, and 2 == 3 is
false. The scanf() function is being used to read in characters
typed by the user, to convert those characters to a value of
type float, and to place the value at the address of x. If
scanf() is successful in doing this, then one successful conversion has been made, and the value 1 is returned by the function. If for some reason the conversion process fails, then the
value 0 is returned; if no more data is available, then the value
−1 is returned. Thus the expression

```
scanf("%f", &x) == 1
```

tests to see whether scanf() succeeded in its task. If it did, then the expression is *true*; otherwise it is *false*.

```
while (scanf("%f", &x) == 1) {
   sum = sum + x;
   cnt = cnt + 1;
}
```

■ We can think of this as

```
while (scanf() succeeds in making a conversion) {
     . . . . .
```

As long as the expression scanf("%f", &x) == 1 is *true*, the body of the while loop is repeatedly executed. Each time through the loop, scanf() reads in a number and places its value at the address of x. Then sum is assigned the old value of sum plus x, and cnt is assigned the old value of cnt plus 1. Thus sum keeps a running total of all the numbers processed so far, and cnt keeps a count of those numbers. When does the process stop? Well, there are two typical things that can happen. First, the user may type in something that cannot be converted to a float. For example, if a letter is typed instead of a digit, then scanf() will fail to make a successful conversion and will return the value 0, causing the expression

```
scanf("%f", &x) == 1
```

to be *false*. Another way to stop the process is for the user to indicate to the program that all the data has been entered. To do this, the user must type an end-of-file mark. What must be typed to effect an end-of-file mark is system dependent. On our system a newline immediately followed by a control-d must be typed.

```
printf("\n%s%5d\n%s%12f\n\n",
   "Count:", cnt,
   " Sum:", sum);
```

■ Suppose this program is executed and the numbers

    1.1 2.02 3.003 4.0004 5.00005

are entered, followed by a newline and a control-d. Here is what appears on the screen:

```
The sum of your numbers will be computed.

Input some numbers: 1.1  2.02  3.003  4.0004  5.00005

Count:    5
  Sum:   15.123451
```

If you carefully count spaces, you will see that the value of cnt has been printed in a field of 5 characters, and that sum has been printed in a field of 12 characters. This was caused by the %5d and %12f formats. Notice that the digit in the sixth place of sum is wrong. See the exercises for a discussion of this.

1.9 STYLE

A good coding style is essential to the art of programming. It facilitates the reading, writing, and maintenance of programs. A good style will use white space and comments so that the code is more easily read and understood, and is visually attractive. The proper use of indentation is crucial, as it indicates to the reader the intended flow of control. For example, in the construct

```
while (expression)
    statement
```

the indentation of *statement* indicates that its execution is under the control of the while loop. Another important stylistic point is to choose names for variables that convey their use in the program. This is a further aid to understanding. A good style will avoid error-prone coding habits.

Our choice of layout for a C program is to place main() starting in column 1. The left brace { that begins the body of main() is placed in column 1 just below the m of main(). All the declarations and statements that follow are indented, and the final right brace } that ends the body of main() is again placed in column 1. This visually highlights the beginning and end of the function body. Inside the body of main() a blank line is used to separate the declarations from the statements that follow.

An indentation of 3, 4, 5, or 8 spaces is commonly used. We are using 3 spaces. Whatever is chosen as an indentation should be used consistently. To heighten readability, we are putting a blank space on each side of the binary operators, although not all programmers bother with this.

There is no single agreed upon "good style." As we proceed in this text, we will often point out alternate styles. Once a style has been chosen, it should be used consistently. Good habits reinforce good programming.

1.10 COMMON PROGRAMMING ERRORS

When you first start programming you will make many frustrating simple errors. One such error is to leave off a closing double quote character to mark the end of a string. When the compiler sees the first ", it starts collecting all the characters that follow as a string. If the closing " is not present, then the string continues to the next line, causing the compiler to complain. In this case most compilers flag the correct offending line.

Another common error is to misspell a variable name, or to forget to declare it. Compilers readily catch this kind of error and properly inform you of what is wrong. However, if you misspell the name of a function, such as prinf() instead of printf(), the compiler will inform you that the function cannot be found. If you do not notice that the error message refers to prinf instead of printf, you may be quite mystified.

Even elementary errors, such as forgetting to place a semicolon at the end of a statement or leaving off a closing brace, can result in rather mystifying error messages from compilers. As you become more experienced, some of the error messages produced by your compiler will begin to make sense. Exercise 4 at the end of this chapter suggests some programming errors you may want to introduce on purpose in order to experiment with the error message capability of your compiler.

1.11 OPERATING SYSTEM CONSIDERATIONS

The precise steps that have to be followed to create a file containing C code and to compile and execute it vary from one operating system to another. However, the general outline is similar. Let us describe how it is done in a UNIX environment.

Steps to be followed in writing and running a C program

1 Create a text file, or more explicitly a source file, with its name ending in *.c* and type a C program into it; for example

  vi example.c

  vi is the name of a UNIX text editor. A knowledge of editor commands to insert and modify text is necessary in order to make use of an editor.

2 After a program has been typed into the file *example.c*, compile the program with the command

  cc example.c

  The *cc* command invokes the C compiler. The input to the compiler is the code in the file *example.c*. If there are no errors in the code, then the executable file *a.out* is automatically created, and the program is ready to be executed; if there are errors, then the process must start again at Step 1 with the re-editing of the source file. Errors that occur at this stage are called syntax errors or compile-time errors. A program called *lint* can be used to find syntax errors and to make other checks:

lint example.c

3 Execute the program. This is done with the command

a.out

If the program compiled successfully, it will start to execute. Typically, if the program has no run-time errors, it will complete execution and a system prompt will reappear on the screen. If for some reason the program needs to be changed, the process must start again at Step 1 with the re-editing of the source file.

If we compile a different program, then the file *a.out* will be overwritten and its previous contents lost. If the contents of the executable file *a.out* are to be saved, then the file must be moved (renamed). Suppose that we have given the command

cc sea.c

This will cause executable code to be written automatically into *a.out*. To save this file, we can give the command

mv a.out sea

This causes *a.out* to be moved to *sea*. Now the program can be executed by giving the command

sea

It is a common practice to give the executable file the same name as the corresponding source file, except to drop the .c suffix. Instead of using the *mv* command, we could have typed

cc −o sea sea.c

The −*o* option causes *cc* to put its output directly into the file name that follows the −*o*, leaving whatever is in *a.out* intact.

Different kinds of errors can occur in a program. Syntax errors are caught by the compiler; other errors manifest themselves only when the program is executed. This second kind of error is called a *run-time* error. For example, if an attempt to divide by zero is encoded into a program, the program will exhibit a run-time error. One of the exercises at the end of this chapter suggests that you find out what happens when division by zero is attempted. Error messages produced during run-time typically do not help to find the trouble.

REDIRECTING THE STANDARD INPUT FILE

Ordinarily the standard input file is connected to the keyboard. When scanf() is looking for characters to convert to a value, it reads the characters from the standard input file. If this file is connected to the keyboard (as it normally is), then scanf() reads its characters from the keyboard. MS-DOS, PC-DOS, UNIX, and other operating systems have the capability of redirecting the standard input file. If redirection is available to you, do the following. Create a file called *data* and put some numbers into it. Then give the command

> *compute_sum < data*

The symbol < causes the operating system to redirect the standard input file from the keyboard to the file *data*. The effect of this is that scanf() now gets its characters from the file *data* instead of the keyboard. In this context one thinks of < as a left pointing arrow.

1.12 SUMMARY

1   An algorithm is a computational procedure consisting of elementary steps. Programming is the art of communicating algorithms to computers.

2   A simple program consists of the function main(). The body of the function consists of declarations and statements within the braces { and }. All variables must be declared. The declarations must occur before the statements.

3   The simplest expressions consist of just a constant or a variable or a function call. In general, expressions consist of combinations of operators and other expressions. Most expressions have value. The assignment operator = is used to assign the value of an expression to a variable.

4   When a variable is declared, it may also be initialized. Only constants or constant expressions can be used as initializers.

5   The C compiler has a built in preprocessor. Lines that begin with a # in column 1 are called control lines. They are used to communicate commands to the preprocessor. A control line of the form

#define   *identifier   replacement_string*

causes the preprocessor to change every occurrence of *identifier* to *replacement_string* before compilation takes place. Control lines are usually placed at the beginning of a file. A #define line affects only the lines in the file that occur after it.

6   The function printf() in the standard library is used for output. The arguments to this function consist of a control string followed by other arguments. The control string consists of ordinary text and conversion specifications, or formats. The ordinary text is simply printed, whereas a format causes the value of an associated argument to be printed. A format begins with a % and ends with a conversion character.

7   The function scanf() in the standard library is used for input. It is analogous to printf(). Both functions take a variable number of arguments, the first one being a control string. For printf() the other arguments are expressions; for scanf() they are addresses. The address of the variable v is written &v.

8   Statements are ordinarily executed sequentially. The special flow of control statements such as a while statement can alter the sequential execution of a program.

1.13 EXERCISES

1   Write on the screen the words

she sells sea shells by the seashore

(i) all on one line, (ii) on seven lines, (iii) inside a box.

2   The following program has a run-time error in it.

```
main()
{
    int   x, y = 0;

    x = 1 / y;
}
```

Check to see that it compiles without any error messages. Run the program to see what the effect of the error is. Error messages produced during run-time usually are not much help in locating the trouble. Try to rewrite the program without the variable y, but keeping the error in the program. What happens when you try to compile it?

3   The following program writes a large letter I on the screen.

```
#define   HEIGHT   17

main()
{
    int   i = 0;

    printf("\n\nIIIIIIII\n");
    while (i < HEIGHT) {
        printf("   III\n");
        i = i + 1;
    }
    printf("IIIIIIII\n\n\n");
}
```

Execute this program so you understand its effect. Write a similar program that prints a large letter C on the screen.

4   The purpose of this exercise is to help you become familiar with some of the error messages produced by your compiler. You can expect some error messages to be helpful and others less so. First check to see that the following program compiles with no error messages.

```
main()
{
   int   a = 1, b = 2, c = 3;

   printf("Some output:  %d %d %d\n", a, b, c);
}
```

Now introduce each of the following programming errors in turn, compile the program, and record the error messages generated:

change the first comma in the declaration to a semicolon
change `printf` to `prinf`
remove the second `"` in the control string
replace the list `a, b, c` by `a, b, c, c`
remove the semicolon at the end of the `printf()` statement
remove the closing brace

5   Write an interactive program that asks the user to input the length and width of a rectangular lawn. The dimensions should be in yards. The program should compute the number of square yards and convert this to square feet and to square inches and print all the information neatly on the screen. Make use of the following declaration:

```
int   conversion_factor = 36 * 36;   /* square inches per square yard */
```

An equivalent declaration is

```
int   conversion_factor = 1296;   /* square inches per square yard */
```

but since most people know that there are 36 inches in a yard, the first declaration is preferable. One can tell at a glance that the right conversion factor is being used. *Caution:* If your lawn is large and you are working on a small machine, you may not get the right number of square inches, even though you wrote a correct program. There are limitations on the size of an integer that can be stored in an `int`; see Chapter 6.

6   Here is part of an interactive program that computes the value
     of some coins. The user is asked to input the number of half
     dollars, quarters, dimes, etc.

```
main()
{
    int    h,      /* number of half dollars */
           q,      /* number of quarters     */
           d,      /* number of dimes        */
           n,      /* number of nickels      */
           p;      /* number of pennies      */

    .  .  .  .  .


    printf("The value of your change will be computed.\n\n");
    printf("How many half dollars do you have?  ");
    scanf("%d", &h);
    printf("How many quarters do you have?  ");
    scanf("%d", &q);

    .  .  .  .  .
```

Complete the program, causing it to print out relevant information. For example, you may want to create output that looks
like this:

```
You entered:     0 half dollars
                 3 quarters
                 2 dimes
                17 nickels
                 1 pennies

The value of your 23 coins is equivalent to 181 pennies.
```

Notice that pennies is plural, not singular as it should be.
After you learn about the if-else statement in Chapter 3, you
will be able to modify your program so that its output is gram-
matically correct.

7   Modify the program that you wrote in the previous exercise so
     that the last line of the output looks like this:

The value of your 23 coins is $1.81

Hint: Declare value to be a variable of type float, and make use of the format %.2f in your printf() statement.

8   The function scanf() returns the number of successful conversions as an int. Consider the statement

```
printf("%d\n", scanf("%d%d%d", &a, &b, &c));
```

When this statement is executed, an integer will be printed. What are the possible values for the integer? Explain. *Hint:* Write a test program and execute it using redirection. If you do not use redirection, then input and output can be intermixed on the screen in such a way as to cause confusion. When scanf() reads an end-of-file mark, the value −1 is returned.

9   Write an interactive program that prints the line

```
1 + 2 = 3
```

Do this without using any digits in your code. *Hint:* One way to do this is to use the idea presented in the previous problem. Can you think of another way?

10   Except for a printf() statement, the following program is complete. It makes use of integer division and the modulus operator to convert seconds to minutes and seconds.

```
/* Convert seconds to minutes and seconds. */

main()
{
    int    input_value, minutes, seconds;

    printf("Input the number of seconds:  ");
    scanf("%d", &input_value);
    minutes = input_value / 60;
    seconds = input_value % 60;
    printf( .  .  . );
}
```

Complete the program by writing an appropriate `printf()` statement. For example, if 123 is entered after the prompt, the program might print the line

```
123 seconds is equivalent to 2 minutes and 3 seconds
```

11 Modify the program that you completed in the previous exercise so that seconds are converted to hours, minutes, and seconds. For example, if 7384 is entered after the prompt, your program might print the line

```
7384 seconds is equivalent to 2 hours, 3 minutes, and 4 seconds
```

12 Repetitive action is essential to most programs. Therefore a programmer must know precisely how a `while` loop works. Study the following code in detail, writing down what you think gets printed. Then write a test program to check your answer.

```
int   i = 1, sum = 0;

while (i < 10) {
    sum = sum + i;
    i = i + 1;
    printf("sum = %d   i = %d\n", sum, i);
}
```

13   Do two variations of the last exercise. For the first variation the line

```
sum = sum + i;
```

should be replaced by

```
sum = sum + 2 + i;
```

For the second variation the line should be replaced by

```
sum = (sum / 3) + (i * i);
```

14   How is an end-of-file mark entered at the keyboard on your system? Experiment with the *compute_sum* program to see that the program terminates when either an inappropriate character is typed or an end-of-file mark is typed. What happens when the program is executed and no numbers are entered?

15   Unlike integer arithmetic, floating arithmetic need not be exact. Very small errors can occur in computations with floating data. Moreover, what actually occurs is machine dependent. Often this is of no concern to the user. With the data that we used as input for the *compute_sum* program, the sum had an error in the sixth decimal place. Modify the program so that the variable sum is a double instead of a float. Since a double usually (but not always; see Chapter 6) represents real numbers more accurately than a float does, with the same input the result may be more accurate. Check to see if this is the case on your machine.

16   Any text editor can be used to write C code. However, a text editor that has special features can make your work much easier. The text editor *vi* provides several facilities to aid in writing code. For example, when the cursor is sitting on a ⦃ character, typing the % key causes the cursor to go to the matching brace symbol, if there is one. This facility allows you to conveniently check if your left and right braces are properly matched. The facility works in a similar fashion for brackets and parentheses. If *vi* is available to you, check this feature. Also, find out how to set and make use of "autoindent" and

"shiftwidth" and "showmatch" in *vi*. If you are using some other text editor, find out what special features, if any, the editor provides to help you write code.

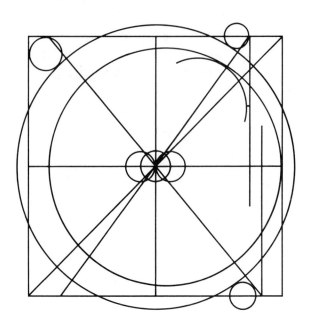

2

FUNDAMENTALS

The purpose of this chapter is to explain the fundamental elements of the C programming language. C is a language. Like other languages it has an alphabet and rules for putting together words and punctuation to make correct or legal programs. These rules are the *syntax* of the language. The program that checks on the legality of C code is called the *compiler*.

Compilers are very precise in their requirements. Unlike human readers of English who are able to understand the meaning of a sentence with an extra punctuation mark or a misspelled word, most C compilers will fail to provide a translation of a syntactically incorrect program, no matter how trivial the error. Hence, the programmer must learn to be precise when writing code.

The programmer should strive to write understandable code. A key part of this is to have well-commented code using meaningful identifier names. The chapter will illustrate these important concepts, including a discussion of commenting style.

2.1 CHARACTERS AND LANGUAGE ELEMENTS

A C program is constructed as a sequence of characters. Among the characters that can be used in a program are

lowercase letters	a b c . . . z
uppercase letters	A B C . . . Z
digits	0 1 2 3 4 5 6 7 8 9
other characters	+ - * / = ( ) { } [ ] < > ' "
	! # $ % & _ | ^ ~ \ . , ; : ?

white space characters such as *blank*, *newline*, and *tab*

These characters are used to produce the language elements of C. The basic language elements are identifiers, keywords, constants, operators, and other separators. Let us look at a simple program and pick out some of these elements.

```
/* Read in two integers and print their sum. */

main()
{
    int    a, b, sum;

    printf("Input two integers:  ");
    scanf("%d%d", &a, &b);
    sum = a + b;
    printf("\nThe sum of %d and %d is %d.\n\n", a, b, sum);
}
```

■ DISSECTION OF THE *sum* PROGRAM

```
/* Read in two integers and print their sum. */
```

■ Comments are delimited by /* and */ and are treated as white space by the compiler.

```
main()
{
    int   a, b, sum;
```

- The function name `main` is an identifier, the characters (and)
  and { are separators, `int` is a keyword, `a` and `b` and `sum` are
  identifiers, and the characters , and ; are separators.

```
printf("Input two integers:  ");
scanf("%d%d", &a, &b);
```

- The function names `printf` and `scanf` are identifiers and the
  parentheses following them tell the compiler that they are functions. These functions are in the standard library. A programmer would not normally redefine these identifiers.

```
"Input two integers:  "
```

- A series of characters enclosed in double quotes is a string constant.

```
&a, &b
```

- The character & is an operator.

```
sum = a + b;
```

- The characters = and + are operators. White space here will be
  ignored, so we could have written

```
    sum=a+b;
```

  or

```
    sum   =   a   +   b ;
```

  but not

```
s   u   m  =  a  +  b;
```

Our style is to put one blank space on each side of binary operators to heighten the readability of the code.

The keyword int is used in this example. It specifies that the identifiers in the list that follows the keyword take only integer values. Characters such as = and + are operators. The character ; is punctuation used to terminate declarations and statements. White space is used by the compiler in many instances to determine how to separate elements of the language. Also, white space is used by programmers to provide more legible code. To the compiler program, text is implicitly a single stream of characters, but to the human reader it is a two-dimensional tableau.

2.2 IDENTIFIERS

An identifier is a sequence of letters, digits, and the special character _ , which is called an underscore. A letter or underscore must be the first character of an identifier. In most implementations of C the upper- and lowercase letters are treated as distinct. It is good programming practice to choose identifiers that have mnemonic significance so that they contribute to the readability and documentation of the program.

Some examples of identifiers are

```
n
_id
iamanidentifier
i_am_an_identifier
```

but not

```
not#me          /* special character # not allowed */
101_south       /* must not start with a digit */
-plus           /* do not mistake - for _ */
```

Identifiers are created to give unique names to various objects in a program. Some words are reserved as special to the C language; these are called *keywords*. Although not technically part of the C language, the identifiers scanf and printf are already known to the C system as input/output functions in the standard library. The identifier main is also special in that C programs always begin execution at the function called main().

Good programming style requires the programmer to choose names that are meaningful. If you were to write a program to figure out various taxes, you might have identifiers such as tax_rate, price, and tax, so that the statement

```
tax = price * tax_rate;
```

would have an obvious meaning. The underscore _ is used to create a single identifier from what would normally be a string of words separated by spaces. Meaningfulness and avoiding confusion go hand in hand with readability to constitute the main guidelines for a good programming style.

2.3 KEYWORDS

Keywords are explicitly reserved identifiers that have a strict meaning in C. They cannot be redefined or used in other contexts.

Keywords

auto	default	extern	int	sizeof	union
break	do	float	long	static	unsigned
case	double	for	register	struct	void
char	else	goto	return	switch	while
continue	enum	if	short	typedef	

Some implementations may have additional keywords such as

```
const        far        near         volatile
```

In comparison to other major languages, C has only a small number of keywords. Ada, for example, has 62 keywords. It is a characteristic of C that it does a lot with relatively few special symbols and keywords.

2.4 OPERATORS AND SEPARATORS

There are many special characters that have particular meanings. Examples include the arithmetic operators

```
+        -        *        /        %
```

which stand for the usual arithmetic operations of addition, subtraction, multiplication, division, and modulus, respectively. In a C program these will often separate identifiers.

```
a+b        /* this is the expression a plus b */
a_b        /* this is a three character identifier */
```

Some symbols have meanings that depend on context. An example of this is the % symbol. In the statement

```
printf("%d", a);
```

the % symbol is a format control character. In an arithmetic expression such as

```
a % 7
```

the % symbol is the modulus operator.

Special characters along with white space serve to separate language elements, and some special characters are used in many different contexts. The context itself can determine which use is intended. For example, the expressions

```
a + b        ++a        a += b
```

all use + as a character, but ++ is a single operator, as is +=. Having the meaning of a symbol depend on context makes for a small symbol set and a terse language.

2.5 PRECEDENCE AND ASSOCIATIVITY OF OPERATORS

Operators have rules of *precedence* and *associativity* that determine precisely how expressions are evaluated. Since expressions inside parentheses are evaluated first, parentheses can be used to clarify or change the order in which operations are performed. Consider the expression

```
1 + 2 * 3
```

In C the operator * has higher precedence than +, causing the multiplication to be performed first, and then the addition. Hence the value of the expression is 7. An equivalent expression is

```
1 + (2 * 3)
```

On the other hand, since expressions inside parentheses are evaluated first, the expression

```
(1 + 2) * 3
```

is different. It has value 9. Now consider the expression

```
1 + 2 - 3 + 4 - 5
```

Because the operators + and - have the same precedence, the associativity rule "left to right" is used to determine how it is evaluated. The "left to right" rule means that the operations are performed from left to right. Thus

```
(((1 + 2) - 3) + 4) - 5
```

is an equivalent expression.

The following table gives the rules of precedence and associativity for some of the operators of C. In addition to the operators we have already seen, the table includes operators that will be discussed in this chapter.

Operators	Associativity
- *(unary)* ++ --	right to left
* / %	left to right
+ -	left to right
= += -= *= /= *etc.*	right to left

All the operators on a given line, such as * and / and %, have equal precedence with respect to each other, but have higher precedence than all the operators that occur on the lines below them. The associativity rule for all the operators on a given line appears on the right side of the table. Whenever we introduce new operators, we will give their rules of precedence and associativity, and often we will encapsulate the information by augmenting the above table. These rules are essential information for every programmer.

In addition to the binary minus, which represents subtraction, there is a unary minus, and both these operators are represented by a minus sign. The precedence of a unary minus is higher than * and / and %, and its associativity is "right to left". In the expression

```
- a * b - c
```

the first minus sign is unary and the second binary. Using the rules of precedence, we see that

```
((- a) * b) - c
```

is an equivalent expression.

2.6 INCREMENT AND DECREMENT OPERATORS

The increment operator ++ and decrement operator −− are unary operators with the same precedence as the unary minus, and they all associate from right to left. Both ++ and −− can be applied to variables, but not to constants or ordinary expressions. Moreover, they can occur in either prefix or postfix position, with possibly different effects occurring. Some examples are

```
++i
i++
--cnt
cnt--
```

but not

```
777++            /* constants cannot be incremented */
++(a * b - 1)    /* ordinary expressions cannot be incremented */
```

Each of the expressions ++i and i++ has a value, and moreover, each causes the stored value of i in memory to be incremented by 1. Each of the expressions takes as its value the value of i, but with ++i the stored value of i is incremented *before* the value of i is computed, whereas with i++ the stored value of i is incremented *after* the value of i is computed. The following code illustrates the situation.

```
int   a, b, c = 0;

a = ++c;
printf("%d %d\n", a, c);    /* 1 1 is printed */
b = c++;
printf("%d %d\n", b, c);    /* 1 2 is printed */
```

In a similar fashion −−i causes the stored value of i in memory to be decremented by 1 first, and this new value is the value of the expression. In contrast, the expression i−− takes as its value the current value of i, and it is only after the value of the expression has been computed that the stored value of i is decremented by 1.

Note carefully that ++ and -- are unlike other operators in that they cause the value of a variable in memory to be changed. For example, the operator + does not do this. An expression such as a + b has value, but the stored values in memory of the variables a and b are left unchanged. These ideas are expressed by saying that ++ and -- have a *side effect*; not only do these operators yield a value, but also the stored value of a variable in memory is changed.

In some cases we can use ++ in either prefix or postfix position with both uses producing equivalent results. For example, each of the two statements

++i;   and   i++;   is equivalent to   i = i + 1;

In a similar fashion each of the two statements

--i;   and   i--;   is equivalent to   i = i - 1;

In simple situations one can consider ++ and -- as operators that provide concise notation for the incrementing and decrementing of a variable. In other situations careful attention must be paid as to whether prefix or postfix position is desired.

Declarations and initializations		
int a = 1, b = 2, c = 3;		
Expression	**Equivalent expression**	**Value**
a * b / c	(a * b) / c	0
a * b % c + 1	((a * b) % c) + 1	3
++ a * b - c --	((++ a) * b) - (c --)	1
7 - - b * ++ c	7 - ((- b) * (++ c))	15

2.7 ASSIGNMENT OPERATORS

To change the value of a variable, we have already made use of assignment statements such as

a = b + c;

Unlike other languages, C treats = as an operator. Its precedence is lower than all the operators we have discussed so far, and its associativity is "right to left." In this section we want to explain in detail the significance of this.

To understand = as an operator, let us first consider + for the sake of comparison. The binary operator + takes two operands, as in the expression a + b. The value of the expression is just the sum of the values of a and b. In comparison, a simple assignment expression is of the form

> *variable = right_side*

where *right_side* is itself an expression. Notice that a semicolon placed at the end would have made this an assignment statement. The assignment operator = has the two operands *variable* and *right_side*. The value of *right_side* is assigned to *variable*, and that value becomes the value of the assignment expression as a whole. To illustrate this, consider

```
int   x, y, z;

y = 2;
z = 3;
x = y + z;
```

The first two assignment statements assign the values 2 and 3 to y and z, respectively. Then the value of y + z is computed and assigned to x. By using assignment expressions, this can be condensed to

```
int   x, y, z;

x = (y = 2) + (z = 3);
```

The assignment expression y = 2 assigns the value 2 to the variable y, and the assignment expression itself takes on this value. Similarly, the assignment expression z = 3 assigns the value 3 to the variable z, and the assignment expression itself takes on this value. Finally, the values of the two assignment expressions are added and the resulting value is assigned to x.

Although the above example is artificial, there are many situations where assignment occurs naturally as part of an expression. A frequently occurring situation is multiple assignment. Consider the statement

```
x = y = z = 0;
```

Since the operator = associates from right to left, an equivalent statement is

```
x = (y = (z = 0));
```

First z is assigned the value 0 and the expression z = 0 has value 0. Then y is assigned the value 0 and the expression y = (z = 0) has value 0. Finally, x is assigned the value 0 and the expression x = (y = (z = 0)) has value 0. Many languages do not use assignment in such an elaborate way. In this respect C is different.

In addition to = there are other assignment operators such as += and -=. An expression such as

```
k = k + 2
```

will add 2 to the old value of k and assign the result to k, and the expression as a whole will have that value. The expression

```
k += 2
```

accomplishes the same task. The following list contains all the assignment operators.

Assignment Operators

=	+=	-=	*=	/=	%=	>>=	<<=	&=	^=	|=

All these operators have the same precedence, and they all have "right to left" associativity. The semantics is specified by

variable op= expression

being equivalent to

variable = variable op (expression)

with the exception that if *variable* is itself an expression, it is evaluated only once. An assignment expression such as

j*= 2 + k   is equivalent to   j = j * (2 + k)

rather than

j = j * 2 + k

The following table illustrates how assignment expressions are evaluated.

Declarations and initializations			
int i, j = 2, k = 3, m = 4;			
Expression	**Equivalent expression**	**Equivalent expression**	**Value**
i += j + k	i += (j + k)	i = (i + (j + k))	6
j *= k = m + 5	j *= (k =´(m + 5))	j = (j * (k = (m + 5)))	18

2.8 COMMENTS

Comments are arbitrary strings of symbols placed between the delimiters /* and */. We have already seen examples such as

/* a comment */   /*** another comment ***/   /*****/

Another example is

```
/***
 ***    A very long comment
 ***    can be written in this fashion
 ***    to set it off from the surrounding
 ***    code.
 ***/
```

The following illustrates one of many styles that can be used to give prominence to comments.

```
/*****************************
 *   If you wish, you can     *
 *   put comments in a box.   *
 *****************************/
```

Comments are not part of the executable program, but are used by the programmer as a documentation aid. The aim of documentation is to explain clearly how the program works and how it is to be used. Comments frequently contain an informal argument demonstrating the correctness of the program.

Comments should be written simultaneously with program text. Frequently beginners leave the inserting of comments as a last step. There are two problems with this. The first is that once the program is running, the tendency is either to omit or abbreviate the comments. The second is that ideally the comments should serve as an ongoing dialogue with the programmer, indicating program structure and contributing to program clarity and correctness. They cannot serve this purpose if they are inserted after the coding is finished.

2.9 CONSTANTS

As we have seen in some simple introductory programs, C manipulates various kinds of values, some of them constants and some of them variables. Integers such as 7 and floating numbers such as 3.14159 are examples of constants. Also, there are character constants such as 'a', 'b', and 'c', and there are string constants such as "i am a string". Note carefully that character and string constants are different. For example, 'a' and "a" are not the same.

Some character constants are of a special kind, such as the newline character written '\n'. The backslash has a special meaning in this context and '\n' is a single character constant even though the two characters \ and n are being used to describe it.

In addition to having value, a constant also has an associated data type. For example, the constant 100 is an int whereas 100.0 is a double. This distinction can be important. For example, the expression 3/100 is an int divided by an int. Because integer division causes any fractional part to be discarded, the value of the expression is 0. In contrast to this the expression 3/100.0 is an int divided by a double. In a mixed expression such as this the value of the int is first converted to a double, and the expression as a whole has type double. Thus 0.03 is the value of the expression. Mixed expressions are discussed in detail in Chapter 6.

2.10 STRINGS

A sequence of characters enclosed in a pair of double quote marks is a string. Note that a double quote mark " is just one character, not two. If the character " itself is to occur in a string, it must be preceded by a backslash character \ . If the character \ is to occur in a string, it too must be preceded by a backslash. Some examples of strings are

```
"a string of text"
""                      /* the null string */
"     "                 /* a string of blank characters */
"   a = b + c;   "      /* nothing is executed */
"   /* this is not a comment */   "
"a string with double quotes \" within"
"a single backslash \\ is in this string"
"by using a backslash at the end of the line \
a string can be extended from one line to the next"
```

but not

```
/* "this is not a string" */
"and
neither is this"
```

Strings are constants. Character sequences that would have meaning if outside a string are just a sequence of characters when surrounded by double quotes. In the above examples one string contains what appears to be the statement a = b + c; however, since it occurs surrounded by double quotes, it is explicitly this sequence of characters. Within a C program a string is a particular type of constant, technically an array of characters; see Chapter 10.

2.11 AN EXAMPLE: COMPUTING POWERS OF TWO

To illustrate some of the ideas presented in this chapter we will write a program that prints on a line some powers of 2. Here is the program.

```
/* Some powers of 2 are printed. */

main()
{
    int   i = 0, power = 1;

    while (++i <= 10)
        printf("%6d", power *= 2);
    printf("\n");
}
```

The output of the program is

```
   2    4    8   16   32   64  128  256  512 1024
```

■ DISSECTION OF THE *powers_of_2* PROGRAM

```
/* Some powers of 2 are printed. */
```

■ Programs often begin with a comment that explains the intent or the use of the program. If the program is large, the comment may be very extensive, perhaps extending for hundreds of lines. The compiler treats comments as white space.

```
int   i = 0, power = 1;
```

■ The variables i and power are declared to be of type int. They are initialized to 0 and 1, respectively.

```
while (++i <= 10)
```

■ As long as the value of the expression ++i is less than or equal to 10, the body of the while loop is executed. The first time through the loop ++i has the value 1; the second time through the loop ++i has the value 2; and so forth. Thus the body of the loop is executed 10 times.

```
printf("%6d", power *= 2);
```

■ The body of the while loop consists of this statement. The string "%6d" is passed as the first argument to the printf() function. The string contains the format %6d, which indicates that the value of the expression power *= 2 is to be printed as a decimal with field length 6.

```
power *= 2
```

■ This assignment expression is equivalent to

```
power = power * 2
```

which causes the old value of power to be multiplied by 2 and the resulting value assigned to power. The value assigned to power is the value of the assignment expression as a whole. The first time through the loop the old value of power is 1 and the new value is 2; the second time through the loop the old value of power is 2 and the new value is 4; and so forth.

2.12 STYLE

Each of the statements

```
++i;        and        i++;
```

has the effect of incrementing the stored value of i in memory by 1. No use is made of the value of the expression; only the side effect of the operator ++ is being used. Which of these two statements is used is a matter of personal taste.

A correct style strives for code that is readable. Although the statement

```
x = (y = 2) + (z = 3);
```

is both correct and concise, it is not as readable as

```
y = 2;
z = 3;
x = y + z;
```

It is important not to condense code just for the sake of using less space. Readability is an attribute that should not be sacrificed.

If we want to add 7 to the variable a, we can write either

```
a += 7;        or        a = a + 7;
```

Which gets used is largely a matter of taste.

Crucial to programming readability is commenting style. There is no one correct style. Comments, properly used, give an arbitrary reader of the code the ability to understand both what the program does and how it works. One should adopt and consistently stay with a given commenting style. This is true both for individuals and organizations. Style becomes habit, and it reinforces good programming practice.

Comments should occur at the head of major structural groupings within code, including at the head of the entire program and of each function that constitutes the program. Short comments should occur to the right of individual statements when the effect of the statement is not obvious.

The lead comment should be visually set off and should include information such as the name of the organization, the programmer's name, the date, and the purpose of the program.

```
/*
 *   Organization:  SOCRATIC SOLUTIONS (Trade Mark)
 *   Programmer:    Constance B. Diligent
 *   Date:          3 September 1991
 *
 *   Purpose:       Birthday greetings
 */

main()
{
    printf("\nHAPPY BIRTHDAY TO YOU!\n\n");
}
```

While in practice the overcommenting of code almost never occurs, comments should, nevertheless, not clutter the program. Comments should illuminate what the program is doing. For example,

```
tax = price * rate;     /* sales tax formula */
```

gives insight into the program, but

```
tax = price * rate;     /* multiply price by rate */
```

is redundant, and therefore useless. It is very important to choose identifiers that describe their own use and to avoid extraneous commenting.

2.13 COMMON PROGRAMMING ERRORS

Programming errors discussed in this section will be chiefly syntactic. These errors are caught by the compiler, and in general they
keep the compiler from producing an executable output file.

Consider the following code contained in file *example_1.c.*

```
main()
{
   int   a = 1, b = 2;

   c = a + b;
   printf("c = %d\n", c);
)
```

On our system, the *cc* or *lint* command produces the following error
messages:

```
example_1.c(5): c undefined
example_1.c(7): syntax error
```

The name of the file containing the code is listed, along with the
line number in which the error occurs. The first error is easily
understood; namely, c is used but not declared. The second error
on line 7 is that a right parenthesis was used instead of a right
brace. The second message is too general to be directly suggestive
of the problem. Unfortunately, many C compilers have imprecise
syntactic error detection capability. A further example shows this.

```
main()
{
   int   a, b = 2, c = 3;     /* a, b, and c will be used
                                 to illustrate arithmetic /

   a = (4 * b + 5 * c) / 6;
   printf("a = %d   b = %d   c = %d\n", a, b, c);
}
```

If this is in the file *example_2.c*, then the *cc* compiler on our system yields the incomprehensible message

```
example_2.c: 9: missing endif
```

And *lint* is only slightly better. It yields the error messages

```
example_2.c(9): unexpected EOF
example_2.c(9): syntax error
```

What has happened is that the comment starting on line 4 is never closed. Looking at line 9 at the end of the program does not reveal where the trouble is. This type of misleading advice by the compiler is frequent. Automatic error detection by the compiler is no substitute for great care in program preparation.

2.14 OPERATING SYSTEM CONSIDERATIONS

One major difference among operating systems and C compilers is the length of discriminated identifiers. On some systems an identifier with more than 8 characters will be accepted, but only the first 8 characters will be used. The remaining characters are simply disregarded. On such a system, for example, the variable names

```
i_am_an_identifier       and       i_am_an_elephant
```

will be considered the same.

On a given system a programmer learns the length of discriminated identifiers by experimenting, reading the local manual, or asking someone. This is not a problem. On the other hand, if a programmer is writing C code to run on a spectrum of systems, then the limitations of all the systems must be known and respected.

On our system, which runs Berkeley 4.2 UNIX, the length of discriminated identifiers is 255.

2.15 SUMMARY

1   The basic elements of C are identifiers, keywords, constants, operators, and other separators. Blanks, tabs, newlines, and comments are separators that otherwise are ignored.

2   Identifiers are used to name variables and functions. They begin with a letter or an underscore _ and are chosen to be meaningful to the human reader.

3   Operators and separators are numerous in C, but are often overloaded. For example, the symbol % can mean different things in different contexts.

4   In C precise rules are used in evaluating expressions. The rules of precedence and associativity for operators determine how an equivalent parenthesized expression would look.

5   The increment operator ++ and decrement operator -- have a side effect. In addition to having a value, an expression such as ++i causes the stored value of i in memory to be incremented by 1.

6   The operators ++ and -- can be used in both prefix and postfix position with possibly different effects. The value of ++i is the value of i in memory *before* i is incremented by 1; the value of i++ is the value of i in memory *after* i is incremented by 1.

7   Unlike other languages, assignment is an operator in C. An expression, such as a = b + c assigns the value of b + c to a, and the expression as a whole takes on this value.

8   Comments are written between /* and */. They are critical to good program documentation. Comments should help the reader to both use and understand the program.

9   In addition to numerical constants such as 1 and 3.14159 there are character constants such as 'A' and string constants such as "i am a string". The constant 'A' is not the same as "A".

10 Strings are composed of characters between double quotes, as in "i am a string". Among the many uses of strings is their use as arguments to printf() and scanf(), where they act to control input and output.

2.16 EXERCISES

1   Is main a keyword? Explain.

2   Which of the following are not identifiers and why?

```
3id        __yes        o_no_o_no    OO_go        star*it
1_i_am     one_i_aren't me_to-2      xYshouldI    int
```

3   List five keywords and explain their use.

4   Design a standard form of introductory comment that will give a reader information about who wrote the program and why.

5   Can you have the following as a comment?

```
/* This is an attempt /* to nest */ a comment */
```

6   The purpose of this exercise is to show that the compiler sees only a stream of characters. Although the compiler is not interested in neatness, to the human reader, properly formatted code is crucial. Sloppy code is hard to read and maintain. The following program, although not very readable, should compile and execute. Test it to see if this is true.

```
main(
){
float qx,
      zz,
   tt;
      printf("gimme 3"
     );
scanf
      (   "%f%f       %f",&qx,&zz

  ,&tt)
     ;printf("averageis=%f",(qx+tt+zz)/3.0);
}
```

7   Rewrite the program given in exercise 6. Use different identifiers, and use white space and comments to make the program more readable and well documented.

8   Use the rules of precedence and associativity of operators to complete the following table.

Declarations and initializations		
int a = 1, b = 2, c = 3, d = 4, e = 5;		
Expression	**Equivalent expression**	**Value**
a + b - c + d		
a * b - c * - d		
a / b * c + d + ++ e		

9   Write an interactive program that converts pounds and ounces to kilograms and grams. Use symbolic constants that are defined before main().

10   This question illustrates one place where white space around operators is important. Since both + and ++ are operators, the expression a+++b can be interpreted as either

    a++ + b   or   a + ++b

depending on how the plus symbols are grouped. Normally, the first two plusses would be grouped and passed to the compiler to see if this were syntactically correct. Write a short program to see which interpretation is made by your compiler.

11   In the *powers_of_2* program explain what the effect would be if the expression ++i were changed to i++ .

12   What gets printed? First study the following code and write down what you think gets printed. Then write a test program to check your answers.

```
int    a, b = 0, c = 0;

a = ++b + ++c;
printf("%d %d %d\n", a, b, c);
a = b++ + c++;
printf("%d %d %d\n", a, b, c);
a = ++b + c++;
printf("%d %d %d\n", a, b, c);
a = b-- + --c;
printf("%d %d %d\n", a, b, c);
```

13   Are parentheses necessary in the following statement? Explain.

```
x = (y = 2) + (z = 3);
```

14   Consider the code

```
int    a = 1, b = 2, c = 3;

a += b += c += 7;
```

Write an equivalent statement that is fully parenthesized. What are the values of the variables a, b, and c? First write down your answer. Then write a test program to check your answer.

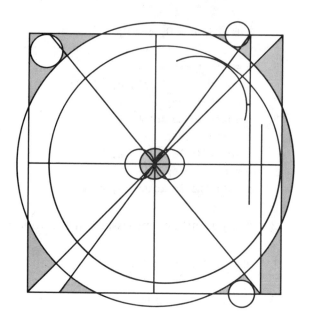

3

FLOW OF CONTROL

Statements in a program are normally executed one after another. This is called sequential flow of control. Often it is desirable to alter the sequential flow of control to provide for a choice of action, or a repetition of action. By means of if and if-else statements a selection among alternative actions can be made. By means of while, for, and do statements iterative actions can be taken. These flow of control constructs are explained in this chapter.

Since the relational, equality, and logical operators are heavily used in flow of control constructs, we begin with a thorough discussion of these operators. These operators are used in expressions that we think of as being *true* or *false*. We explain how *true* and *false* are implemented in C. We also discuss the compound statement. It is used to group together statements that are to be treated as a unit.

3.1 RELATIONAL, EQUALITY, AND LOGICAL OPERATORS

In Chapter 1 we used the "less than or equal" operator <= in the expression i <= 10 to control a while loop. This is an example of a relational expression. The natural interpretation is that this expression is *true* when the value of i is less than or equal to 10, and *false* when the value of i is larger than 10. The relational, equality and logical operators are used in expressions in flow of control constructs that control the order in which statements in a program are executed. These expressions have either the value 0 or the value 1. The reason for this is that in C the value zero is used to represent *false* and any nonzero value is used to represent *true*. In this chapter we will carefully explain how these operators work, how they combine with other operators to make expressions, and how they are used in flow of control constructs.

The names of the relational, equality, and logical operators, along with the symbols that represent them, are given in the following table.

Relational, Equality, and Logical Operators		
relational operators:	less than:	<
	greater than:	>
	less than or equal:	<=
	greater than or equal:	>=
equality operators:	equal:	==
	not equal:	!=
logical operators:	(unary) negation:	!
	logical and:	&&
	logical or:	||

As with all operators in C, the relational, equality, and logical operators have rules of precedence and associativity that determine precisely how expressions involving these operators are evaluated.

Operators	Associativity
– (*unary*) ++ –– !	right to left
* / %	left to right
+ –	left to right
< <= > >=	left to right
== !=	left to right
&&	left to right
||	left to right
= += –= *= /= *etc*	right to left

All the relational, equality, and logical operators are binary, except for !, which is unary. Notice that the precedence of ! is the same as all the other unary operators. The precedence of all the relational, equality, and logical operators other than ! is below the arithmetic operators, but above the assignment operators. Intuitively, an expression such as a < b is either *true* or *false*. C evaluates *true* expressions to the int value 1 and *false* expressions to the int value 0. As we shall see, any nonzero value is considered *true*.

3.2   RELATIONAL OPERATORS AND EXPRESSIONS

The relational operators <, <=, >, and >= are all binary. They each take two expressions as operands and yield either the int value 0 or the int value 1. Some examples are

```
a < 3
a > b + c
-13.7 >= (20.0 * x + 33.1)
```

but not

```
a =< b       /* out of order */
a < = b      /* space not allowed */
a >> b       /* this is a shift operation */
```

Consider the relational expression a < b. If the value of a is less than the value of b, then the expression has the int value 1, which we think of as *true*. If the value of a is not less than the value of b, then the expression has the int value 0, which we think of as *false*. Observe that the value of a < b is the same as the value of a - b < 0. Because the precedence of the relational operators is less than that of the arithmetic operators, the expression

a - b < 0   is equivalent to   (a - b) < 0

Let *e1* and *e2* be arbitrary arithmetic expressions. The following truth table shows how the value of *e1* - *e2* determines the logical value of a relational expression such as *e1* < *e2*.

Values of:

e1 - e2	e1 < e2	e1 > e2	e1 <= e2	e1 >= e2
positive	F	T	F	T
zero	F	F	T	T
negative	T	F	T	F

However, since all the relational, equality, and logical operators yield either the value 0 or 1, the above table can be rewritten to show more accurately the semantics of the relational operators. The new table reinforces the concept of how C uses zero for *false* and nonzero for *true*.

Values of:

e1 − e2	e1 < e2	e1 > e2	e1 <= e2	e1 >= e2
positive	0	1	0	1
zero	0	0	1	1
negative	1	0	1	0

The following table illustrates the use of the rules of precedence and associativity to evaluate relational expressions.

Declarations and initializations		
int i = 1, j = 2; float x = 3.3, y = 4.4;		
Expression	**Equivalent expression**	**Value**
i < j + 3	i < (j + 3)	1
2 * i - 7 <= j - 8	((2 * i) - 7) <= (j - 8)	0
- x + y >= 2.0 * y	((- x) + y) >= (2.0 * y)	0

3.3 EQUALITY OPERATORS AND EXPRESSIONS

The equality operators == and != are binary operators acting on expressions. They yield either the int value 0 or the int value 1. Some examples are

```
c == 'A'
k != -2
x + y == 2 * z - 3
```

but not

```
a = b            /* an assignment statement */
a = = b - 1      /* space not allowed */
x =! 44          /* equivalent to x = (!44) */
x + y =! 44      /* equivalent to (x + y) = (!44)  -  syntax error */
```

Intuitively, an equality expression such as a == b is either *true* or
false. An equivalent expression is a - b == 0. If the value of a
equals the value of b, then a - b has value 0 and 0 == 0 is *true*. In
this case the expression a == b will yield the int value 1. If the
value of a is not equal to the value of b, then a == b will yield the
int value 0. The expression a != b makes use of the "not equal"
operator. It is evaluated in a similar fashion, except that the test
here is for inequality rather than for equality. The operator semantics is given by the following table.

Values of:		
exp1 - exp2	**exp1 == exp2**	**exp1 != exp2**
zero	1	0
nonzero	0	1

The following table shows how the rules of precedence and associativity are used to evaluate some expressions with equality operators:

Declarations and initializations		
int i = 1, j = 2, k = 3;		
Expression	**Equivalent expression**	**Value**
i == j	j == i	0
i != j	j != i	1
i + j + k == - 2 * - k	((i + j) + k) == ((- 2) * (- k))	1

3.4 LOGICAL OPERATORS AND EXPRESSIONS

The three logical operators are !, &&, and || . Of these, ! is unary, whereas && and || are binary. All of these operators when applied to expressions yield either the int value 0 or the int value 1.

Logical negation can be applied to an arbitrary arithmetic expression. If an expression has value zero, then its negation will yield the int value 1. On the other hand, if the expression has a nonzero value, then its negation will yield the int value 0. Some examples are

```
!5
!a
!'z'
!(x + 7.7)
```

but not

```
a != b    /* this is the "not equal" operator */
```

The semantics for the operator ! is given by the following table.

Values of:	
exp	!exp
zero	1
nonzero	0

While logical negation is a very simple operator, there is one subtlety. This operator is unlike the *not* operator in ordinary logic. If *s* is a logical statement, then

not (*not s*) = *s*

whereas in C the value of !!5, for example, is 1. Since ! associates from right to left,

!!5   is equivalent to   !(!5)

and !(!5) is equivalent to !(0), which has the value 1. The following table shows how some expressions with logical negation are evaluated.

Declarations and initializations		
int i = 7, j = 7;		
float x = 0.0;		
Expression	**Equivalent expression**	**Value**
! (i - j)	! (i - j)	1
! i - j	(! i) - j	-7
! x * ! x	(! x) * (! x)	1

The binary logical operators && and || also act on expressions and yield either the int value 0 or the int value 1. Some examples are

```
2 || 3
a && b
a < b || a == c
x >= 2.2 && x <= 7.7 * y
```

but not

```
a &&          /* one operand missing */
a | b         /* this is a bitwise operation */
a | | b       /* extra space not allowed */
&a            /* address of a */
a & b         /* this is a bitwise operation */
```

The operator semantics is given by the following table.

Values of:			
exp1	**exp2**	**exp1 && exp2**	**exp1 || exp2**
zero	*zero*	0	0
zero	*nonzero*	0	1
nonzero	*zero*	0	1
nonzero	*nonzero*	1	1

This table, although completely accurate, does not reflect the way that programmers usually think when dealing with logical expressions. Even experienced programmers think in terms of truth values.

Values of:			
exp1	exp2	exp1 && exp2	exp1 || exp2
F	F	F	F
F	T	F	T
T	F	F	T
T	T	T	T

The precedence of && is higher than ||, but both operators are of lower precedence than all unary, arithmetic, and relational operators. Their associativity is "left to right." The following table shows how the rules of precedence and associativity are used to compute the value of some logical expressions.

Declarations and initializations		
int i = 7, j = 8, k = 9;		
float x = 0.0;		
Expression	**Equivalent expression**	**Value**
i && j && k	(i && j) && k	1
i || j - 3 && 0	i || ((j - 3) && 0)	1
i < j && 2 >= k	(i < j) && (2 >= k)	0
i < j || 2 >= k	(i < j) || (2 >= k)	1
i == 2 || j == 4 || k == 6	((i == 2) || (j == 4)) || (k == 6)	0
i = 2 || j == 4 || k == 6	i = ((2 || (j == 4)) || (k == 6))	1
x <= 5.0 && x != 1.0 || i > j	((x <= 5.0) && (x != 1.0)) || (i > j)	1

In the evaluation of expressions that are the operands of && and ||, the evaluation process is from left to right, and the process stops as soon as the outcome *true* or *false* is known. Suppose that *exp1* and *exp2* are expressions and that *exp1* has value zero. In the evaluation of the logical expression

exp1 && *exp2*

the evaluation of *exp2* will not occur, because the value of the logical expression as a whole is already determined to be 0. Similarly, if *exp1* has nonzero value, then in the evaluation of

   exp1 || exp2

the evaluation of *exp2* will not occur, because the value of the logical expression as a whole is already determined to be 1. The following code illustrates this.

```
int   i, j = 2;

i = 0 && (j = 3);
printf("%d  %d\n", i, j);       /* 0  2 is printed */
i = 4 || (j = 5);
printf("%d  %d\n", i, j);       /* 1  2 is printed */
i = 0 || (j = 6);
printf("%d  %d\n", i, j);       /* 1  6 is printed */
```

3.5 THE COMPOUND STATEMENT

A compound statement is a series of statements surrounded by the braces { and }. The chief use of the compound statement is to group statements into an executable unit. When declarations come at the beginning of a compound statement, it is called a block. In C wherever it is possible to place a statement, it is also possible to place a compound statement. *A compound statement is itself a statement.* An example of a compound statement is

```
{
    ++i;
    sum += x;
    printf("Count: %d\nRunning sum: %d\n", i, sum);
}
```

Grouping of statements is used to achieve the desired flow of control in such constructs as the if statement and the while statement.

3.6 THE NULL STATEMENT

The null statement is written as a single semicolon. It causes no action to take place. An example is

```
a = b + c;
;                    /* this is a null statement */
```

This is not a typical example of the use of a null statement, because here it serves no useful purpose. Usually a null statement is used where a statement is required syntactically, but no action is desired. This situation sometimes occurs in statements that affect the flow of control. An example of a while statement making use of a null statement occurs in Section 5.6 in Chapter 5.

3.7 THE if AND THE if-else STATEMENTS

The general form of an if statement is

> if (*expression*)
>   *statement*

If *expression* is nonzero (*true*), then *statement* is executed; otherwise *statement* is skipped. After the if statement has been executed, control passes to the next statement. In the example

```
if (grade >= 90)
    printf("Congratulations!\n");
printf("Your grade is %d.\n", grade);
```

a congratulatory message is printed only when grade is greater than or equal to 90. The second printf() statement is always executed. Usually the expression in an if statement is a relational or equality or logical expression, but an expression from any domain is permissible. Some other examples of if statements are

```
if (z != 0)
   x = y / z;

if (c == ' ') {
   ++blank_cnt;
   printf("found another blank\n");
}
```

but not

```
if  b == a              /* parentheses missing */
   area = a * a;
```

Where appropriate, compound statements should be used to group a series of statements under the control of a single if expression. The following code consists of two if statements.

```
if (j < k)
   min = j;
if (j < k)
   printf("j is smaller than k\n");
```

The code can be written more efficiently and more understandably by making use of a single if statement with its body consisting of a compound statement.

```
if (j < k) {
   min = j;
   printf("j is smaller than k\n");
}
```

In the first version, the relational expression j < k is evaluated twice, whereas in the second version it is evaluated only once with a compound statement grouping all of the actions needed when the expression is *true*.

Closely related to the if statement is the if-else statement. It has the general form

```
if (expression)
    statement1
else
    statement2
```

If *expression* is nonzero, then *statement1* is executed and *statement2* is skipped; if *expression* is zero, then *statement1* is skipped and *statement2* is executed. After the if-else statement has been executed, control passes to the next statement. Consider the code

```
if (x < y)
    min = x;
else
    min = y;
printf("min = %d\n", min);
```

If x < y is *true*, then min will be assigned the value of x, and if it is *false*, then min will be assigned the value of y. After the if-else statement is executed, the printf() statement is executed, causing the value of min to be printed. Another example of an if-else statement is

```
if ('a' <= c && c <= 'z') {
    ++lc_cnt;
    printf("another lowercase letter\n");
}
else {
    ++other_cnt;
    printf("%c is not a lowercase letter\n", c);
}
```

but not

```
if (i != j) {
    i = 1;
    j = 2;
};
else            /* syntax error */
    i += j;
```

The syntax error occurs because the semicolon following the right brace creates a null statement, leaving the else with nowhere to attach.

Since an if statement is itself a statement, it can be used as the statement part of another if statement. Consider the code

```
if (a == 1)
   if (b == 2)
      printf("***");
```

This is of the form

```
if (a == 1)
   statement
```

where *statement* is the following if statement

```
if (b == 2)
   printf("***");
```

In a similar fashion an if-else statement can be used as the statement part of another if statement. Consider, for example,

```
if (a == 1)
   if (b == 2)
      printf("***");
   else
      printf("###");
```

Now we are faced with a semantic difficulty. This code illustrates the *dangling else problem*. It is not clear how the else part gets associated. Do not be fooled by the format of the code. As far as the machine is concerned, the following code is equivalent.

```
if (a == 1)
   if (b == 2)
      printf("***");
else
   printf("###");
```

The rule is:

> *an* else *attaches to the nearest* if

Thus the code is correctly formatted as we first gave it. It has the form

```
if (a == 1)
   statement
```

where *statement* is the if-else statement

```
if (b == 2)
   printf("***");
else
   printf("###");
```

To illustrate the use of the if and if-else statements, we will write an interactive program that finds the minimum of three values entered at the keyboard.

```
/* Find the minimum of three values. */

main()
{
   int   x, y, z, min;

   printf("Input three integers:  ");
   scanf("%d%d%d", &x, &y, &z);
   if (x < y)
      min = x;
   else
      min = y;
   if (z < min)
      min = z;
   printf("The minimum value is %d\n", min);
}
```

■ DISSECTION OF THE *find_minimum* PROGRAM

```
printf("Input three integers:  ");
```

- In an interactive environment, the program must prompt the user for input data.

```
scanf("%d%d%d", &x, &y, &z);
```

- The input function scanf() from the standard library is used to read in three integer values that are stored at the address of x, the address of y, and the address of z, respectively.

```
if (x < y)
   min = x;
else
   min = y;
```

- This whole construct is a single if-else statement. The values of x and y are compared. If x is less than y, then min is assigned the value of x; if x is not less than y, then min is assigned the value of y.

```
if (z < min)
   min = z;
```

- This is an if statement. A check is made to see if the value of z is less than the value of min. If it is, then min is assigned the value of z; otherwise the value of min is left unchanged.

Just as an if-else statement can be used as the statement part of another if statement, so can it be used as the statement part following an else. Here is an example of this.

```
if (a == 1)
   printf("a is 1\n");
else if (a == 2)
   printf("a is 2\n");
else
   printf("a is not 1 or 2\n");
```

Because long chains of if-else statements can occur, they are usually formatted as shown above, rather than

```
if (a == 1)
   printf("a is 1\n");
else
   if (a == 2)
      printf("a is 2\n");
   else
      printf("a is not 1 or 2\n");
```

Even though this shows the flow of control more clearly, it is not the preferred formatting style. We will discuss these ideas again in Chapter 7.

3.8 THE while STATEMENT

Repetition of action is one reason we rely on computers. When there are large amounts of data, it is very convenient to have control mechanisms for repeatedly executing specific statements. The most basic such iterative statement is the while statement.

The general form of a while statement, or while loop, is

while (*expression*)
    statement

First *expression* is evaluated. If it is nonzero (*true*), then *statement* is executed and control passes back to the beginning of the while loop. The effect of this is that the body of the while loop, namely *statement*, is executed repeatedly until *expression* is zero (*false*). At that point control passes to the next statement. The effect of this is that *statement* can be executed zero or more times.

An example of a while statement is

```
while (i <= 10) {
    sum += i;
    ++i;
}
```

Assume that just before this loop the value of i is 1 and the value of sum is 0. Then the effect of the loop is to repeatedly increment the value of sum by the current value of i and then to increment i by 1. After the first time through the loop the value of sum is 0 + 1, after the second time through the loop the value of sum is 0 + 1 + 2, after the third time through the loop the value of sum is 0 + 1 + 2 + 3, and so forth. After the body of the loop has been executed 10 times, the value of i is 11 and the value of the expression i <= 10 is 0 (*false*). Thus the body of the loop is not executed and control passes to the next statement. When the while loop is exited, the value of sum is 55. Note again that a compound statement is used to group statements together, with the compound statement itself syntactically representing a single statement.

3.9 AN EXAMPLE: FINDING THE MAXIMUM VALUE

A task that programmers often encounter is to find an item having a particular property from among a given collection of items. We will illustrate such a task by finding the maximum value of some real numbers entered interactively at the keyboard. Our program will make use of if and while statements to do this.

```
/* Find the maximum of n real values. */

main()
{
   int      i, n;
   float    max, x;

   printf("The maximum value will be computed.\n");
   printf("How many numbers do you wish to enter?  ");
   scanf("%d", &n);
   while (n <= 0) {
      printf("\nERROR:  A positive integer is required.\n\n");
      printf("How many numbers do you wish to enter?  ");
      scanf("%d", &n);
   }
   printf("\nEnter %d real numbers:  ", n);
   scanf("%f", &x);
   max = x;
   i = 1;
   while (i < n) {
      scanf("%f", &x);
      if (max < x)
         max = x;
      ++i;
   }
   printf("\nMaximum value:  %g\n\n", max);
}
```

Suppose that we execute this program, enter 5 when prompted, and
then enter the numbers 1.01, −3, 2.2, 7.07000, and 5. Here is
what appears on the screen:

```
The maximum value will be computed.
How many numbers do you wish to enter?  5

Enter 5 real numbers:  1.01  -3  2.2  7.07000  5

Maximum value:  7.07
```

■ DISSECTION OF THE *find_maximum* PROGRAM

```
int     i, n;
float   max, x;
```

- The variables i and n are declared to be of type int, and the variables max and x are declared to be of type float.

```
printf("The maximum value will be computed.\n");
```

- A line of text is printed explaining the purpose of the program. This is an important documentation aid. The program in effect is self-documenting in its own output. This is good programming style.

```
printf("How many numbers do you wish to enter?  ");
scanf("%d", &n);
```

- The user is prompted to input an integer. The function scanf() is used to store the value of the integer entered by the user at the address of n.

```
while (n <= 0) {
    printf("\nERROR:  A positive integer is required.\n\n");
    printf("How many numbers do you wish to enter?  ");
    scanf("%d", &n);
}
```

- If n is negative or zero, then the value of the expression n <= 0 is 1 (*true*), causing the body of the while loop to be executed. An error message and another prompt is printed, and a new value is stored at the address of n. As long as the value of n is negative or zero, the body of the loop is repeatedly executed. The purpose of this while loop is to provide the program with some input error detection capability. Other input errors, such as typing the letter a instead of a digit, still cause the program to fail. For more robust error detection, we need to look at the actual characters typed by the user. To do this we need character-processing tools and strings; see Chapters 5 and 10.

```
printf("\nEnter %d real numbers: ", n);
scanf("%f", &x);
max = x;
```

■ The user is prompted to input n real numbers. The scanf()
function uses the format %f to convert the characters in the
input stream to a floating point number and to store its value
at the address of x. The variable max is assigned the value of
x.

```
i = 1;
while (i < n) {
   scanf("%f", &x);
   if (max < x)
      max = x;
   ++i;
}
```

■ We begin by assigning to i the value 1. As long as i is less
than n, the following is done repeatedly:

1. Read in a real number and store its value at the address of x.
2. If x is less than min, assign its value to min.
3. Increment i by 1.

The body of a while statement is a single statement, in this case
a compound statement. The compound statement aids flow of
control by grouping several statements to be executed as a unit.

```
printf("\nMaximum value: %g\n\n", max);
```

■ The value of min is printed in the %g format. Notice that
7.07000 was entered at the keyboard, but 7.07 was printed.
With the %g format, extraneous zeros are not printed.

3.10 THE for STATEMENT

The `for` statement is closely related to the `while` statement, and is used just about as much. As an example, the following code makes use of a `for` statement to sum the integers from 1 to 10.

```
int   i, sum = 0;

for (i = 1; i <= 10; ++i)
   sum += i;
```

Code that is equivalent to this is

```
int   i, sum = 0;

i = 1;
while (i <= 10) {
   sum += i;
   ++i;
}
```

More generally, the construction

```
for (expression1; expression2; expression3)
   statement
next statement
```

is equivalent to

```
expression1;
while (expression2) {
   statement
   expression3;
}
next statement
```

provided that *expression2* is nonempty, and provided that a `continue` statement is not in the body of the `for` loop. From our understanding of the `while` statement, we can deduce the semantics of the `for` statement. First *expression1* is evaluated. Typically, *expression1* is used to initialize a variable used in the loop. Then *expression2* is evaluated. If it is nonzero (*true*), then *statement* is executed and *expression3* is evaluated and control passes back to the beginning of the for loop again, except that evaluation of *expression1* is skipped. Typically, *expression2* is a logical expression controlling the iteration. This process continues until *expression2* is zero (*false*), at which point control passes to *next statement*. Some examples are

```
for (i = 1; i <= n; ++i)
   factorial *= i;

for (j = 1; scanf("%d", &val) == 1; ++j) {
   printf("Count:%3d        Value:%5d\n", j, val);
   sum += val;
}
```

but not

```
for (i = 0, i < n, ++i)      /* semicolons must separate expressions */
   sum += i;
```

Any or all of the expressions in a for statement can be missing, but the two semicolons must remain. If *expression1* is missing, then no initialization step is performed as part of the for loop. The code

```
i = 1;
sum = 0;
for ( ; i <= 10; ++i)
   sum += i;
```

will compute the sum of the integers from 1 to 10, and so will the code

```
i = 1;
sum = 0;
for ( ; i <= 10 ; )
   sum += i++;
```

The special rule for when *expression2* is missing, is that the test is always *true*. Thus the for loop in the code

```
i = 1;
sum = 0;
for ( ; ; ) {
   sum += i++;
   printf("%d\n", sum);
}
```

is an infinite loop.

3.11 AN EXAMPLE: PRINTING A TABLE OF POWERS

To illustrate the use of a for loop, we will write a program to print a table of powers. The computational ideas are straightforward. The part that the programmer must think about the most is the formatting of the table.

```
/* Print a table of powers. */

#define   LIMIT   10

main()
{
   int   i;

   printf("\n%s\n%s\n%7s%12s%12s%12s%12s\n\n",
      "A table of powers",
      "------------------",
      "integer", "square", "cube", "quartic", "quintic");

   for (i = 1; i <= LIMIT; ++i)
      printf("%7d%12d%12d%12d%12d\n",
         i, i*i, i*i*i, i*i*i*i, i*i*i*i*i);
}
```

Here are the first few lines of output from this program.

```
A table of powers
------------------

   integer      square        cube     quartic     quintic

         1           1           1           1           1
         2           4           8          16          32
         3           9          27          81         243

       .     .     .     .     .
```

■ DISSECTION OF THE *tbl_of_powers* PROGRAM

```
printf("\n%s\n%s\n%7s%12s%12s%12s%12s\n\n",
   "A table of powers",
   "------------------",
   "integer", "square", "cube", "quartic", "quintic");
```

■ A general heading and column headings are printed. The format %7s is used because the string "integer" contains 7 letters. The formats %12s are used to get spacing in the table that looks acceptable to the eye. Formatting is often a trial and error process. We leave it as an exercise to try other formats.

```
for (i = 1; i <= LIMIT; ++i)
   printf("%7d%12d%12d%12d%12d\n",
      i, i*i, i*i*i, i*i*i*i, i*i*i*i*i);
```

■ The body of this for loop is a single printf() statement. It is executed repeatedly with i going from 1 to LIMIT. Notice that the numbers specifying the field widths in the formats correspond to those in the previous printf() statement. These formats cause the entries in our table to line up in columns.

3.12 THE do STATEMENT

The do statement can be considered a variant of the while statement. Instead of making its test at the top of the loop, it makes it at the bottom. An example is

```
do {
    sum += i;
    scanf("%d", &i);
} while (i > 0);
```

Consider a construction of the form

```
do
    statement
while (expression);
    next statement
```

First *statement* is executed, and then *expression* is evaluated. If it is nonzero (*true*), then control passes back to the beginning of the do statement and the process repeats itself. When the value of *expression* is zero (*false*), then control passes to *next statement*. As an example, suppose we want to read in a positive integer, and we want to insist that the integer is positive. The following code will accomplish this.

```
do {
    printf("Input a positive integer:  ");
    scanf("%d", &n);
} while (n <= 0);
```

The user will be prompted for a positive integer. A negative or zero value will cause the loop to be executed again, asking for another value. Control will exit the loop only after a positive integer has been entered.

3.13 STYLE

The placement of braces to reflect flow of control is crucial to a good programming style. For `if`, `if-else`, `while`, and `for` statements that have a compound statement as their body, we have been using the following style:

```
while (i < 10) {
   .  .  .  .  .
}
```

The statements in the body of the loop are indented three spaces, and the closing brace `}` is lined up directly under the `while`. The indentation serves to visually set off those statements making up the body of the loop. The placement of the `while` and the `}` one above the other in the same column serves to visually mark the beginning and end, respectively, of the loop. A variation of this style would be to choose a different indentation, such as four, five, or eight spaces. Another style is to place beginning and ending braces in the same column. For example,

```
while (i < 10)
{
   .  .  .  .  .
}
```

Which style is used is a matter of taste. However, after an individual or organization chooses a style, it should be followed consistently.

If the body of a loop is a single statement, braces are not necessary. Nonetheless, as a matter of style, some programmers *always* use braces.

```
while (i < 10) {
    a single statement
}
```

This is an acceptable practice.

Only a small percentage of loops in C code tend to be `do` loops. Because of this, it is considered good programming style to use braces even when they are not needed. The braces in the construct

```
do {
    a single statement
} while ( . . . );
```

make it easier for the reader to realize that this is a do statement rather than a while statement followed by an empty statement.

In many situations either a while loop or a for loop can be used. Which one is used is a matter of personal taste.

3.14 COMMON PROGRAMMING ERRORS

We will discuss four common programming errors. The first common programming error is the confusion between the two expressions

```
a == b        and        a = b
```

Although they are *visually* similar, they are radically different in function. The expression a == b is a test for equality, whereas a = b is an assignment expression. One of the more common programming mistakes is to code something like

```
if (i = 1)
    . . . . .
```

instead of

```
if (i == 1)
    . . . . .
```

The assignment expression i = 1 is always *true*, because its value is 1. An error like this can be very difficult to find.

The second common programming error occurs when an expression that controls an iterative statement causes an unwanted infinite loop. Care should be taken to avoid this difficulty. As an example, consider the code

```
printf("Input an integer:  ");
scanf("%d", &n);
while (--n) {
    .  .  .  .  .
}
```

The intent is for a positive integer to be entered and its value stored at the address of n. Then the statements in the body of the while loop are to be executed repeatedly until the expression --n is eventually zero. However, if a negative integer is inadvertently assigned to n, then the loop will be infinite. To guard against this possibility, it would be better to code instead

```
while (--n > 0) {
    .  .  .  .  .
}
```

The third common programming error occurs with the use of an inappropriate test in a loop. An example of this is

```
float   sum = 0.0, x;

for (x = 0.0; x != 9.9; x += 0.1)      /* test not robust */
    sum += x;
```

On most machines this code results in an infinite loop. The reason for this is that floating values such as 0.1 are stored in memory with a value that is very close to one-tenth, but not exactly. The technical details are beyond the scope of this text, but programmers need to be aware of this general phenomenon. If we use the expression

```
x <= 9.9        instead of        x != 9.9
```

the test is robust and the code performs as expected. As a general rule it is better to use a relational expression, when appropriate, rather than an equality expression. In many cases the resulting code will be more robust.

A fourth common programming error involves the use of an unwanted semicolon after an if or while or for. For example, the code

```
for (i = 1; i <= 10; ++i);
   sum += i;
```

does not behave as expected. The reason for this is that the semicolon at the end of the first line creates an unwanted null statement. The code is equivalent to

```
for (i = 1; i <= 10; ++i)
   ;
sum += i;
```

and this is clearly not what the programmer intended.

3.15   OPERATING SYSTEM CONSIDERATIONS

It is often useful in interactive programming to deliberately use infinite loops. However, if a program makes use of an infinite loop, then the user will have to interrupt the program to stop it. What must be typed to interrupt a program is system dependent. On our system a control-c must be typed. On other systems there is a special key marked delete. You will have to find out what is needed on your system to effect an interrupt.

Two conventional styles of infinite loop are

```
while (1) {
   .  .  .  .  .
}
```

and

```
for ( ; ; ) {
   .  .  .  .  .
}
```

Suppose that a programmer wishes to experiment. Rather than running a program over and over, it may be more convenient to put the essential code into an infinite loop. Here is an example.

```
printf("The sum from 1 to limit with step 0.1 will be computed.\n\n");
for ( ; ; ) {
    printf("Input limit:  ");
    scanf("%f", &limit);
    for (x = 1.0; x <= limit; x += 0.1)
        sum += x;
    printf("sum = %f\n\n", sum);
}
```

3.16   SUMMARY

1   Relational, equality, and logical expressions have an int value of 0 or 1.

2   All the relational, equality, and logical operators are binary, except !, which is unary. This means that they make a comparison of two expressions. A chief use of all of these operators, including !, is to test data to affect flow of control.

3   The grouping construct { . . . } is a compound statement. It allows enclosed statements to be treated as a single unit.

4   An if statement provides a means of choosing whether or not to execute a statement. An if-else statement provides a means of choosing which of two statements gets executed. The else part of an if-else statement associates with the nearest available if. This resolves the "dangling else" problem.

5   The ability to perform actions repeatedly is one reason that we use computers. The while, for, and do statements provide looping mechanisms in C. The body of a while or for statement is executed zero or more times. The body of a do statement is executed one or more times.

3.17   EXERCISES

1   Give equivalent logical expressions that do not mak   _se of negation.

```
!(a == b)              !(a < b && c < d)
!(a + 1 < b - 2)       !(a < 1 || b < 2 && c < 3)
```

2   What are the values of the expressions in the following table?

Declarations and initializations	
int a = 1, b = 2, c = 3; float x = 7.61;	
Expression	**Value**
a >= b + 3	
(a < b) || c	
a = b + c < !(a || b) && c	
! !(x <= 7 + 2/3)	

3   Write a program that contains the loop

```
while (scanf("%d", &salary) == 1) {
    .  .  .  .  .
}
```

Within the loop compute a 17% federal withholding tax and a 3% state withholding tax, and print these values along with the corresponding salary. Accumulate the sums of all salaries and taxes printed. Print these sums after the program exits the while loop.

4   What gets printed?

```
int  i = 1, j = 2, k = 3;

printf("%d %d %d\n", !i - j, !i + !!j, !!!k);
printf("%d %d %d\n", i == !j, j != -k, !-i == j * k);
printf("%d %d %d\n", i / j == !k, !i || j, !(i && j));
```

5   Complete the following table.

Declarations and initializations		
int a = 1, b = 2, c = 3;		
Expression	**Equivalent expression**	**Value**
a && b && c	(a && b) && c	
a && b || c		
a || b && c		
a || ! b && ! ! c + 4		
a += ! b && c == ! 5		

6   Assume that i is a variable of type int. First explain the effect of the following code:

```
while (i = 2) {
   printf("Some even numbers: %d %d %d\n", i, i + 2, i + 4);
   i = 0;
}
```

Now contrast this with

```
if (i = 2)
   printf("Some even numbers: %d %d %d\n", i, i + 2, i + 4);
```

Both pieces of code are logically wrong. The run-time effect of one of them is so striking that the error is easy to spot, whereas the other piece of wrong code has a subtle effect that is much harder to spot. Explain.

7   What gets printed?

```
int   i = 1, j = 2;

if (i == 1)
   if (j == 2)
      printf("%5d", i = i + j);
else
   printf("%5d", i = i - j);
printf("%5d\n", i);
```

8   In some programming languages a "do" is required to effect a
while loop. Because of this, a programmer experienced in
another language might make the following kind of mistake
when learning C:

```
while (++k < LIMIT) do {      /* syntax error */
   j = 2 * k + 3;
   printf("%d\n", j);
}
```

The syntax error does not really show up on the line listed.
Run a test program with this piece of code in it, find out which
line is flagged with a syntax error, and explain why.

9   We have already explained that

```
while (1) {
   . . . . .
}
```

is an infinite loop. What happens when the following program
is executed? If you are not quite sure, try it.

```
main()
{
   while (-33.777) {
      printf("run forever, if you can");
   }
}
```

10   Let *e1* and *e2* be arithmetic expressions. We want to establish
     that

     e1 != *e2*   is equivalent to   !(*e1* == *e2*)

     Do this by completing the following table:

Values of:			
e1 – e2	**e1 != e2**	**e1 == e2**	**!(e1 == e2)**
zero			
nonzero			

11   Run the program *find_maximum* and enter 1 when first
     prompted. Then you will see on the screen

     Enter 1 real numbers:

     This is, of course, improper English. Change the program so
     that number is printed if n has the value 1, and numbers is printed
     otherwise.

12   Suppose that you love even integers and detest odd ones.
     Rewrite the *find_maximum* program so that all the variables are
     of type int, and so that only even integers are processed. Of
     course, you will have to explain all of this to the user via
     appropriate printf() statements.

13   What happens when you run the following program on your
     system? If it does not run correctly, change it so that it does.

```
main()
{
    float   sum = 0.0, x;

    for (x = 0.0; x != 9.9; x += 0.1) {    /* test not robust */
        sum += x;
        printf("x = %f   running sum = %f\n", x, sum);
    }
}
```

14 Mixing up the order of expressions that control a for loop is a mistake frequently made by beginners. What is the effect of the following code? An attempt is being made to sum the integers from 1 to 25. First hand simulate what happens, and then write a test program to find out if you were correct.

```
int   i, sum = 0;

for (i = 0; ++i; i < 25)
    printf("i = %d   sum = %d\n", i, sum += i);
```

15 Write an interactive program that asks the user to supply three integers, k, m, and n, with k being greater than 1. Your program should compute the sum of all the integers between m and n which are divisible by k.

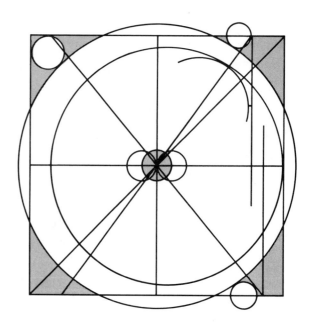

4

FUNCTIONS
AND STRUCTURED
PROGRAMMING

Structured programming is a problem-solving strategy and a programming methodology that includes the following two guidelines:

1   The flow of control in a program should be as simple as possible.
2   The construction of a program should embody top-down design.

Top-down design, also referred to as stepwise refinement, consists of repeatedly decomposing a problem into smaller problems. Eventually, one has a collection of small problems or tasks, each of which can be easily coded.

The function construct in C is used to write code for the bottommost directly solvable problems. These functions are combined into other functions and ultimately used in main() to solve the original problem. The function mechanism is provided in C to perform distinct programming tasks. Some functions, such as printf() and scanf(), are provided by the system. Others can be written by the programmer.

We will illustrate structured programming and top-down design in this chapter, but first we want to describe the function mechanism.

4.1 FUNCTION INVOCATION

A program is made up of one or more functions, with one of these being main(). Program execution always begins with main(). When program control encounters a function name, the function is called, or invoked. This means that program control passes to the function. After the function does its work, program control is passed back to the calling environment, which then continues with its work. As a simple example, consider the following program, which prints a message.

```
main()
{
    prn_message();
}

prn_message()
{
    printf("Message for you:  ");
    printf("Have a nice day!\n");
}
```

Execution begins in main(). When program control encounters prn_message(), the function is invoked and program control is passed to it. After the two printf() statements in prn_message() have been executed, program control passes back to the calling environment, which in this example is main() . Since there is no more work to be done in main(), the program ends.

4.2 FUNCTION DEFINITION

The C code that describes what a function does is called the function definition. It has the following general form:

> *type name(parameter list)*
> *declarations of the parameters*
> {
>   *declarations*
>   *statements*
> }

Everything before the first brace comprises the *header* of the function definition, and everything between the braces comprises the *body* of the function definition. In the function definition for prn_message() above, the parameter list is empty, so there are no declarations of parameters. The body of the function consists of two printf() statements. Since the function does not return a value, the type of the function was not specified.

The *type* of a function depends on the type of the value that the function returns, if any. If no value is returned, or an int value is returned, the type of the function can be omitted. The return mechanism is explained in Section 4.3 below. There we will give an example that shows how the type of the function is used in a function definition. As we shall see in Chapter 6, it is important to properly declare the function type whenever a value having a type other than int is returned. The type void can be used if a function does not return a value.

Parameters are syntactically identifiers, and they can be used within the body of the function. Sometimes the parameters in a function definition are called *formal parameters* to emphasize their role as place holders for actual values that are passed to the function when it is called. Upon function invocation, the value of the argument corresponding to a formal parameter is used within the body of the executing function.

To illustrate these ideas, let us rewrite the above program so that prn_message() has a formal parameter. The parameter will be used to specify how many times the message is printed.

```
main()
{
   int   n;

   printf("Input a small positive integer:  ");
   scanf("%d", &n);
   prn_message(n);
}



prn_message(k)
int   k;
{
   int   i;

   printf("Message for you:\n");
   for (i = 0; i < k; ++i)
      printf("   Have a nice day!\n");
}
```

■ DISSECTION OF THE *message* PROGRAM

```
main()
{
   int   n;

   printf("Input a small positive integer:  ");
   scanf("%d", &n);
```

■ The variable n is declared to be an int. The function printf()
is used to prompt the user for a small integer. The function
scanf() is used to store the value typed in by the user in the
variable n.

```
prn_message(n);
```

■ This statement causes the function `prn_message()` to be called. The value of n is passed as an argument to the function.

```
prn_message(k)
int   k;
```

■ This is the header of the function definition for `prn_message()`. The identifier k is a parameter that is declared to be of type int. One can think of the parameter k as representing the value of the actual argument that is passed to the function when it is called. A call to this function occurred in `main()` in the statement

```
prn_message(n);
```

In `main()` suppose that the value of n is 2. Then when program control passes to `prn_message()`, the variable k will have the value 2. Since no value is returned by the function, we can, if we wish, specify void as the function type. To do this we would have to replace the first line of the function definition by

```
void prn_message(k)
```

The remaining code in the function definition would not be changed.

```
{
   int   i;

   printf("Message for you:\n");
   for (i = 0; i < k; ++i)
      printf("   Have a nice day!\n");
}
```

■ This is the body of the function definition for `prn_message()`. If we think of k as having the value 2, then the message is printed twice. When program control reaches the end of the function, control is passed back to the calling environment.

Note carefully that parameters and local variables used in one function definition have no relation to those in another. For example, if the variable i had been used in main(), it would have had no relationship to the variable i used in prn_message().

4.3 THE return STATEMENT

The return statement is used for two purposes. When a return statement is executed, program control is immediately passed back to the calling environment. In addition, if an expression follows the keyword return, then the value of the expression is returned to the calling environment as well. This value must agree in type with the function definition header. If no type is explicitly declared, the type is implicitly int. A return statement has one of the following two forms:

```
return;
return expression;
```

Some examples are

```
return (3);
return (a + b);
```

Although it is not necessary, it is considered good programming practice to enclose in parentheses the expression being returned so that it is more clearly visible.

As an example let us write a program that computes the minimum of two integers.

```
main()
{
    int   j, k, m;

    printf("Input two integers:  ");
    scanf("%d%d", &j, &k);
    m = min(j, k);
    printf("\n%d is the minimum of %d and %d\n\n", m, j, k);
}


min(x, y)
int   x, y;
{
    if (x < y)
        return (x);
    else
        return (y);
}
```

■ DISSECTION OF THE *minimum* PROGRAM

```
main()
{
    int   j, k, m;

    printf("Input two integers:  ");
    scanf("%d%d", &j, &k);
```

■ The variables j, k, and m are declared to be of type int. The user is asked to input two integers. The function scanf() is used to store the values in j and k.

```
m = min(j, k);
```

■ The values of j and k are passed as arguments to min(). The function min() is expected to return a value, and that value is assigned to m.

```
printf("\n%d is the minimum of %d and %d\n\n", m, j, k);
```

- The values of m, j, and k are printed out.

```
min(x, y)
int    x, y;
```

- This is the header of the function definition for min(). The parameter list consists of x and y. They are declared to be of type int.

```
{
    if (x < y)
        return (x);
    else
        return (y);
}
```

- This is the body of the function definition for min(). If the value of x is less than the value of y, then the value of x is returned to the calling environment; otherwise the value of y is returned.

Even a small function such as min() provides useful structuring to the code. If we now want to write a function max() that computes the maximum of two values, then we can copy min() and modify it slightly. Let us write that function as well.

```
max(x, y)
int    x, y;
{
    if (x > y)
        return (x);
    else
        return (y);
}
```

We have designed min() and max() to work with integer values. Suppose instead that we want these functions to work with values of type double. We will rewrite min() and leave the rewriting of max() as an exercise.

```
double min(x, y)
double   x, y;
{
    if (x < y)
        return (x);
    else
        return (y);
}
```

Since min() now returns a value of type double, we must put this type in the header of the function definition, just before the name of the function. Moreover, other functions that make use of min() must declare it as a function that returns a double. For example,

```
main()
{
    double   min(), max(), x, y, z;
    .  .  .  .  .
```

The declaration in main() tells the compiler that min() and max() are functions that return a value of type double. We will emphasize these ideas again in Chapter 6.

4.4 TOP-DOWN DESIGN

Imagine that we have the problem of analyzing some company data that is represented by a file of integers. As we read each integer we want to print out the count, the integer, the sum of all the integers seen up to this point, the minimum integer seen up to this point, and the maximum integer seen up to this point. In addition to this, suppose that a banner should be printed at the top of the page, and that all the information should be neatly printed in columns under appropriate headings. To construct this program, we will use a top-down design.

We can decompose the problem into

print a banner
print the headings
read and print the data

Each of these subproblems can be coded directly as functions. Then these functions can be used in main() to solve the overall problem. Note that by designing the code this way further functions analyzing the data can be added without affecting the program structure.

```
main()
{
   prn_banner();
   prn_headings();
   read_and_prn_data();
}
```

This illustrates in a very simple way the idea of top-down design. The programmer thinks of the tasks to be performed and codes each task as a function. If a particular task is complicated, then that task in turn can be subdivided into other tasks, each coded as a function. A further benefit of this is that the program as a whole is more readable and self-documenting.

Coding the individual functions is straightforward. The first function contains a single printf() statement.

```
prn_banner()
{
   printf("\n%s%s%s\n",
      "*******************************************\n",
      "*   RUNNING SUMS, MINIMUMS, AND MAXIMUMS   *\n",
      "*******************************************\n");
}
```

The next function writes headings over columns. The format %5s is used to print a string in 5 spaces. The format %12s is used four times to print four strings, each in 12 spaces.

```
prn_headings()
{
    printf("%5s%12s%12s%12s%12s\n\n",
        "Count", "Item", "Sum", "Minimum", "Maximum");
}
```

Most of the work is done in read_and_prn_data(). We will dissect
this program below to show in detail how it works.

```
read_and_prn_data()
{
    int   cnt = 0, item, sum, smallest, biggest;

    if (scanf("%d", &item) == 1) {
        ++cnt;
        sum = smallest = biggest = item;
        printf("%5d%12d%12d%12d%12d\n",
            cnt, item, sum, smallest, biggest);
        while (scanf("%d", &item) == 1) {
            ++cnt;
            sum += item;
            smallest = min(item, smallest);
            biggest = max(item, biggest);
            printf("%5d%12d%12d%12d%12d\n",
                cnt, item, sum, smallest, biggest);
        }
    }
    else
        printf("No data was input - BYE.\n\n");
}
```

Suppose that this program is compiled and that the executable code
is put into the file named *running_sums*. Now suppose that we create a file called *data* containing the following integers:

19   23   -7   29   -11   17

When we run the program *running_sums* with the file *data* as input,
the following is printed on the screen.

```
********************************************
*   RUNNING SUMS, MINIMUMS, AND MAXIMUMS   *
********************************************
```

Count	Item	Sum	Minimum	Maximum
1	19	19	19	19
2	23	42	19	23
3	-7	35	-7	23
4	29	64	-7	29
5	-11	53	-11	29
6	17	70	-11	29

■ DISSECTION OF THE read_and_prn_data() FUNCTION

```
read_and_prn_data()
{
    int   cnt = 0, item, sum, smallest, biggest;
```

■ The header of the function definition is the single line before the brace. The parameter list is empty. In the body of the function definition the local variables cnt, item, sum, smallest, biggest are declared to be of type int. The variable cnt is initialized to zero. The value of the variable item is taken as input. The values of the variables sum, smallest, and biggest are to be computed.

```
if (scanf("%d", &item) == 1) {
    ++cnt;
    sum = smallest = biggest = item;
    printf("%5d%12d%12d%12d%12d\n",
        cnt, item, sum, smallest, biggest);
    .   .   .   .   .
}
else
    printf("No data was input - BYE.\n\n");
```

■ The function scanf() returns the number of successful conversions made. Here scanf() is attempting to read characters from the standard input stream (keyboard), to convert them to a decimal integer, and to store the result at the address of item. If this conversion process is successful, then the expression

```
scanf("%d", &item) == 1
```

will be *true* and the body of the if statement will be executed. That is, cnt will be incremented, and the variables sum, smallest, and biggest will be assigned the value of item, and these values will be printed out in appropriate columns. Notice that the formats in the printf() statement are similar to those found in prn_headings(). If scanf() is unsuccessful in its conversion attempt, then the else part of the if-else statement will be executed. The conversion process can fail for two reasons. One, there might be an inappropriate character, for example a letter, say x, before any digits occur in the input stream. Since scanf() cannot convert the character x to a decimal integer, the value returned by scanf() would be 0. Second, there may be no characters at all in the input stream, or only white space characters. Since scanf() skips white space, it would come to the end of the file. When the end-of-file mark is read, then scanf() returns the value EOF. This value, although system dependent, is typically −1.

```
while (scanf("%d", &item) == 1) {
   ++cnt;
   sum += item;
   smallest = min(item, smallest);
   biggest = max(item, biggest);
   printf("%5d%12d%12d%12d%12d\n",
       cnt, item, sum, smallest, biggest);
}
```

■ After the first integer has been obtained from the input stream, we use scanf() in this while loop to find others. Each time a successful conversion is made by scanf(), the body of this while loop is executed. This causes cnt to be incremented by 1, sum to be incremented by the current value of item, smallest to be assigned the minimum of the current values of item and smallest, biggest to be assigned the maximum of the current values of item and biggest, and all these values to be printed in appropriate columns. Eventually, scanf() will encounter an inappropriate character in the input stream or encounter the end-of-file mark. In either case scanf() will return a value different from 1, causing program control to exit from the while loop.

4.5 AN EXAMPLE: RANDOM NUMBERS

Random numbers have lots of uses on computers. One use is to serve as data to test code. We will generate some random numbers, find the minimum and maximum values, and display everything neatly on the screen.

A random number generator is a function that returns integers which appear to be randomly distributed in some interval 0 to n, where n is system dependent. The function rand() in the standard library is provided by the C system to do this. Let us begin to write a program that displays some random numbers generated by rand().

```
main()
{
   int   n;

   printf("Some random numbers are to be printed.\n");
   printf("How many would you like to see?  ");
   scanf("%d", &n);
   prn_random_numbers(n);
}
```

The user is asked how many random numbers are wanted. The function scanf() is used to convert the characters typed at the keyboard to a decimal integer and to store the value at the address of n. The value of n is passed as an argument to the function prn_random_numbers().

```
prn_random_numbers(k)      /* print k random numbers */
int   k;
{
   int   i, r, smallest, biggest;

   r = smallest = biggest = rand();
   printf("\n%12d", r);
   for (i = 1; i < k; ++i) {
      if (i % 5 == 0)
         printf("\n");
      r = rand();
      smallest = min(r, smallest);
      biggest = max(r, biggest);
      printf("%12d", r);
   }
   printf("\n\n%d random numbers printed.\n", k);
   printf("Minimum:%12d\nMaximum:%12d\n\n", smallest, biggest);
}
```

We want to dissect this function definition, but before we do so, let us show what the output of the program looks like. Suppose we run this program and input 19 when prompted. Here is what appears on the screen.

```
Some random numbers are to be printed.
How many would you like to see?  19

    1103527590    377401575    662824084   1147902781   2035015474
     368800899   1508029952    486256185   1062517886    267834847
     180171308    836760821    595337866    790425851   2111915288
    1149758321   1644289366   1388290519   1647418052

19 random numbers printed.
Minimum:    180171308
Maximum:   2111915288
```

■ DISSECTION OF THE prn_random_numbers()
FUNCTION

```
prn_random_numbers(k)
int   k;
{
    int   i, r, smallest, biggest;
```

■ The first two lines are the header of the function definition.
The variable k is a parameter. It is declared to be an int. The
local variables i, r, smallest, and biggest are all declared to be
of type int.

```
r = smallest = biggest = rand();
printf("\n%12d", r);
```

■ The function rand() from the standard library is used to generate a random number. That number is assigned to the variables r, smallest, and biggest. The function printf() is used to
print the value of r in 12 spaces as a decimal integer.

```
for (i = 1; i < k; ++i) {
  if (i % 5 == 0)
    printf("\n");
  r = rand();
      .  .  .  .  .
}
```

■ This for loop is used to print the remaining random numbers.
Because one random number has already been printed, the
variable i at the top of the loop is initialized to 1 rather than
0. Whenever i is divisible by 5 (the values 5, 10, 15, . . .),
the expression

```
i % 5 == 0
```

controlling the if statement is *true*, causing a newline to be printed. The effect of this is to print at most five random numbers on each line.

4.6 AN EXAMPLE: THE GAME OF HEADS OR TAILS

To provide a further example of the use of functions, we wish to implement a computer game that simulates the children's game of calling heads or tails. In this game the first child tosses a coin and the second child calls heads or tails. If the second child guesses the outcome correctly, then he wins; otherwise he loses. The game can be played repeatedly with a count kept of the number of wins and losses.

The machine will use rand() to simulate tossing a coin. If the integer returned by rand() is even, it will be considered heads, and if it is odd, it will be considered tails. The program begins by printing instructions to the player. These instructions contain some of the design considerations for the program. After each toss of the coin, a report of the outcome is printed. At the conclusion of the program a final report is printed.

Top-down design reveals the need for a number of different functions. Each function is short, making the overall program easy to read.

```
main()
{
    int   n;

    prn_instructions();
    printf("How many times do you want to play?  ");
    scanf("%d", &n);
    play(n);
}
```

```
prn_instructions()
{
   printf("\n%s\n%s\n%s\n%s\n%s\n\n",
      "This is the game of calling heads or tails.",
      "I will flip a coin; you call it.",
      "If you call it correctly, you win; otherwise, I win.",
      "To call heads, type 0; to call tails, type 1.",
      "As I toss my coin I will tell you to \"call it\".");
}



play(n)      /* machine does the tossing, user does the calling */
int   n;
{
   int   coin, i, lose = 0, win = 0;

   for (i = 0; i < n; ++i) {
      printf("Call it:  ");
      coin = toss();
      if (get_call_from_user() == coin) {
         ++win;
         report_a_win(coin);
      }
      else {
         ++lose;
         report_a_loss(coin);
      }
   }
   prn_final_report(win, lose, n);
}



toss()      /* return 0 for heads and 1 for tails */
{
   return (rand() % 2);
}
```

```
get_call_from_user()      /* return 0 for heads and 1 for tails */
{
   int   guess;

   scanf("%d", &guess);
   while (guess != 0 && guess != 1) {
      printf("ERROR: type 0 for heads and 1 for tails\n");
      scanf("%d", &guess);
   }
   return (guess);
}



report_a_win(coin)
int   coin;
{
   if (coin == 0)
      printf("I have heads, you win.\n");
   else
      printf("I have tails, you win.\n");
}



report_a_loss(coin)
int   coin;
{
   if (coin == 0)
      printf("I have heads, you lose.\n");
   else
      printf("I have tails, you lose.\n");
}
```

```
prn_final_report(win, lose, n)
int   win, lose, n;
{
    printf("\n%s\n%s%3d\n%s%3d\n%s%3d\n\n",
        "Final report:",
        "   Number of games that you won:   ", win,
        "   Number of games that you lost:  ", lose,
        "   Total number of games:          ", n);
}
```

There are only a few new ideas in this program. In the printf()
statement in prn_instructions() the format %s is being used to print
strings. Notice that in the last string \" is used to represent the
double quote character within the string. This construct will be
explained in the next chapter. The value of the expression

```
rand() % 2
```

is returned by toss(). Recall that a modulus expression of the form
a % b has the value of the remainder after b is divided into a. For
example, 4 % 2 has the value 0 and 5 % 2 has the value 1. Thus
rand() % 2 has the value 0 if the integer returned by rand() is even,
and it has the value 1 if the integer returned by rand() is odd.

The user of this program has to type 0 for heads and 1 for tails.
A better strategy would be to type h for heads and t for tails. One
way to do this is to use scanf() with the format %c to read characters. A better strategy, however, is to use the character processing
tools presented in the next chapter. We leave this change to an
exercise at the end of that chapter.

4.7 INVOCATION AND CALL BY VALUE

Functions are invoked by writing their name and an appropriate list
of arguments within parentheses. Typically these arguments will
match in number and type the parameters in the parameter list in
the function definition. All arguments are passed "call by value."
This means that each argument is evaluated and its value is used
locally in place of the corresponding formal parameter. Thus if a

variable is passed to a function, the stored value of that variable in the calling environment will not be changed.

Here is a simple example that clearly illustrates the concept of "call by value."

```
main()
{
    int    n = 3, sum;

    printf("%d\n", n);          /* 3 is printed */
    sum = compute_sum(n);
    printf("%d\n", n);          /* 3 is printed */
    printf("%d\n", sum);        /* 6 is printed */
}


compute_sum(n)        /* sum the integers from 1 to n */
int    n;
{
    int    sum = 0;

    for ( ; n > 0; --n)
        sum += n;
    printf("%d\n", n);          /* 0 is printed */
    return (sum);
}
```

Even though n is passed to compute_sum() and the value of n in the body of that function is changed, the value of n in the calling environment remains unchanged. It is the *value* of n that is being passed, not n itself.

The "call by value" mechanism is in contrast to "call by reference." In Chapter 8, we will explain how to accomplish the effect of "call by reference." It is a way to pass addresses (references) of variables to a function that then allows the body of the function to make changes to the values of variables in the calling environment.

4.8 STYLE

Breaking a problem into small subproblems that are then coded as functions is critical to good programming style. So as to be easily readable, a function should be at most a page of code. Where it is not transparent from a choice of identifier names, functions should be commented as to their purpose. Furthermore, each parameter should be an identifier that clearly indicates its own purpose, or else a comment as to its purpose is needed.

A common style for the placement of the declarations of parameters in a function definition is to write them beginning in column 1. This is the style that we have been using. Other styles are possible.

The order in which functions occur in a file is not important. It is usually a matter of taste whether one writes main() followed by the function definitions, or vice versa. If one is doing a top-down development, however, it is natural to start with main(). Of course, for large projects a good deal of program organization might be done on paper first, so even in a top-down development effort the coding of the functions can occur first.

It is considered good style to have only a few return statements in a given function. If there are many return statements, then the logic of the code may be difficult to follow.

The names read, write, and print are commonly used as parts of names for systems functions. For example, printf() makes use of the name print. To clearly distinguish our names from systems names we often use prn and wrt as parts of names. Even though we could write a function named print(), it would be confusing to do so. The name print is visually too close to printf.

Whenever something is being counted inside a loop, it is a good idea to count it as soon as it is possible to do so. This rule is followed in the incrementing of cnt in the function definition for read_and_prn_data().

4.9 COMMON PROGRAMMING ERRORS

Passing incorrect arguments to a function is a most common error. It is the programmer's responsibility to see that all arguments are of the proper type and value. Consider the following example.

```
f(n)
int  n;
{
    return (3 * n + 1);
}

main()
{
    printf("%d\n", f(2));       /*    7 is printed */
    printf("%d\n", f(2.0));     /* 49921 is printed */
}
```

The second call to the function f() causes an unexpected value to be printed. Instead of an integer value, a floating value has been passed to f(). The floating value 2.0 is not converted to an integer value, but instead has a machine-dependent interpretation giving an unexpected result. On our machine the compiler does not complain about this program, but *lint* does.

Another common error is to mistakenly assume that a function is changing the value of a variable. Since the function mechanism in C is strictly "call by value," it is not possible to change the value of a variable in the calling environment by invoking a function with the variable as an argument. If f() is a function and v is a variable, then the statement

```
    f(v);
```

cannot change the value of v in the calling environment. However, in contrast to this, if f() returns a value, then the statement

```
    v = f(v);
```

can change the value of v.

4.10 OPERATING SYSTEM CONSIDERATIONS

The function rand() in the standard library must be tested carefully to see if its use is appropriate in a particular application. In some cases it may have repetitive patterns that undermine a particular use. In that case it may be necessary to write your own random number generator having the required properties. Newer versions of UNIX provide an expanded and improved standard library of C functions. One of the new functions in it is random(), a much improved random number generator. This function, however, returns a long rather than an int.

A random number generator typically returns integers in the range from 0 to *n*, where *n* is system dependent. Usually, *n* is the largest int available on the system. On our system the number is 2147483647, approximately 2 billion. On small systems the number is typically 32767, approximately 32 thousand.

4.11 SUMMARY

1   Structured programming is a problem-solving strategy and a programming methodology that strives for simple flow of control and uses top-down design.

2   Top-down design, also referred to as stepwise refinement, consists of repeatedly decomposing a problem into smaller problems.

3   A long program should be written as a collection of functions, each one being no longer than, say, a page in length. Each function should capture some small task of the overall problem.

4   A programmer creates a function by writing a function definition. A function definition consists of a header and a body. If the parameter list in the header is nonempty, then the declarations for the parameters occur before the left brace that marks the beginning of the body. The body of a function definition consists of declarations and statements. If a function returns a value having a type other than int, then the type must be specified in the header of the function definition just before the function name.

5   In the body of a function the compiler recognizes a name followed by parentheses, such as prn_message() or min(x, y), as a call to a function.

6   The execution of a program always begins with main(). When a function is called, program control is passed to the function. When a return statement is executed, or the end of the function is reached, control is passed back to the calling environment. If a return statement contains an expression, the value of the expression is passed back to the calling environment as well.

4.12   EXERCISES

1   Rewrite the *message* program so that the output looks like

```
Message for you:  Have a nice day!
                  Have a nice day!
                  Have a nice day!

                  .   .   .   .   .
```

2   Write a function square() that will take an integer and return its square. Write another function cube() that will take an integer and return its cube.

3   Using the functions written in the previous exercise, write a program to produce a neatly printed table containing a list of integers, their squares, and their cubes. The integers should run from 1 to 25.

4   The program *prn_random_numbers* does not work right if the user types in 0 when asked for the number of random numbers desired. Correct the program so that it works correctly for this case too.

5   Consider the for loop in the function prn_random_numbers() that begins

```
for (i = 1; i < k; ++i) {
  if (i % 5 == 0)
    printf("\n");
        .   .   .   .   .
```

Suppose that we rewrite the first line as

```
for (i = 2; i <= k; ++i) {
```

Will the same number of random numbers be printed? This modification causes the format of the output to change. Try it and see. Make a further program modification in the body of the for loop to get the output formatted correctly.

6   Test the *heads_or_tails* program and see if you can easily guess a rule that shows you how to win constantly. Modify the function toss() to return a value between 0 and 99. Then change the program so that numbers less than 50 are considered heads and numbers greater than or equal to 50 are considered tails. Is it still easy to win?

7   If the standard library function random() is available to you, modify the *heads_or_tails* program so that random() is used instead of rand(). Does the new version of the program act any differently than the old version? (It should be more difficult for you to win.) *Hint:* You should remember to use the declaration

```
long    random();
```

in any function that calls random().

8   Run the program that prints random numbers. Notice that each time the program is executed, the same sequence of numbers is printed. The function srand() in the standard library can be used to supply a seed to the random number generator, causing a different sequence of numbers to be printed. The code

```
int    seed = 13579;

srand(seed);
rand();
```

shows how srand() might be used. Different values for seed will result in the random number generator starting in a different place. Modify the program that prints random numbers so that the user supplies a seed first.

9   Investigate how to write your own random number generator.

10 In Section 4.3 we wrote an interactive program that computes the minimum of two integers. Rewrite the code to work with type double.

11 Modify the *heads_or_tails* program given in Section 4.6 by explicitly declaring the type of each function. In each of the function definitions put either int or void in the header just before the function name, whichever is appropriate. If, after having done this, you run the code through *lint*, you will see that *lint* complains. Now you must add appropriate function declarations to some of the bodies of the function definitions. Here is how the beginning of your code should look:

```
void main()
{
   int    n;
   void   prn_instructions(), play();

   prn_instructions();
   .   .   .   .   .
}

void prn_instructions()
{
   .   .   .   .   .
```

By default, any function that is not declared is assumed to return a value of type int. The purpose of this exercise is to declare everything. After you have done so, *lint* should not complain. Compile and execute your program to see that it

behaves just as before. (See Chapter 6 for further explanation
concerning function declarations.)

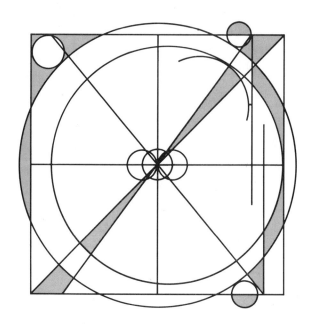

5

CHARACTER
PROCESSING

In this chapter we will introduce some of the basic ideas involved in character processing. We want to discuss how characters are stored and manipulated in a machine, how characters can be treated as small integers, and how use is made of certain standard header files. To illustrate the ideas, we present simple character-processing programs that accomplish useful work. These example programs make use of the character input/output functions getchar() and putchar(). For anyone trying to master a new language, getting data into and out of a machine is a skill that has to be developed early.

A number of important concepts are covered in this chapter. The use of the symbolic constant EOF is explained. When getchar() detects an end-of-file mark, it returns the value EOF, which makes it possible for the programmer to detect when the end of a file has been reached. The use of the header file *ctype.h* is explained. This file provides the programmer with a set of macros that can be used to process character data. To the programmer, these macros are used in the same manner as functions are used. The use of system header files such as *ctype.h* allows the programmer to write portable code. The programs, such as *capitalize*, presented in this chapter are quite simple, but we are able to use them to explain the essential ideas of character processing.

5.1 THE DATA TYPE char

The type char is one of the fundamental types of the C language. Constants and variables of this type are used to represent characters. Each character is stored in a machine in 1 byte. We will assume throughout that a byte is composed of 8 bits, which is the case for most machines. A byte composed of 8 bits is capable of storing $2^8 = 256$ distinct values.

When a character is stored in a byte, the contents of that byte can be thought of as either a character or as a small integer. Although 256 distinct values can be stored in a byte, only a subset of these values represent actual printing characters. These include the lowercase letters, uppercase letters, digits, punctuation, and special characters such as +, *, and %. The character set also includes the white space characters blank, tab, and newline. Examples of nonprinting characters are newline and bell. We will illustrate the use of the bell in this chapter.

A constant of type char is written between single quotes as in 'a' or 'b' or 'c'. A typical declaration for a variable of type char is

```
char    c;
```

Character variables can be initialized as in the example

```
char    c1 = 'A', c2 = 'B', c3 = '*';
```

A character is stored in memory in one byte according to a specific encoding. Most machines use either ASCII or EBCDIC character codes, and in the discussion that follows we will be using the ASCII code. For any other code the numbers will be different, but the ideas are analogous. A table of ASCII codes appears in an appendix. A character is considered to have the integer value corresponding to its ASCII encoding. Some examples are given in the following table.

Some constants of type char and their corresponding integer values

Constants of type char	:	'a'	'b'	'c'	. . .	'z'
Corresponding integer values:		97	98	99	. . .	112
	:	'A'	'B'	'C'	. . .	'Z'
	:	65	66	67	. . .	90
	:	'0'	'1'	'2'	. . .	'9'
	:	48	49	50	. . .	57
	:	'&'	'*'	'+'		
	:	38	42	43		

Observe that there is no particular relationship between the value of the character constant representing a digit and the digit's intrinsic integer value. That is, the value of '7' is *not* 7. The fact that the values of 'a', 'b', 'c', and so forth, occur in order is an important property. It makes convenient the sorting of characters, words, lines, etc., into lexicographical order.

In the functions printf() and scanf() a %c is used to designate the character format. For example, the statement

```
printf("%c", 'a');    /* a is printed */
```

causes the character constant 'a' to be printed in the format of a character. Similarly,

```
printf("%c%c%c", 'A', 'B', 'C');    /* ABC is printed */
```

causes ABC to be printed.

Constants and variables of type char can be treated as small integers. The statement

```
printf("%d", 'a');    /* 97 is printed */
```

causes the value of the character constant 'a' to be printed in the format of a decimal integer. Thus 97 is printed. On the other hand the statement

```
printf("%c", 97);    /* a is printed */
```

causes the value of the decimal integer constant 97 to be printed in the format of a character. Thus a is printed.

Some nonprinting and hard-to-print characters require an escape sequence. For example, the newline character is written as '\n' in a program, and even though it is being described by the two characters \ and n, it represents a single ASCII character. The backslash character \ is also called the *escape character* and is used to escape the usual meaning of the character that follows it. The following table contains some nonprinting and hard-to-print characters.

Name of Character	Written in C	Integer Value
null	\0	0
backspace	\b	8
tab	\t	9
newline	\n	10
formfeed	\f	12
carriage return	\r	13
double quote	\"	34
single quote	\'	39
backslash	\\	92

The character " has to be escaped if it is used as a character in a string. An example is

```
printf("\"ABC\"");    /* "ABC" is printed */
```

However, inside single quotes one would write '"', although '\"' is also accepted. In general, escaping an ordinary character has no effect. Inside a string the single quote is just an ordinary character.

```
printf("'ABC'");    /* 'ABC' is printed */
```

Another way to write a constant of type char is by means of a one-, two-, or three-octal-digit escape sequence as in '\007'. This character is the *bell* and it also can be written as '\07' or '\7', but it cannot be written as '7'.

5.2 THE USE OF getchar() AND putchar()

The system provides getchar() and putchar() for the input and output of characters. To read a character from the keyboard getchar() is used. To write a character to the screen putchar() is used. For example, a program that prints the line

```
she sells sea shells by the seashore
```

on the screen can be written as follows:

```
main()
{
    putchar('s');
    putchar('h');
    putchar('e');
    putchar(' ');
        .   .   .   .   .
    putchar('e');
    putchar('\n');
}
```

Of course, this is a tedious way to accomplish the task; the use of a printf() statement would be much easier.

In the next program getchar() gets a character from the input stream (keyboard) and assigns it to the variable c. Then putchar() is used to print the character twice on the screen.

```
main()
{
    char    c;

    while (1) {
        c = getchar();
        putchar(c);
        putchar(c);
    }
}
```

Note that the variable c is of type char. In the next version of this program we will change this. Also, because 1 is nonzero, as an expression it is always *true*. Thus the construct

```
while (1) {
    .  .  .  .  .
}
```

is an infinite loop. The only way to stop this program is with an interrupt, which on our system is effected by typing a control-c. However, since an interrupt is system dependent, you may have to type something different to effect it. The "delete" or "rubout" key is sometimes used to effect an interrupt.

For a number of reasons the above program is not really acceptable. Let us rewrite the program and call the new version *double_out*.

```
#include   <stdio.h>

main()
{
    int   c;

    while ((c = getchar()) != EOF) {
        putchar(c);
        putchar(c);
    }
}
```

■ DISSECTION OF THE *double_out* PROGRAM

```
#include   <stdio.h>
```

■ Lines that begin with a # in column one are control lines for the preprocessor. A control line of the form

```
#include   <file_name>
```

causes the preprocessor to include a copy of the named file into the source code at that point before passing the code to the compiler. The angle brackets around stdio.h tell the system to look for this file in the "usual place." The location of this place is system dependent. The file *stdio.h* is a standard header file supplied with the C system, and this file is typically included in functions that make use of certain standard input/output constructs. One line of this header file is

```
#define   EOF   (-1)
```

The identifier EOF is mnemonic for "end-of-file." What is actually used to signal an end-of-file mark is system dependent. Although the int value −1 is often used, different systems can have different values. By including the file *stdio.h* and using the symbolic constant EOF, we have made the program portable. This means that the source file can be moved to a different system and run with no changes.

```
int   c;
```

■ The variable c has been declared in the program as an int rather than a char. Whatever is used to signal the end of a file, it cannot be a value that represents a character. Since c is an int, it can hold all possible character values as well as the special value EOF. Although one usually thinks of a char as a very short int type, one can also think of an int as a very long char type.

```
while ((c = getchar()) != EOF) {
```

■ The expression

```
(c = getchar()) != EOF
```

is composed of two parts. The subexpression

```
c = getchar()
```

gets a value from the keyboard and assigns it to the variable c, and the value of the subexpression takes on that value as well. The symbols != represent the "not equal" operator. As long as the value of the subexpression c = getchar() is not equal to EOF, the body of the while loop is executed. Typically, an EOF value can be entered at the keyboard by typing a control-d immediately following a carriage return. This is system dependent. The parentheses around the subexpression c = getchar() are necessary. Suppose that we had typed

```
c = getchar() != EOF
```

Because of operator precedence this is equivalent to

```
c = (getchar() != EOF)
```

This has the effect of getting a character from the input stream, testing to see if it is not equal to EOF, and assigning the result of the test (either 0 or 1) to the variable c. See exercise 10.

5.3 AN EXAMPLE: CAPITALIZE

Characters have an underlying integer-valued representation that on most C systems is the numeric value of their 7-bit ASCII representation. For example, the constant char 'a' has value 97. If one thinks of characters as small integers, then arithmetic on characters makes sense. Since the values of the letters in both the lowercase and uppercase alphabet occur in order, the expression 'a' + 1 has the value 'b', the expression 'b' + 1 has the value 'c', and the expression 'Z' - 'A' has the value 25. Moreover, 'A' - 'a' has a value that is the same as 'B' - 'b', which is the same as 'C' - 'c', etc. Because of this, if the variable c has the value of a lowercase letter, then the expression c + 'A' - 'a' has the value of the corresponding uppercase letter. These ideas are incorporated into the next program, which capitalizes all lowercase letters and doubles the newline characters.

```
/* capitalize lowercase letters and double space */

#include    <stdio.h>

main()
{
    int    c;

    while ((c = getchar()) != EOF)
        if ('a' <= c && c <= 'z')
            putchar(c + 'A' - 'a');
        else if (c == '\n') {
            putchar('\n');
            putchar('\n');
        }
        else
            putchar(c);
}
```

■ DISSECTION OF THE *capitalize* PROGRAM

```
while ((c = getchar()) != EOF)
```

■ The function getchar() gets a character and assigns it to the variable c. As long as the value of c is not EOF, the body of the while loop is executed.

```
if ('a' <= c && c <= 'z')
    putchar(c + 'A' - 'a');
```

■ Because of operator precedence the expressions

   'a' <= c && c <= 'z'   and   ('a' <= c) && (c <= 'z')

are equivalent. The symbols <= represent the operator "less than or equal." The subexpression 'a' <= c tests to see if the value 'a' is less than or equal to the value of c. The subexpression c <= 'z' tests to see if the value of c is less than or equal to the value `'z'`. The symbols `&&` represent the operator "logical and." If both subexpressions are *true*, then the expression

```
'a' <= c && c <= 'z'
```

is *true*; otherwise it is *false*. Thus the expression is *true* if and only if c is a lowercase letter. If the expression is *true*, then the statement

```
putchar(c + 'A' - 'a');
```

is executed, causing the corresponding uppercase letter to be printed.

```
else if (c == '\n') {
   putchar('\n');
   putchar('\n');
}
```

■ The symbols `==` represent the operator "equals." If c is not a lowercase letter, a test is made to see if it is equal to a newline character. If it is, two newline characters are printed.

```
else
   putchar(c);
```

■ If the value of c is not a lowercase letter and it is not a newline character, then the character corresponding to the value c is printed. An else is always associated with the immediately preceding if.

Although the *capitalize* program is portable to any ASCII machine, it will not work as expected on an EBCDIC machine. The reason for this is that the uppercase letters are not all contiguous in the EBCDIC code. Here is a version of the *capitalize* program that can be expected to work on all machines.

```
/* capitalize lowercase letters and double space */

#include    <stdio.h>
#include    <ctype.h>

main()
{
    int   c;

    while ((c = getchar()) != EOF)
        if (islower(c))
            putchar(toupper(c));
        else if (c == '\n') {
            putchar('\n');
            putchar('\n');
        }
        else
            putchar(c);
}
```

■ DISSECTION OF THE PORTABLE *capitalize* PROGRAM

```
#include    <stdio.h>
#include    <ctype.h>
```

■ The file *ctype.h*, along with *stdio.h*, is a standard header file provided with the C system. This file contains macros, which can be used when processing characters. A macro is code that gets expanded by the preprocessor. In Chapter 11 we will explain in detail how macros work. For the purposes of this chapter we will treat the macros in *ctype.h* just as if they were functions. Although there are technical differences between a macro and a function, they both are used in a similar fashion. The macros islower() and toupper(), which are used in this program, are found in *ctype.h*.

```
while ((c = getchar()) != EOF)
  if (islower(c))
    putchar(toupper(c));
```

■ A character is obtained from the input stream and assigned to
c. As long as the value of c is not EOF, the body of the while
loop is executed. The macro islower() is defined in *ctype.h*. If
c is a lowercase letter, then islower(c) has value 1, otherwise
value 0. The macro toupper() is defined in *ctype.h*. If c is a
lowercase letter, then toupper(c) has the value of the corresponding uppercase letter. Therefore, the if statement has the
effect of testing to see whether or not c has the value of a lowercase letter. If it does, then the corresponding uppercase letter is written on the screen. Note carefully that the stored
value of c itself is not changed by invoking isupper(c) or
toupper(c).

A novice C programmer need not know exactly how the macros
in *ctype.h* are implemented. Along with printf() and scanf(), they
can be treated as a system-supplied resource. The important point
to remember is that by using these macros one is writing portable
code that will run in any environment, not just an ASCII environment.

Why learn about a construct such as c + 'A' - 'a' at all? Well, a
lot of C code is written just for an ASCII environment, and even
though the construct is not considered good programming practice,
one commonly sees it. Since a programmer must learn to read code
as well as write it, this particular construct should be mastered. In
order to avoid nonportable code, it is good programming practice to
use the macros in *ctype.h* wherever appropriate.

5.4 THE MACROS IN *ctype.h*

The system provides a standard header file *ctype.h*, which contains a
set of macros that are used to test or convert characters. They are
made accessible by the preprocessor control line

```
#include    <ctype.h>
```

Those macros that only test a character return an `int` value that is nonzero (*true*) or 0 (*false*).

Macro	Nonzero (true) is returned if:
isalpha(c)	c is a letter
isupper(c)	c is an uppercase letter
islower(c)	c is a lowercase letter
isdigit(c)	c is a digit
isxdigit(c)	c is a hexadecimal digit
isspace(c)	c is a white space character
isalnum(c)	c is a letter or digit
ispunct(c)	c is a punctuation character
isprint(c)	c is a printable character
iscntrl(c)	c is a control character
isascii(c)	c is an ASCII code

Other macros provide for the appropriate conversion of a character value. Note carefully that these macros do not change the value of c stored in memory.

Macro	Effect
toupper(c)	changes c from lowercase to uppercase
tolower(c)	changes c from uppercase to lowercase
toascii(c)	changes c to ASCII code

5.5 AN EXAMPLE: REPEATING CHARACTERS

In the program *double_out*, which we presented above, we showed how every character read in can be printed out twice. Here we want to generalize that simple idea by writing a function that prints out a given character *n* times.

```
repeat(c, n)
char    c;
int     n;
{
    int    i;

    for (i = 0; i < n; ++i)
        putchar(c);
}
```

Notice that the variable `c` is declared as a `char`, not an `int`. Since a test for `EOF` is not made in this function, there is no need to declare `c` an `int`. Suppose that we invoke the function with the statement

```
repeat('B' - 1, 2 + 3);
```

The arguments of this function call are `'B' - 1` and `2 + 3`. The respective values of these arguments are passed and associated with the formal parameters of the function. The effect of the function call is to print the letter A five times. Here is a `main()` function that can be used to test `repeat()`.

```
main()
{
    int     i;
    char    bell = '\007', c = 'A';

    repeat('B' - 1, 2 + 3);
    putchar(' ');
    for (i = 0; i < 10; ++i) {
        repeat(c + i, i);
        putchar(' ');
    }
    repeat(bell, 100);
    putchar('\n');
}
```

When we compile the program and run it, here is what we see on the screen.

AAAAA B CC DDD EEEE FFFFF GGGGGG HHHHHHH IIIIIIII JJJJJJJJ

The function repeat() can be used to draw simple figures on the screen. A diamond is suggested in the exercises.

5.6 AN EXAMPLE: COUNTING WORDS

Suppose that we want to count the number of words being input at the keyboard. Again, top-down design leads us to break up the problem into small pieces. To do this we need to know the definition of a word, and we need to know when to end our task. For our purposes we will assume that words are separated by white space. Thus any word is a contiguous string of nonwhite space characters. As usual, we will end the processing of characters when we encounter the end-of-file sentinel. The heart of our program is a function that detects a word. We will explain this function in some detail.

```
#include   <stdio.h>
#include   <ctype.h>

main()
{
   int   word_cnt = 0;

   while (found_next_word() == 1)
      ++word_cnt;
   printf("Number of words = %d\n\n", word_cnt);
}
```

```
found_next_word()
{
    int    c;

    while (isspace(c = getchar()))
        ;      /* skip white space */
    if (c != EOF) {      /* found a word */
        while ((c = getchar()) != EOF && !isspace(c))
            ;       /* skip everything except EOF and white space */
        return (1);
    }
    return (0);
}
```

■ DISSECTION OF THE *word_cnt* PROGRAM

```
int    word_cnt = 0;
```

■ The int variable word_cnt is initialized to zero.

```
while (found_next_word() == 1)
    ++word_cnt;
```

■ As long as the function found_next_word() returns the value 1, the body of the while loop is executed, causing word_cnt to be indexed.

```
printf("Number of words = %d\n\n", word_cnt);
```

■ Just before exiting the program, we print out the number of words found.

```
found_next_word()
{
    int    c;
```

■ This is the beginning of the function definition for found_next_word(). The function has no parameters in its parameter list. In the body of the function the int variable c is declared. Although we are going to use c to take on character values, we declare c as an int, not a char. Eventually c will hold the special value EOF and on some systems that value may not fit in a char.

```
while (isspace(c = getchar()))
    ;      /* skip white space */
```

■ A character is gotten from the input stream and assigned to c. The value of the subexpression c = getchar() takes on this value as well. As long as this value is a white space character, the body of the while loop is executed. However, the body of the while loop is just the empty statement. Thus the effect of the while loop is to skip white space. Notice that the empty statement is clearly displayed on a line by itself. Good programming practice requires this. If we had written

```
    while (isspace(c = getchar()));
```

the visibility of the empty statement would be reduced.

```
if (c != EOF) {      /* found a word */
    while ((c = getchar()) != EOF && !isspace(c))
        ;      /* skip everything except EOF and white space */
    return (1);
}
```

■ After white space has been skipped, the value of c is either EOF or the first "letter" of a word. If the value of c is not EOF, then a word has been found. The test expression in the while loop consists of three parts. First a character is gotten from the input stream and assigned to c, and the subexpression c = getchar() takes on the value of c as well. A test is then made to see if that value is EOF. If it is, then the body of the while loop is not executed and control passes to the next statement. If the value is not EOF, then a test is made to see if the value is a white space character. If it is, then the body of the while loop is not executed and control passes to the next statement. If the value is not a white space character, then the body of the while loop is executed. However, the body is just the empty statement. Thus the effect of this while loop is to skip everything except EOF and white space characters. That is, the word that has been found has now been skipped.

```
return (1);
```

- After a word has been found and skipped, the value 1 is returned.

```
return (0);
```

- If a word was not found, then the value 0 is returned.

5.7 STYLE

Simple character variables are often given the identifier c, or identifiers starting with c such as c1, c2, and c3. Functions that do character manipulation frequently have char as part of their name, or the name ends with the letter c. Examples are getchar() and putchar(), and as we shall see in Chapter 14, getc() and putc(). The choice of identifiers for the macros in *ctype.h* is instructive. Those macros that answer a true/false question, such as isalpha() and isupper(), all have names that start with is. Those macros that have the sense of changing a character value, such as toupper(), all have names that start with to. Proper choice of identifier names is crucial to readability and documentation.

For character-processing tasks we can use either getchar() or scanf() to read characters. Similarly, we can use either putchar() or printf() to write characters. In many instances whichever one gets used is a matter of personal taste. However, if there is a great deal of character processing being done, then the use of getchar() and putchar() along with the standard header file *stdio.h* can result in faster code. This is because getchar() and putchar() may be implemented as *macros* in *stdio.h*. As we shall see in Chapter 11, macros are a code substitution mechanism that can be used to avoid a function call.

One difference between putchar() and printf() is that putchar() returns the value of the character gotten from the input stream as an int, whereas printf() returns no useful value. Sometimes this dictates the use of putchar().

A common C programming idiom is to perform both an assignment and a test in the expression that controls a while or for loop. Although this is a general practice, one most often sees it in code used to process characters. As an example, the code

```
while ((c = getchar()) != EOF) {
     .   .   .   .   .
}
```

uses this idiom. In contrast to this, we could write

```
c = getchar();
while (c != EOF) {
     .   .   .   .   .
    c = getchar();
}
```

but now, if the body of the loop is long, the last statement, which affects the control of the loop, is a long way from the test expression. On the other hand, a construct such as

```
while (isspace(c = getchar()))
    ;     /* skip white space */
```

can just as well be written

```
c = getchar();
while (isspace(c))
    c = getchar();
```

Here the body of the loop is very short. So short, in fact, that if we put the control all at the top, the body of the loop is empty. Which form is used is largely a matter of taste.

5.8 COMMON PROGRAMMING ERRORS

We have already explained that if a program uses a variable to read in characters and to test for the value EOF, then that variable should be an int, not a char. This is a portability consideration, and *lint* will give a warning if a char is used instead of an int.

Suppose that we have text files that are double- or triple-spaced, and our task is to copy the files, except that multiple occurrences of newlines are to be reduced to a single newline. For example, we want to be able to change a double-spaced file into one that is only single-spaced. Here is a program that will do this.

```
/* copy stdin to stdout, except single space only */

#include   <stdio.h>

main()
{
    int  c, last_c = '\0';

    while ((c = getchar()) != EOF) {
        if (c == '\n') {
            if (last_c != '\n')
                putchar('\n');
        }
        else
            putchar(c);
        last_c = c;
    }
}
```

At the start of this program the variable last_c is initialized to the null character, but thereafter, that variable holds the last character gotten from the input stream (keyboard). There is nothing special about the use of the null character here. We just need to initialize last_c with some character other than a newline character. There are two common errors that can be made in this program. Suppose that we had typed

```
if (c = '\n') {
```

using = instead of ==. Since the expression c = '\n' is always true, the else part will never get executed and the program will fail badly. Here is another error. Supposed that we had typed

```
if (c == '\n')
    if (last_c != '\n')
        putchar(c);
else
    putchar(c);
```

The indentation shows the logic that we want, but not what we are actually getting. Because an else statement always attaches to the nearest preceding if, the above code is equivalent to

```
if (c == '\n')
    if (last_c != '\n')
        putchar(c);
    else
        putchar(c);
```

and this is clearly in error. The programmer must always remember that the compiler sees only a stream of characters.

5.9 OPERATING SYSTEM CONSIDERATIONS

What you see on your screen when the *double_out* program is executed depends on how your operating system is configured. Typically, when a character is typed on the keyboard that character is echoed on the screen, but the operating system waits until a line of characters ending with a newline has been received before it processes those characters. A newline character is passed to the operating system when the carriage return key on the keyboard is pressed. At that point the current line of characters, including the newline character, is processed by the operating system. If we run the *double_out* program and then type

abc *<CR>*

where $<CR>$ represents a carriage return, the program will print on the screen on a new line

    aabbcc

This line is being printed by the program. The carriage return caused a newline character to be passed to the machine, so two newline characters are printed as well.

Some operating systems process a character as soon as it is typed on the keyboard. If this is the case, when the above program is run and the letter a is typed, the letters

    aaa

appear on the screen. The first a is the echo of the character that was typed; the next two are printed by the program. If abc is typed, then

    aaabbbccc

appears on the screen.

It is more common for an operating system to process characters a line at a time, because this gives the user a chance to correct typing mistakes. The UNIX operating system normally processes a line at a time, but it can be changed to process each character as it is typed. The command to do this is

   stty cbreak

After this command has been given, the effects of the *double_out* program are strikingly different. The keyboard is now "hot." The UNIX command

   stty −cbreak

will reset the operating system to its usual state.

In Chapter 1 we discussed redirecting the standard input. Here we will give a more complete discussion of redirection that includes redirecting the standard output. Many operating systems, including UNIX and recent versions of MS-DOS, can redirect the standard input and the standard output. The standard input stream consists of the characters typed on the keyboard. The standard output stream consists of the characters written to the screen. Let us illustrate how this redirection facility works in UNIX.

Suppose that the source code for the program that capitalizes lowercase letters is in the file *capitalize.c.* To compile the program, we give the command

   cc   − o capitalize   capitalize.c

Suppose that *infile* is one of our files. If we give the command

   capitalize   <   infile

then the contents of *infile* will be printed on the screen with all lowercase letters capitalized. The symbol < is used to redirect the input. Instead of taking its input from the keyboard, the program now takes its input from the file *infile.* In a similar fashion we can redirect the output. The command

   capitalize   >   outfile

will redirect the output of the program from the screen to the file *outfile.* If the file does not exist, it will be created. If it exists, it will be overwritten. These facilities can be used together. For example, the command

   capitalize   <   infile   >   outfile

will cause the *capitalize* program to take its input from *infile* and write its output in *outfile.*

Most operating systems have a command that copies one file to another. The following program can be considered a simple version of such a command.

```
#include   <stdio.h>

main()
{
   int   c;

   while ((c = getchar()) != EOF)
      putchar(c);
}
```

If we compile this program and put the executable code in *copy*, then the command

> *copy* < *infile* > *outfile*

will copy the contents of *infile* to *outfile*.

5.10 SUMMARY

1   A char is stored in 1 byte according to its ASCII code, and is considered to have the corresponding integer value. For example, the value of the character constant 'a' is 97.

2   There are nonprinting characters. Examples are the newline character '\n' and the bell '\07'. The newline character is used extensively to format output.

3   Basic input/output for characters is accomplished readily with the standard functions getchar() and putchar().

4   When using certain input/output constructs, the system header file *stdio.h* should be included. This is done by means of the control line

```
#include   <stdio.h>
```

5   When doing character input, it is frequently necessary to test for the end-of-file mark. This is accomplished by using the symbolic constant EOF in a program. The symbolic constant EOF is defined in the system header file *stdio.h*. Typically, the value of EOF is -1.

6 There are a number of system-supplied macros which test or convert character values. These macros are made available to the programmer by including the system header file *ctype.h*.

5.11 EXERCISES

1 Write a program using putchar() and getchar() that reads characters from the keyboard and writes to the screen. Every letter that is read should be written three times and followed by a newline. Any newline that is read should be disregarded. All other characters should just be copied to the screen.

2 Write a program using getchar() that reads characters from the standard input stream (keyboard) until the sentinel character # is encountered. The program should count the number of occurrences of the letters a, b, and c.

3 Change the program in the previous exercise so that characters are read until EOF is encountered. If redirection is available to you, use it to test the program.

4 Write a program that reads characters from the keyboard and writes to the screen. Write all vowels as uppercase letters, and write all nonvowels as lowercase letters.

5 Among the characters backspace, newline, space, and tab, which are considered "printable"? Take as the authority in this matter the macro isprint() in *ctype.h*.

6 Write a program that formats text files so that most lines contain approximately N characters. Start with the control line

```
#define  N  30
```

Count the characters as they are written. As long as the count is less than N, change any newline character to a space. When the count is N or more, write any white space character as a newline and change the count to zero. If we assume that most words contain less than 10 characters, then the effect of the program will be to write lines containing between N and $N + 10$ characters. Typists usually follow such an algorithm. Assume that the program has been compiled and put into the file *format*. If redirection is available to you, test the program by giving the command

format < *text*

Of course, you can get different length lines by changing the value of the symbolic constant N.

7   Write a program that indents all the lines in a text file. Each line should be preceded by N blank spaces, where N is a symbolic constant.

8   The function repeat() can be used to draw simple figures on your screen. For example, the following program draws a triangle:

```
#define   N   33

main()
{
   char   c = 'X';
   int    i;

   for (i = 1; i < N; i += 2) {
      repeat(c, i);
      putchar('\n');
   }
}
```

Compile and run this program so that you understand its effects. Write a similar program that prints a diamond in the middle of your screen.

9   One difference between putchar() and printf() is that putchar() returns the value of the character written to the output stream as an int, whereas printf() returns no useful value. What gets printed by the following code?

```
for (putchar('0'); putchar('1'); putchar('2'))
   putchar('3');
```

Does the following make sense? Explain.

```
printf("%c%c%c\n", putchar('A'), putchar('B'), putchar('C'));
```

10   To copy the standard input file to the standard output file, a programmer can make use of the loop

```
while ((c = getchar()) != EOF)
    putchar(c);
```

Suppose that by mistake the inner parentheses are left out, causing the loop to be written instead as

```
while (c = getchar() != EOF)
    putchar(c);
```

Write a test program to see what the effect is. If the input file has *n* characters, are *n* characters written to the output file? Explain.

11   The game of calling heads or tails, which was presented at the end of Chapter 4, requires the user to input 0 for heads and 1 for tails. Rewrite the program so that the user must input the letter h for heads and the letter t for tails.

12   The ancient Egyptians wrote in hieroglyphics. In this system of writing, vowel sounds are not represented, only consonants. Is written English generally understandable without vowels? To experiment, write a function isvowel() that tests whether or not a character is a vowel. Use your function in a program that reads the standard input file and writes to the standard output file, deleting all vowels. Use redirection on a file containing some English text to test your program.

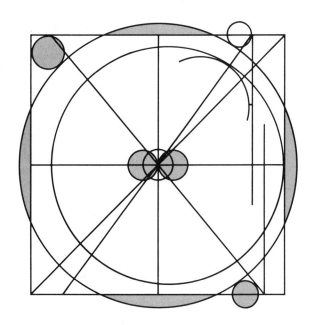

6

THE ARITHMETIC
DATA TYPES

The arithmetic data types are the fundamental data types of the C language. They are called "arithmetic" because operations such as addition and multiplication can be performed on them. Other data types such as arrays, pointers, and structures are derived from the fundamental types. They are presented in later chapters.

In this chapter we discuss in detail the fundamental types, including their memory requirements. The number of bytes used to store a type in memory determines the range of values that can be assigned to a variable of that type. We explain how the sizeof operator can be used to determine the storage requirement for any object, including a fundamental type.

The chapter continues with a discussion of the mathematical library. Although functions such as sin() and cos() are not technically part of the C language, they usually are available in a mathematical library. Examples are given to show how mathematical functions are used. After this we discuss conversions and casts. In expressions with operands of different types certain implicit conversions occur. The rules for conversion are explained, including the cast operator that forces explicit conversion. We end the chapter with a typical business application.

6.1 THE FUNDAMENTAL DATA TYPES

C provides several fundamental types. Many of them we have already seen. For all of them we need to discuss limitations on what can be stored.

Fundamental data types

char	short	int	long
unsigned char	unsigned short	unsigned	unsigned long
float	double		

The keywords short int, long int, and unsigned int may also be used. They are equivalent to short, long, and unsigned, respectively. Also, long float is equivalent to double. The fundamental types can be grouped into two separate categories:

Integral types: char, short, int, long,
                    unsigned char, unsigned short, unsigned, unsigned long

Floating types: float, double

Arithmetic types: *Integral types + Floating types*

These collective names are a convenience. Later, for example, when we discuss arrays, we will explain that only integral expressions are allowed as subscripts, meaning only expressions involving integral types are allowed.

6.2 THE DATA TYPE int

In C the data type int is the principal working type of the language. This type, along with the other integral types such as short and long, is designed for working with the integer values that are representable on a machine. In addition to decimal integer constants, there are hexadecimal and octal constants. We will not use them, but the reader has to know that integers that begin with a leading 0, such as 011 and 0573, are octal numbers, not decimal. Hexadecimal integer constants begin with 0x or 0X, as in 0x22 and 0X684. Some examples of decimal integer constants are

```
0
7
123
123456789123456789          /* too big for the machine? */
```

but not

```
5.0          /* a floating constant */
0x66         /* a hexadecimal integer, not decimal */
077          /* an octal integer, not decimal */
1,890        /* comma not allowed */
-444         /* this is a constant expression */
```

A variable of type int cannot take on all integer values; some integers are too big to be stored in a machine. Moreover, the range of values that an int can hold is machine dependent. Typically, an int is stored in 4 bytes (= 32 bits) on a large machine and in 2 bytes (= 16 bits) on a small machine. Let N_{min_int} represent the smallest integer that can be stored in an int, and let N_{max_int} represent the largest integer that can be stored in an int. If i is a variable of type int, then the range of values that i can take on is given by

$$N_{min\_int} \leq i \leq N_{max\_int}$$

with the end points of the range being machine dependent. The typical situation is

On large machines:
$$N_{min\_int} = -2^{31} = -2147483648 \approx -2 \text{ billion}$$
$$N_{max\_int} = 2^{31} - 1 = +2147483647 \approx +2 \text{ billion}$$

On small machines:
$$N_{min\_int} = -2^{15} = -32768 \approx -32 \text{ thousand}$$
$$N_{max\_int} = 2^{15} - 1 = +32767 \approx +32 \text{ thousand}$$

On any machine the following code is syntactically correct:

```
int   a, b, c;

a = 2000000000;
b = 2000000000;
c = a + b;        /* out of range */
```

However, at run-time the variable c may be assigned an incorrect value. The logical value of the expression a + b is 4 billion, and on most machines that is greater than N_{max_int}. This condition is called an *integer overflow*. Typically, when an integer overflow occurs, the program continues to run, but with logically incorrect results. For this reason the programmer must strive at all times to keep the values of integer expressions within the proper range.

6.3 THE INTEGRAL TYPES short, long, AND unsigned

In C the data type int is considered the "natural" or "usual" type for working with integers. The other integral types: char, short, long, and the unsigned types, are intended for more specialized use. For example, the data type short might be used in situations where storage is of concern. The compiler may provide less storage for a short than for an int, although it is not required to do so. In a similar fashion the type long might be used in situations where large integer values are needed. The compiler may provide more storage for a long than for an int, although it is not required to do so. Typically, on both large and small machines a short is stored in 2 bytes and a long is stored in 4 bytes. Thus on most large machines the size of an int is the same as the size of a long, and on most small machines the size of an int is the same as the size of a short. If s is a variable of type short, then the range of values that s can take on is given by

$$N_{min\_short} \le s \le N_{max\_short}$$

where typically

$$
\begin{aligned}
N_{min\_short} &= -2^{15} &&= -32768 &\approx\ -32 \text{ thousand} \\
N_{max\_short} &= 2^{15} - 1 &&= +32767 &\approx\ +32 \text{ thousand}
\end{aligned}
$$

If v is a variable of type long, then the range of values that v can take on is given by

$$N_{min\_long} \; \le \; v \; \le \; N_{max\_long}$$

where typically

$$
\begin{aligned}
N_{min\_long} &= -2^{31} &&= -2147483648 &\approx\; -2 \text{ billion} \\
N_{max\_long} &= 2^{31} - 1 &&= +2147483647 &\approx\; +2 \text{ billion}
\end{aligned}
$$

A variable of type unsigned is stored in the same number of bytes as an int. However, as the name implies, the integer values stored have no sign. Typically, variables of type int and unsigned are stored in a machine word. If u is a variable of type unsigned, then the range of values that u can take on is given by

$$0 \; \le \; u \; \le \; 2^{wordsize} - 1$$

Arithmetic on unsigned variables is performed modulo $2^{wordsize}$; see exercise 13. On large machines a word is usually 32 bits ($=$ 4 bytes), and on small machines a word is usually 16 bits ($=$ 2 bytes). The typical situation is

On large machines:

$$N_{max\_unsigned} = 2^{32} - 1 = +4294967295 \approx\; +4 \text{ billion}$$

On small machines:

$$N_{max\_unsigned} = 2^{16} - 1 = +65535 \approx\; +64 \text{ thousand}$$

USING THE TYPE long

Since on most small machines an int can store values only up to approximately 32 thousand, the type long is often used. Constants of type long can be specified by appending the letter L or l to the number. For example, 22L is a constant of type long. On systems where an int is stored in less memory than a long, a constant too big to be stored in an int is automatically converted to a long. For example, on small machines the constant 33000 is automatically of type long.

When using printf() and scanf() with variables and expressions of type long, the conversion character d should be preceded by the l or L modifier. Here is an example:

```
long    a, b, c;

printf("Input three integers:  ");
scanf("%ld%ld%ld", &a, &b, &c);
printf("\nHere they are:\n");
printf("a = %ld\nb = %ld\nc = %ld\n", a, b, c);
```

THE USE OF random()

The C system continues to evolve. In Chapter 4 we explained the use of rand(), which is available in the standard library. However, because this random number generator is not adequate for some applications, a new function called random() has been added to the library. It returns a value of type long. Thus wherever the function is used, it should be declared as returning a value of type long. In any serious program requiring a random number generator, this new function should be used; see exercise 14.

6.4 THE sizeof OPERATOR

C provides the unary operator sizeof to find the the number of bytes needed to store an object. It has the same precedence and associativity as all the other unary operators. An expression of the form

sizeof(*object*)

returns an integer that represents the number of bytes needed to store the object in memory. An object can be a type such as int or float, or it can be just a variable such as a, or it can be an expression such as a + b, or it can be an array or structure type. The following program uses this operator. On a given machine it provides precise information about the storage requirements for the fundamental types:

```
/* Compute the size of the fundamental types. */

main()
{
    printf("The size of the fundamental types is computed.\n\n");
    printf("   char:%3d byte \n", sizeof(char));
    printf("  short:%3d bytes\n", sizeof(short));
    printf("    int:%3d bytes\n", sizeof(int));
    printf("unsigned:%3d bytes\n", sizeof(unsigned));
    printf("   long:%3d bytes\n", sizeof(long));
    printf("  float:%3d bytes\n", sizeof(float));
    printf(" double:%3d bytes\n", sizeof(double));
}
```

All that is guaranteed by the C language is that

```
sizeof(char)   =   1
sizeof(short)  ≤   sizeof(int)  ≤   sizeof(long)
sizeof(unsigned)  =  sizeof(int)
sizeof(float)  ≤   sizeof(double)
```

6.5 THE FLOATING TYPES

C provides the two floating types float and double to deal with real numbers such as 3.7 and 0.005 and 3.1415926. Integers are representable as floating constants, but they must be written with a decimal point. For example, the constants 1.0 and 2.0 are both of type double, whereas the constant 3 is an int. All floating constants are of type double; there are no constants of type float.

In addition to the ordinary decimal notation for floating constants, there is an exponential notation as in the example 1.234567e5. This corresponds to the scientific notation 1.234567×10^5. Recall that

$$1.234567 \times 10^5 = 1.234567 \times 10 \times 10 \times 10 \times 10 \times 10$$
$$= 1.234567 \times 100000$$
$$= 123456.7 \qquad \textit{(decimal point shifted 5 places)}$$

In a similar fashion, the number 1.234567e-3 calls for shifting the decimal point 3 places to the left to obtain the equivalent constant 0.001234567.

Now we want to describe accurately the exponential notation. After we give the precise rules, we will show some examples. A floating constant such as 333.77777e-22 may not contain any embedded blanks or special characters. Each part of the constant is given a name:

> 333   is the integer part
> 77777   is the fractional part
> e-22   is the exponential part

A floating constant may contain an integer part, a decimal point, a fractional part, and an exponential part. A floating constant *must* contain either a decimal point or an exponential part or both. If a decimal point is present, either an integer part or fractional part or both *must* be present. If no decimal point is present, then there must be an integer part along with an exponential part. Some examples of floating constants are

```
3.14159
314.159e-2
0.0
0e0          /* equivalent to 0.0 */
1.0
1.           /* equivalent to 1.0, but harder to read */
```

but not

```
3.14,159     /* comma not allowed */
314159       /* decimal point or exponential part needed */
.e0          /* integer part or fractional part needed */
-3.14159     /* this is a floating constant expression */
```

Typically, a C compiler will provide more storage for a variable of type double than for one of type float, although it is not required to do so. On most machines a float is stored in 4 bytes and a double is stored in 8 bytes. The effect of this is that a float stores about 6 decimal places of accuracy, and a double stores about 16 decimal places of accuracy. All floating constants are of type double.

The range of values that a floating variable can be assigned is machine dependent. Typically, positive values range from about 10^{-38} to 10^{+38} for both a float and a double. The main points that one must be aware of are that not all real numbers are representable, and that floating arithmetic operations, unlike the integer arithmetic operations, need not be exact.

6.6 MATHEMATICAL FUNCTIONS

In C there are no built-in mathematical functions. Functions such as

```
sqrt()    pow()    exp()    log()    sin()    cos()    tan()
```

usually occur in a special library. If a programmer wishes to use these functions, the library must be made available to the compiler. We will explain in Section 6.11 of this chapter how this is done on most UNIX systems. All of the above functions, except the power function pow(), take a single argument of type double and return a value of type double. The power function takes two arguments of type double and returns a value of type double. Later in this chapter we will illustrate the use of pow(). Here, we will show how sqrt() can be used.

Let us recall the definition of square root. If x is a nonnegative number, then the square root of x is a nonnegative number y having the property that y times y yields x. For example, the square root of 4 is 2, because 2 times 2 is 4. The following interactive program asks the user to input a number, and then prints out the number along with its square root.

```
/* Compute square roots. */

main()
{
   double   sqrt(), x;

   printf("\nSquare roots of x are computed.\n\n");
   for ( ; ; ) {      /* do it forever */
     printf("Input x:  ");
     scanf("%lf", &x);
     if (x >= 0.0)
       printf("\n%10s%.16f\n%10s%.16f\n\n",
          "x = ", x,
          "sqrt(x) = ", sqrt(x));
     else
       printf("\nSorry, your number must be nonnegative.\n\n");
   }
}
```

Notice that sqrt() is declared as a function returning a double. This declaration is necessary. Although the system will obtain the object code for the sqrt() function from the mathematical library, the programmer must supply the correct declaration. As an alternative, we could have written

```
#include   <math.h>

main()
{
   double   x;


      .   .   .   .   .

```

The included file <math.h> contains the declarations of all the functions in the mathematical library. This file does *not* contain the sqrt() function itself.

Now let us suppose that we execute this program. If we input the number 2 when prompted, the following appears on the screen:

```
Square roots of x are computed.

Input x:  2

        x = 2.000000000000000
  sqrt(x) = 1.4142135623730951

Input x:
```

■ DISSECTION OF THE *compute_square_roots* PROGRAM

```
double   sqrt(), x;
```

■ This declaration tells the compiler that sqrt() is a function that returns a value of type double and that x is a variable of type double. Even though the function sqrt() is obtained from a library supplied by the system, it must be declared properly in the program. If it is not declared, the compiler will assume that it is a function returning an int.

```
for ( ; ; ) {     /* do it forever */
    . . . . .
}
```

■ This is an infinite loop. When the program is to be exited, an interrupt must be effected. What must be typed to effect an interrupt is system dependent. On our system this is done by typing a control-c.

```
printf("Input x:  ");
scanf("%lf", &x);
```

■ A prompt for the user is printed. The function scanf() is used to convert the characters typed by the user to a long float, or equivalently a double. The appropriate value is stored at the address of x. Notice that we typed 2 when we illustrated the use of this program. Equivalently, we could have typed 2.0 or 2e0 or 0.2e1. The function call scanf("%lf", &x) would have converted each of these to the same double. In C code 2 and 2.0 are different. The first is of type int, and the second is of type double. The input stream that is read by scanf() is *not* code, so the rules for code do not apply. When scanf() reads in a double, the number 2 is just as good as the number 2.0. For details about scanf() see Chapter 15.

```
if (x >= 0.0)
    .  .  .  .  .
else
    printf("\nSorry, your number must be nonnegative.\n\n");
```

■ Since the sqrt() function is not designed to work with negative numbers, a test is made to see that the value of x is nonnegative. If the test fails, an explanation is printed for the user.

```
printf("\n%10s%.16f\n%10s%.16f\n\n",
    "x = ", x,
    "sqrt(x) = ", sqrt(x));
```

■ The values for x and sqrt(x) are printed. The format %.16f is used because on most systems a double is stored in 8 bytes, and this gives about 16 decimal places of accuracy. Here it would be just as reasonable to use %.16e or %.16g.

6.7 CONVERSIONS AND CASTS

An arithmetic expression such as x + y has both a value and a type. For example, if x and y are both variables of the same type, say int, then x + y is also an int. However, if x and y are of different types, then x + y is a *mixed expression*. Suppose x is a short and y is an int. Then the value of x is converted to an int and the expression x + y has type int. Note carefully that the value of x as stored in memory is unchanged. It is only a temporary copy of x that is converted during the computation of the value of the

expression. Now suppose that both x and y are of type short.
Even though x + y is not a mixed expression, automatic conversions
again take place; both x and y are promoted to int and the expression is of type int. The general rules are straightforward.

Automatic conversion in an arithmetic expression   x op y

First:

Any char or short is promoted to int.
Any unsigned char or unsigned short is promoted to unsigned.

Second:

If after the first step the expression is of mixed type,
then according to the hierarchy of types

    int < unsigned < long < unsigned long < float < double

the operand of lower type is promoted to that of the higher type
and the value of the expression has that type.

This process goes under various names:

    automatic conversion
    implicit conversion
    coercion
    promotion
    widening

To illustrate the idea of automatic conversion, we first make the following declarations:

    char c;   double d;   float f;   int i;
    long v;   short s;   unsigned u;

Now we can list a variety of mixed expressions along with their corresponding types.

Expression	Type	Expression	Type
c − s / i	int	u * 3 − i	unsigned
u * 3.0 − i	double	f * 3 − i	float
c + 1	int	3 * s * v	long
c + 1.0	double	d + s	double

In addition to automatic conversions in mixed expressions, an automatic conversion also can occur across an assignment. For example

```
d = i
```

causes the value of i, which is an int, to be converted to a double and then assigned to d; and double is the type of the expression as a whole. A promotion or widening such as d = i will usually be well behaved, but a narrowing or demotion such as i = d can lose information. Here, the fractional part of d will be discarded. Precisely what happens in each case is machine dependent.

In addition to implicit conversions, which can occur across assignments and in mixed expressions, there are explicit conversions called *casts*. If i is an int, then

```
(double) i
```

will cast the value of i so that the expression has type double. The variable i itself remains unchanged. Casts can be applied to expressions. Some examples are

```
(char) ('A' + 1.0)
x = (float) ((int) y + 1)
(double) (x = 77)
```

but not

```
(double) x = 77      /* equivalent to ((double) x) = 77 */
```

The cast operator (*type*) is a unary operator having the same precedence and "right to left" associativity as other unary operators. Thus the expression

```
(float) i + 3        is equivalent to        ((float) i) + 3
```

because the cast operator (*type*) has higher precedence than + .

Operators						Associativity
−	++	−−	!	sizeof	(*type*)	right to left
		*	/	%		left to right
		+	−			left to right
	<	<=	>	>=		left to right
		==	!=			left to right
		&&				left to right
		||				left to right
=	+=	−=	*=	/=	*etc*	right to left

6.8 AN EXAMPLE: ·COMPUTING INTEREST

Everyone is familiar with putting money into a savings account to earn interest. In the business world many transactions and agreements involve the borrowing and lending of money with interest. To illustrate some of the ideas presented in this chapter, we will show how interest that is compounded yearly is computed. In the exercises at the end of the chapter we indicate how to compute interest compounded quarterly and daily.

Suppose that we put P dollars into a savings account that pays 7% interest compounded yearly. At the end of the first year we have P, our original principal, plus 7% of P, the earned interest. Since 7% of P is $0.07 \times P$, we have in our savings account

$$P + 0.07 \times P \qquad \text{or equivalently} \qquad 1.07 \times P$$

At the end of every year, to find the amount in our savings account, we take the amount that we started with at the beginning of the year and multiply it by 1.07. Thus we have

at the end of the first year $1.07 \times P$
at the end of the second year $1.07 \times (1.07 \times P)$ or $1.07^2 \times P$
at the end of the third year $1.07 \times (1.07^2 \times P)$ or $1.07^3 \times P$
· · · · ·
at the end of the nth year $1.07 \times (1.07^{n-1} \times P)$ or $1.07^n \times P$

We want to use these ideas to write an interactive program to compute interest that is compounded yearly. Values corresponding

to principal, interest rate, and number of years will be supplied by
the user. Our top-down design of this program is to print instructions, read in values, compute a new amount, and print out the
results. Following this structured design, we write the program to
consist of main() and the three functions prn_instructions(),
compute_amount(), and prn_results(). Let us suppose that these function are all in the file *compute_interest.c.* Here are the first two
functions.

```c
/* Compute interest compounded yearly. */

main()
{
    int     nyears;              /* number of years */
    double  amount,             /* principal + interest */
            interest_rate,      /* example:  0.07 is 7% */
            principal,
            compute_amount();

    prn_instructions();
    printf("Input principal, interest, # of years:  ");
    scanf("%lf%lf%d", &principal, &interest_rate, &nyears);
    amount = compute_amount(interest_rate, nyears, principal);
    prn_results(amount, interest_rate, nyears, principal);
}


prn_instructions()
{
    printf("\n%s\n\n%s\n%s\n%s\n%s\n%s\n%s\n\n",
        "This program computes interest compounded yearly.",
        "You need to input three items:",
        "   principal, interest, and number of years.",
        "For example, to find the interest on",
        "   $1000.00 at 5.5% for 15 years",
        "you should input",
        "   1000.00   0.055   15");
}
```

Notice that compute_amount() is declared to be a function that returns a double. If the function definition for compute_amount() occurs before main() in the file *compute_interest.c*, then this declaration is not needed. However, since we are writing main() before compute_amount(), this declaration is necessary. Before we show the code for the rest of the program, it is helpful to see what the program does. Suppose that we execute the program and input 1000.00, 0.07, and 20 when prompted. Here is what appears on the screen:

```
This program computes interest compounded yearly.

You need to input three items:
    principal, interest, and number of years.
For example, to find the interest on
    $1000.00 at 5.5% for 15 years
you should input
    1000.00   0.055   15

Input principal, interest, # of years:  1000.00  0.07  20

Interest rate:  7%
       Period:  20 years

    Principal at start of period:   1000.00
               Interest accrued:    2869.68
Total amount at end of period:      3869.68
```

In main() the value returned by the function call compute_amount() is assigned to the variable amount. This value represents the principal and interest at the end of the period. The computation of this value is at the heart of the program. Let us see how it is done.

```
double compute_amount(interest_rate, nyears, principal)
int      nyears;
double   interest_rate, principal;
{
    int     i;
    double  amount;

    amount = principal;
    for (i = 1; i <= nyears; ++i)
        amount *= 1.0 + interest_rate;
    return (amount);
}
```

■ DISSECTION OF THE compute_amount() FUNCTION

```
double compute_amount(interest_rate, nyears, principal)
int      nyears;
double   interest_rate, principal;
{
    int     i;
    double  amount;
```

■ The first double tells the compiler that this function returns a value of that type. The parameter list contains three identifiers. They are declared before the body of the function definition. In the body itself two variables are declared.

```
amount = principal;
for (i = 1; i <= nyears; ++i)
    amount *= 1.0 + interest_rate;
```

■ First the value of principal is assigned to amount. Suppose that interest_rate has the value 0.07. Then the expression 1.0 + interest_rate has the value 1.07, and amount is multiplied by 1.07 each time through the loop. The first time through the loop amount has the value 1.07 times the value of principal, the second time through the loop its value is 1.07^2 times the value of principal, and so forth. At the end of the loop its value is 1.07^{nyears} times the value of principal.

```
return (amount);
```

■ The value of the variable amount is returned to the calling environment.

Finally, back in main() we want to print the results of our computation on the screen. We pass the relevant variables as arguments to the function prn_results() and call it.

```
prn_results(amount, interest_rate, nyears, principal)
int      nyears;
double   amount, interest_rate, principal;
{
   printf("\n%s%g%c\n%s%d%s\n\n",
      "Interest rate: ", 100.0 * interest_rate, '%',
      "      Period: ", nyears, " years");
   printf("%s%9.2f\n%s%9.2f\n%s%9.2f\n\n",
      " Principal at start of period: ", principal,
      "             Interest accrued: ", amount - principal,
      "Total amount at end of period: ", amount);
}
```

Notice that the format %g was used to suppress the printing of extraneous zeros. Also observe that the format %9.2f was used to align the numbers on the screen.

We want to show how to simplify our program by making use of pow() in the mathematical library. This function takes as arguments two expressions of type double and returns a value of type double. A function call such as pow(x, y) computes the value of x raised to the y power. Here is how we modify our program. Since pow() will take the place of compute_amount(), we discard the code making up the function definition for compute_amount(). Then we must modify main(). First, discard the declaration of compute_amount(). Second, declare pow() to be a function returning a value of type double, or alternatively, include the header file <math.h> at the beginning of the file. Third, replace the statement

```
amount = compute_amount(interest_rate, nyears, principal);
```

with the statement

```
amount = pow(1.0 + interest_rate, (double) nyears) * principal;
```

Notice that nyears has been cast to a double. This is a typical use of the cast operator. We leave as an exercise the problem of seeing what happens if the cast is omitted.

6.9 STYLE

A common programming style is to use the identifiers i, j, k, m, and n as variables of type int, and to use identifiers such as x, y, and z as floating variables. This naming convention is loosely applied in mathematics, and historically, some early programming languages assumed that a variable name beginning with i through n was an integer type by default. This style is still acceptable in simple situations, such as using i as a counter in a for or while loop. In more complicated situations, however, one should use variable names that are descriptive of their use or purpose.

Another stylistic issue concerns the use of floating constants in floating expressions. Suppose that x is a floating variable. Because of automatic conversion, the value of an expression such as

```
x >= 0.0        is equivalent to        x >= 0
```

Nonetheless, the use of the first expression is considered good programming practice. The use of the floating constant 0.0 helps to remind the reader that x is a floating type. Similarly, the expression

```
1.0 / 3.0        is preferable to        1 / 3.0
```

Again, due to automatic conversion, the values of both expressions are the same. However, since in the first expression both the numerator and denominator are of type double, the reader is more likely to recognize immediately that the expression as a whole is of type double.

6.10 COMMON PROGRAMMING ERRORS

The programmer must alway be careful to keep the logical value of integer expressions within the proper range. On small machines the problem of integer overflow can easily occur. For example, the code

```
int   i, j = 32000, k = 1776;

i = j + k;
      .    .    .    .    .
```

may produce unexpected results. The largest integer that can be stored in an int on a small machine is typically about 32 thousand.

Using integer constants in what is meant to be a floating expression can also produce unintended results. Although the two expressions 1/3 and 1.0/3.0 look similar, the first is an int having value zero whereas the second is a double having value 0.333 . . . . To minimize the chance of using the first expression in situations where the second is correct, the programmer should get into the habit of coding floating constants in floating expressions. If, for example, the variable x is a float, and it is desired to assign zero as its value, it is better to code x = 0.0 rather than x = 0.

Another common programming error is to pass an argument of the wrong type to a function. This kind of error can occur easily when using functions from the mathematical library. For example, the function call sqrt(4) is wrong because 4 is an int, whereas a double is needed. In a similar fashion, if k is a variable of type int, then the function call sqrt(k) is wrong. In contrast, sqrt((double) k) is correct. This is a typical use of the cast operator. On our system *cc* will not complain when mathematical functions are passed arguments of the wrong type. However, *lint* can spot this kind of error provided that the mathematical library is made available to it. We will explain this further in the next section.

Finally, we want to emphasize again that in C an undeclared function is assumed to return an int. Therefore, if a mathematical library function such as sqrt() is not declared as returning a double, unexpected results can occur.

6.11 OPERATING SYSTEM CONSIDERATIONS

The size of an int typically varies from 2 bytes on small machines to 4 bytes on large machines. The C programmer must be aware of this. This means that on small machines the largest int is about 32 thousand, whereas on large machines the largest int is about 2 billion. If a programmer is writing code that is sensitive to these limits, and the code is run on many machines, then a symbolic constant such as

```
#define   MAX_INT   32767
```

should be used. When the code moves from one machine to another, all that needs to be changed is this #define line.

How the mathematical library is accessed varies. On most UNIX systems the programmer needs to compile the program with the −lm option. Moreover, the option has to go at the end of the command line. This is because the option is being read by the loader, rather than the compiler. For example, on our system the command

```
cc program.c  −lm
```

makes the mathematical library available. If a call to one or more mathematical functions has been made in *program.c*, then the object code for those functions will be loaded. Although the system provides the object code, the programmer must supply the appropriate function declarations.

When using *lint* on programs that use functions from the mathematical library, it is advisable to provide information about the library to *lint* as well. This is done by using the $-lm$ option as follows:

    lint program.c $-lm$

Lint only cross checks the files given to it. When properly used, *lint* will catch errors such as forgetting to declare sqrt() or passing an argument of the wrong type, as in the function call sqrt(4).

C is a general-purpose language, but at the same time it is aptly suited for writing operating system code. System programmers frequently have to deal with the explicit representation of values stored in a byte or a word. Since hexadecimal and octal integers are useful for these purposes, they were included as part of the C language. However, we will not make explicit use of them in this text.

6.12 SUMMARY

1 The fundamental data types are char, short, int, long, unsigned versions of these, and two floating types. The type int is designed to be the "natural" or "working" integral type. The types short, long, and unsigned are provided for more specialized situations.

2 Except for a char, which is always stored in 1 byte, the amount of memory used to store the fundamental types is machine dependent. Typically, a short takes 2 bytes, an int takes either 2 or 4 bytes, and a long takes 4 bytes. A programmer needs to know what these values are because they determine the size of the largest and smallest integers that can be stored in these types.

3 Two floating types, float and double, are provided to represent real numbers. Typically a float will be stored in 4 bytes, giving about 6 decimal places of accuracy, and a double in 8 bytes, giving about 16 decimal places of accuracy. Unlike integer arithmetic, floating arithmetic is not always exact. The type double, not float, is the "working" type. Floating constants are of type double.

4 Mathematical functions are not part of the C language, but they are usually available in a library. Typically these functions take a single argument of type double and return a value

of type `double`. The power function `pow()` is an exception; it takes two arguments of type `double`.

5   Mathematical functions, like all functions, must be properly declared when they are used. This can be done by putting the control line

```
#include    <math.h>
```

at the beginning of the source code. The system provides this header file as a convenient way to provide declarations for all the functions in the mathematical library.

6   Automatic conversions occur in mixed expressions and across an assignment. Casts can be used to force explicit conversions. A cast is a unary operator with the same precedence and "right to left" associativity as the other unary operators.

6.13   EXERCISES

1   If the number 3.777 is truncated to 2 decimal places, it becomes 3.77, but if it is rounded to 2 places, it becomes 3.78. Write a test program to find out whether `printf()` truncates or rounds when printing a `float` or `double` with fractional part.

2   C has evolved with time. In the beginning, the types `unsigned char`, `unsigned short`, and `unsigned long` were not included as fundamental types of the language. Today, most C systems support these types, although there are some small C systems that do not. Experiment to see if these types are supported by your system.

3   If your machine stores an `int` in 4 bytes, run the following program and explain its output. If your machine stores an `int` in 2 bytes, change the value of the symbolic constant `BIG` to `32000` before running the program.

```
#define   BIG   2000000000     /* 2 billion */

main()
{
    int       i = BIG + BIG;
    unsigned  u = BIG + BIG;

    printf("\n%s%d\n%s%d\n%s%u\n%s%u\n\n",
        "i with %d format is ", i,
        "u with %d format is ", u,
        "i with %u format is ", i,
        "u with %u format is ", u);
}
```

4 The following table shows how many bytes are required on most machines to store some of the fundamental types. What are the appropriate values for your machine? Execute the program suggested in the text and complete the table.

Fundamental type	Memory required on most large machines	Memory required on most small machines	Memory required on your machine
char	1 byte	1 byte	
short	2 bytes	2 bytes	
int	4 bytes	2 bytes	
unsigned	4 bytes	2 bytes	
long	4 bytes	4 bytes	
float	4 bytes	4 bytes	
double	8 bytes	8 bytes	

5 Before the age of computing machines it was common to make tables of square roots, sines, cosines, etc. Write a program that makes a table of square roots and fourth roots of the integers from 1 to 100. Your table should look like this:

Integer	Square root	Fourth root
1	1.000000000e+00	1.000000000e+00
2	1.414213562e+00	1.189207115e+00
3	1.732050808e+00	1.316074013e+00
4	2.000000000e+00	1.414213562e+00

. . . . .

Hint: The fourth root of a number is just the square root of the square root of the number.

6   If functions are not properly declared, a program can misbehave. In the *compute_square_roots* program make the following change:

```
double   x;     /* sqrt() is not declared */
```

On our system neither *cc* nor *lint* will complain. Check to see what happens on your system. Is the square root of 4 computed correctly?

7   A program that has an infinite loop in it may not work as expected with redirection. Put some real numbers into a file called *data*, and try the command

compute_square_roots < data

Now modify the *compute_square_roots* program so that the for loop is replaced by a while loop of the form

```
while (scanf("%lf", &x) == 1) {
    .  .  .  .  .
}
```

After you get the program to work properly in an interactive mode, try redirection again.

8   When writing an interactive program, you should try to anticipate errors that a user might make. If you expect a certain kind of input error to be common, then you should design

your program to handle the error gracefully. Users running the *compute_interest* program can be expected to make a mistake when typing in the interest rate. For example, instead of typing 0.07, a user might type in 7 or 0.7 by mistake. The reason for this is that most people associate "7 percent" in their mind with 7% rather than 0.07. Modify the *compute_interest* program to guard against this kind of user error. Test the value of the interest rate supplied by the user. If the value seems to be out of line with what might be expected, ask the user to confirm it.

9   Rewrite the *compute_interest* program, making use of the function pow() in the mathematical library. Does the modified program yield the same results as before? What happens if in the call to pow() the variable nyears is not cast as a double?

10 We want to modify the *compute_interest* program to reduce further the chance of input errors by the user. The function prn_instructions() causes the lines

```
.   .   .   .   .
you should input
    1000.00   0.055   15
```

to be printed on the screen. Modify the function so that this is changed to

```
.   .   .   .   .
you should input
    $1000.00   5.5%   15
```

Now the instructions indicate that an interest rate is to be entered using the percent notation. For example, "7 percent" is entered as 7%; what could be more natural? All right, let us now suppose that the user types in $1000.00, 7%, and 20 when prompted. We now have the problem of modifying the program in such a way that the two characters $ and % do not get in the way of scanf(). Let us write the function find_next_digit() to help us.

```
#include   <stdio.h>
#include   <ctype.h>

find_next_digit()
{
   int   c;

   while ((c = getchar()) != EOF && !isdigit(c))
      ;                     /* discard everything except a digit */
   if (isdigit(c))
      ungetc(c, stdin);   /* push the digit back */
   else
      printf("\nNo digits found!\n\n");
}
```

When this function is invoked, characters from the standard input stream (keyboard) are read until a digit is found. At that point the function call ungetc(c, stdin) is used to push the character value in c back onto the input stream so that it can be read again. The function ungetc() is in the standard library. The identifier stdin stands for "standard input" and is defined in <stdio.h> as a file. (For details about files see Chapter 14.) In main() we can write

```
find_next_digit();
scanf("%lf", &principal);
```

to read characters in the input stream. First, all characters are skipped until a digit is found, which in our example will be the digit 1, and then the digit is pushed back onto the input stream. Next, scanf() is invoked. It reads the characters 1000.00, converts them to a double, and places the value at the address of principal.

11 Suppose that Constance B. DeMogul has a million dollars to invest. She is thinking of investing the money at 9% compounded yearly, or at 8.75% compounded quarterly, or at 8.7% compounded daily, for a period of either 10 or 20 years. For each of these investment strategies and periods what interest will be earned? Write a program that helps you to advise her. *Hint:* Suppose that *P* dollars is invested at 8.75%

compounded quarterly. The amount of principal and interest is given by

$$(1 \ + \ 0.0875 \ / \ 4)^4 \ \times \ P \qquad \text{at the end of the first year}$$
$$(1 \ + \ 0.0875 \ / \ 4)^{4 \times 2} \ \times \ P \qquad \text{at the end of the second year}$$
$$(1 \ + \ 0.0875 \ / \ 4)^{4 \times 3} \ \times \ P \qquad \text{at the end of the third year}$$

$\cdot \quad \cdot \quad \cdot \quad \cdot \quad \cdot$

For P dollars invested at 8.7% compounded daily, the formulas are similar, except that 0.0875 is replaced by 0.087 and 4 is replaced by 365. These computations can be carried out by writing a function such as

```
double find_accrued_interest(p, ir, cp, period)
double    p,       /* principal */
          ir,      /* interest rate */
          cr,      /* compounding rate */
                   /* example:  if compounded daily, cr is 365.0 */
          period;  /* in years */
{
```

$\cdot \quad \cdot \quad \cdot \quad \cdot \quad \cdot$

12 Occasionally a programmer needs a power function for integers. Because such a function is so easy to write, it typically is not found in a mathematics library. Write the function power() so that if m and n are integers with n being nonnegative, the call power(m, n) will return m raised to the nth power. *Hint:* Make use of the following loop.

```
product = 1;
for (i = 1; i <= n; ++i)
   product *= m;
```

13 On a 24-hour clock the zero hour is midnight and the 23rd hour is 11 o'clock at night, one hour before midnight. On such a clock when 1 is added to 23, we do not get 24, but instead we get 0. There is no 24. In a similar fashion 22 plus 5 yields 3, because 22 plus 2 is 0 and 3 more is 3. This is an example of modular arithmetic, or more precisely, of arithmetic modulo 24. Most machines do modular arithmetic on all the

integral types. This is most easily illustrated with the unsigned types. Run the following program and explain what is printed. If you are working on a small machine, first change 4294967295 to 65535 throughout.

```
#define   MAX_UNSIGNED   4294967295

main()
{
    int       i;
    unsigned  u = MAX_UNSIGNED;

    for (i = 0; i < 10; ++i)
        printf("4294967295 + %d = %u\n", i, u + i);
    for (i = 0; i < 10; ++i)
        printf("4294967295 * %d = %u\n", i, u * i);
}
```

14 On some C systems the following code will produce an alternating sequence of 0s and 1s. See if this is so on your system.

```
for (i = 0; i < 100; ++i)
    printf("%d \n", rand() % 2);
```

Run a similar test where rand() is replaced by random(). Do not forget to declare random() as a function returning a value of type long.

15 This problem is for those readers who are familiar with hexadecimal and octal numbers. In a program an integer written with a leading 0 is an octal number, and an integer written with a leading 0x or 0X is a hexadecimal number. For example

```
int   i = 077, j = 0x77, k = 0xcbd;

printf("Some numbers:%7d%7d%7d\n", i, j, k);
```

causes the line

Some numbers: 63   119   3261

to be printed. Just as the conversion character d is used in a format in printf() to print a decimal integer, the conversion character x is used to print hexadecimal numbers, and the conversion character o is used to print octal numbers. Define a symbolic constant LIMIT and print a table of values containing corresponding decimal, hexadecimal, and octal integers from 0 to LIMIT. *Hint:* Print an appropriate heading, and then use

```
for (i = 0; i <= LIMIT; ++i)
    printf("%12d%12x%12o\n", i, i, i);
```

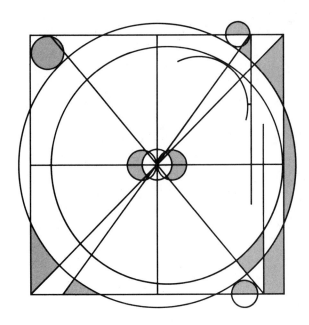

7

BRANCHING
AND NESTED
FLOW OF CONTROL

This chapter begins by treating a variety of flow of control constructs. The `break` and `continue` statements are used to interrupt ordinary iterative flow of control in loops. In addition, the `break` statement is used within a `switch` statement. A `switch` statement can select among several different cases. It can be considered a generalization of the `if-else` statement. Similar in function to an `if-else` statement, the conditional operator provides for the selection of alternative values. The chapter continues with a discussion of nested flow of control structures and a brief discussion of the `goto` statement. After that, there is a discussion of nested blocks and their effect on the "scope" of variables, in conjunction with the different types of storage class attributes.

7.1 THE break AND continue STATEMENTS

To interrupt normal flow of control within a loop, the programmer can use the two special statements

```
break;        and        continue;
```

The break statement, in addition to its use in loops, can also be used in a switch statement. It causes an exit from the innermost enclosing loop or switch statement.

The following example illustrates the use of a break statement. A test for a negative value is made, and if the test is *true*, the break statement causes the while loop to be exited. Program control jumps to the statement immediately following the loop.

```
while (scanf("%lf", &x) == 1) {
   if (x < 0.0) {
      printf("All done - bye.\n");
      break;      /* exit loop if value is negative */
   }
   printf("%f\n", sqrt(x));
}
/* break jumps to here */
   .   .   .   .   .
```

This is a typical use of a break statement. When a special condition is met, an appropriate action is taken and the loop is exited.

The continue statement causes the current iteration of a loop to stop and causes the next iteration of the loop to begin immediately. The following code processes all characters except digits.

```
while ((c = getchar()) != EOF) {
   if (isdigit(c))
      continue;
         .   .   .   .   .   /* process other characters */
   /* continue jumps to here*/
}
```

In this example all characters except digits are processed. When the continue statement is executed, control jumps to just before the closing brace, causing the loop to begin execution at the top again. Notice that the continue statement ends the current iteration, whereas a break statement would end the loop.

A break statement can occur only inside the body of a for, while, do, or switch statement. The continue statement can occur only inside the body of a for, while, or do statement.

7.2 THE switch STATEMENT

The switch statement is a multi-way conditional statement generalizing the if-else statement. Its general form is given by

switch (*expression*)
   statement

where *statement* is typically a compound statement containing case labels and optionally a default label. Typically, a switch is composed of many cases, and the expression in parentheses following the keyword switch determines which, if any, of the cases get executed. The precise details of how a switch works are best explained by looking at a specific example. The following program counts the occurrences of the letters a, b, c, and C, with the letters c and C counted together. A switch statement is used to accomplish this task.

```
/* count a, b, and c-C */

#include    <stdio.h>

main()
{
    int   c, a_cnt = 0, b_cnt = 0, cC_cnt = 0, other_cnt = 0;

    while ((c = getchar()) != EOF)
        switch (c) {
        case 'a':
            ++a_cnt;
            break;
        case 'b':
            ++b_cnt;
            break;
        case 'c':
        case 'C':
            ++cC_cnt;
            break;
        default:
            ++other_cnt;
        }
    printf("\n%9s%5d\n%9s%5d\n%9s%5d\n%9s%5d\n%9s%5d\n\n",
        "a count:", a_cnt, "b count:", b_cnt,
        "cC count:", cC_cnt, "Other:", other_cnt,
        "Total:", a_cnt + b_cnt + cC_cnt + other_cnt);
}
```

■ DISSECTION OF THE *count_abc_C* PROGRAM

```
while ((c = getchar()) != EOF)
```

■ The value of the next character in the input stream is assigned
to c. The loop is exited when the end-of-file sentinel EOF is
detected.

```
switch (c) {
    .   .   .   .   .
}
```

■ This whole construct is a `switch` statement. The integral expression in the parentheses following the keyword `switch` is evaluated with the usual arithmetic conversions taking place. In this program the expression is just the variable c. The value of c is used to transfer control to one of the `case` labels or to the `default` label.

```
case 'a':
    ++a_cnt;
    break;
```

■ When the value of c is 'a', this case is executed, causing the value of a_cnt to be incremented. The `break` statement causes control to exit the `switch` statement.

```
case 'c':
case 'C':
    ++cC_cnt;
    break;
```

■ Multiple `case` labels allow the same actions to be taken for different values of the `switch` expression. Here we wish the same actions to be taken when c has the value 'c' or 'C'.

```
default:
    ++other_cnt;
```

■ If the value of the `switch` expression matches none of the `case` labels, then control passes to the `default` label, if there is one. If there is no `default` label, then the `switch` statement is exited. In this example we use the `default` label to cause the variable other_cnt to be incremented.

A case label is of the form

case *constant integral expression*:

In a switch statement the case labels must all be unique. Typically, the action taken after each case label ends with a break statement. If there is no break statement, then execution "falls through" to the next statement in the succeeding case; see exercise 3.

If no case label is selected, then control passes to the default label, if there is one. A default label is not required. If no case label is selected, and there is no default label, then the switch statement is exited. To detect errors, programmers frequently include a default even when all the expected cases have been accounted for.

The keywords case and default cannot occur outside of a switch.

The effect of a switch

1   Evaluate the integral expression in the parentheses following switch.

2   Execute the case label having a constant value
     that matches the value of the expression found in Step 1,
     or, if a match is not found, execute the default label,
     or, if there is no default label, terminate the switch.

3   Terminate the switch when a break statement is encountered,
     or terminate the switch by "falling off the end."

7.3 THE CONDITIONAL OPERATOR

The conditional operator ?: is unusual in that it is a ternary operator. It takes three expressions as operands. In a construct such as

exp1 ? *exp2* : *exp3*

exp1 is evaluated first. If it is nonzero (*true*), then *exp2* is evaluated and that is the value of the conditional expression as a whole. If *exp1* is zero (*false*), then *exp3* is evaluated and that is the value of the conditional expression as a whole. Thus a conditional expression can be used to do the work of an if-else statement. Consider, for example, the code

```
if (y < z)
    x = y;
else
    x = z;
```

which assigns to x the minimum of y and z. This also can be accomplished by writing

```
x = (y < z) ? y : z;
```

The parentheses are not necessary because the precedence of the conditional operator is just above =. However, parentheses are usually used to make clear what is being tested for.

The type of the conditional expression

exp1 ? *exp2* : *exp3*

is determined by *exp2* and *exp3*. The usual conversion rules are applied. Note carefully that the type of the conditional expression does not depend on which of the two expressions *exp2* or *exp3* is evaluated. The conditional operator ?: has precedence just above the assignment operators, and it associates "right to left."

Declarations and initializations			

`char    a = 'a', b = 'b';    /* a has decimal value 97 */`
`int     i = 1, j = 2;`
`double  x = 7.07;`			

Expression	**Equivalent expression**	**Value**	**Type**
`i == j ? a - 1 : b + 1`	`(i == j) ? (a - 1) : (b + 1)`	99	int
`j % 3 == 0 ? i + 4 : x`	`((j % 3) == 0) ? (i + 4) : x`	7.07	double
`j % 3 ? i + 4 : x`	`(j % 3) ? (i + 4) : x`	5.0	double

7.4 NESTED FLOW OF CONTROL

Flow of control statements such as if, for, while and switch statements can be nested within themselves and within each other. Although such nested control constructs can be quite complicated, some have a regular structure and are easily understood.

One of the more common nested flow of control constructs makes repeated use of if-else statements. Its general form is given by

> if (*expression1*)
>   *statement1*
> else if (*expression2*)
>   *statement2*
> else if (*expression3*)
>   *statement3*
>
>   . . . . .
> else if (*expressionN*)
>   *statementN*
> else .
>   *default statement*
> *next statement*

This whole giant construction, except for *next statement*, is a single if-else statement. Suppose, for example, that *expression1* and *expression2* are both zero (*false*) and that *expression3* is nonzero (*true*). Then *statement1* and *statement2* will be skipped and *statement3* will be executed and then control will pass to *next statement*. No other intervening statement will be executed. If we suppose that all of the expressions are zero, then only *default statement* will be executed. In some circumstances the execution of a default statement is not wanted. In this case a construction such as the above would be used except that the two lines

> else
>   *default statement*

would not appear.

These ideas are illustrated in the following program.

```
/* Count digits, letters, newlines, and others. */

#include   <stdio.h>
#include   <ctype.h>

main()
{
    int    c, digit_cnt = 0, letter_cnt = 0,
           newline_cnt = 0, other_cnt = 0;

    while ((c = getchar()) != EOF)
       if (isdigit(c))
          ++digit_cnt;
       else if (isalpha(c))
          ++letter_cnt;
       else if (c == '\n')
          ++newline_cnt;
       else
          ++other_cnt;
    printf("\n%12s%12s%12s%12s%12s\n\n",
       "digits", "letters", "newlines", "others", "total");
    printf("%12d%12d%12d%12d%12d\n\n",
       digit_cnt, letter_cnt, newline_cnt, other_cnt,
       digit_cnt + letter_cnt + newline_cnt + other_cnt);
}
```

Note carefully that since only a single if-else statement is under the control of the while loop, braces are not necessary. A construct composed of nested if-else statements has in it many statements, yet syntactically the construct as a whole is just a single statement. Suppose that this program is in the file *cnt_char.c*, and that we compile it into *a.out*. To test the program we give the command

  a.out < cnt_char.c

This causes the following to appear on the screen:

digits	letters	newlines	others	total
24	320	25	271	640

A nested if-else statement in this program was used to test a series of conditions. We could have used a switch statement, although to do so would have required much more code. We will discuss this further in the exercises.

Just as an if-else statement can be one of the statement parts of another if-else statement, so can a for statement be the statement part of some other control statement. That is, a for statement can be used as the statement part of an if, if-else, while, or another for statement. In particular, nested for statements occur often. A construction of the form

```
for ( . . .)
    for ( . . .)
        for ( . . .)
            statement
```

is a single for statement. Let us illustrate this with a specific example.

We want to consider a problem that comes from the domain of combinatorics, the art of enumerating combinations and permutations. The problem is to list all triples of nonnegative integers that add up to a given number. For example, suppose they add up to 7. Here is a program that does this.

```
/* Find triples of integers that add up to N */

#define   N   7

main()
{
   int   cnt = 0, i, j, k;

   for (i = 0; i <= N; ++i)
      for (j = 0; j <= N; ++j)
         for (k = 0; k <= N; ++k)
            if (i + j + k == N) {
               ++cnt;
               printf("%d %d %d\n", i, j, k);
            }
   printf("\nCount:   %d\n\n", cnt);
}
```

When we execute this program, here is what appears on the screen:

```
0 0 7
0 1 6
0 2 5

 .    .    .

6 0 1
6 1 0
7 0 0

Count:  36
```

■ DISSECTION OF THE *combinatorics* PROGRAM

```
#define   N   7
```

■ We use the symbolic constant N so that we can easily experiment with the program.

```
for (i = 0; i <= N; ++i)
```

- This for controls the outermost loop. First i is assigned 0 and the entire inner loop is executed with this value. Then i is incremented and again the entire inner loop is executed. This process continues until the value of i is greater than N.

```
for (j = 0; j <= N; ++j)
   for (k = 0; k <= N; ++k)
```

- For each outermost value of i, all values of j within the inner loop get cycled through. For each value of j, all values of k within the innermost loop get cycled through. This is similar to an odometer where the lower digits are first cycled through before a higher digit is changed.

```
if (i + j + k == N) {
   ++cnt;
   printf("%d %d %d\n", i, j, k);
}
```

- This is the body of the innermost loop. A check is made to see if i plus j plus k add up to N. If they do, cnt is incremented and the triple of integers is printed.

7.5 AN EXAMPLE: BOOLEAN VARIABLES

Boolean algebra plays a major role in the design of computer circuits. In this algebra all variables have only the values zero or one. Transistors and memory technologies implement zero-one value schemes with currents, voltages, and magnetic orientations. Frequently the circuit designer has a function in mind and needs to check whether for all possible zero-one inputs the output has the desired behavior.

We will use int variables b1, b2, b3, b4, and b5 to represent five boolean variables. They will be allowed to take on only the values 0 and 1. A boolean function of these variables is one that returns only 0 or 1. A typical example of a boolean function is the majority function; it returns 1 if a majority of the variables have value 1, and 0 otherwise.

```
majority(b1, b2, b3, b4, b5)
int   b1, b2, b3, b4, b5;
{
    return (b1 + b2 + b3 + b4 + b5 >= 3);
}
```

Let us write three more boolean functions, making use of the logical operators !, &&, and ||. Recall that expressions with these operators always have the int value 0 or 1.

```
fct1(b1, b2, b3, b4, b5)
int   b1, b2, b3, b4, b5;
{
    return (b1 && b2 || b3 || b4 || b5);
}
```

```
fct2(b1, b2, b3, b4, b5)
int   b1, b2, b3, b4, b5;
{
    return (b1 || b2 && b3 && b4 || b5);
}
```

```
fct3(b1, b2, b3, b4, b5)
int   b1, b2, b3, b4, b5;
{
    return (!b1 || b2 && !b3 || b4 && !b5);
}
```

Now we will write main() to print a table of values for all possible inputs and corresponding outputs. First we print the column headings, and then we make use of a nested for loop to print the entries in the table.

```
/* Print a table of values for some boolean functions. */

main()
{
    int    b1, b2, b3, b4, b5;     /* boolean variables */
    int    cnt = 0;

    printf("%3s%5s%5s%5s%5s%5s%7s%7s%7s%11s\n\n",
        "cnt", "b1", "b2", "b3", "b4", "b5",
        "fct1", "fct2", "fct3", "majority");

    for (b1 = 0; b1 <= 1; ++b1)
        for (b2 = 0; b2 <= 1; ++b2)
            for (b3 = 0; b3 <= 1; ++b3)
                for (b4 = 0; b4 <= 1; ++b4)
                    for (b5 = 0; b5 <= 1; ++b5)
                        printf("%3d%5d%5d%5d%5d%5d%7d%7d%7d%11d\n",
                            ++cnt, b1, b2, b3, b4, b5,
                            fct1(b1, b2, b3, b4, b5),
                            fct2(b1, b2, b3, b4, b5),
                            fct3(b1, b2, b3, b4, b5),
                            majority(b1, b2, b3, b4, b5));
}
```

Here are some of the lines of the output of the program:

cnt	b1	b2	b3	b4	b5	fct1	fct2	fct3	majority
1	0	0	0	0	0	0	0	1	0
2	0	0	0	0	1	1	1	1	0
3	0	0	0	1	0	1	0	1	0

.   .   .   .   .

In this table a pattern appears that comes from the boolean variables cycling through the values 0 and 1 repeatedly. However, the printout does not show enough of the output of the program for this pattern to be appreciated. We leave it as an exercise to run the program and to see the cycling pattern.

7.6 THE goto STATEMENT

The goto statement is the most primitive method of interrupting ordinary control flow. It is an unconditional branch to an arbitrary labeled statement in the function. The goto statement is considered a harmful construct in most accounts of modern programming methodology. Thus it can undermine all the useful structure provided by other flow of control mechanisms (for, while, do, if, switch). Here is a program that uses a goto statement to create an infinite loop that prints integers. Keep in mind that such a program must be terminated by a control-c or a delete key on most systems.

```
main()
{
    int   i = 0;

    loop:  printf("%d\n", i++);
    goto loop;
}
```

In this example loop is a label and

```
loop:  printf("%d\n", i++);
```

is a labeled statement. Whenever the goto statement is reached, it passes control to the labeled statement. The program has no means of exiting this loop.

A label is a unique identifier. Some examples of labeled statements are

```
spot1:  a = b + c;
error_one:  printf("error_one\n");
bug1:  bug2:  bug3:  printf("bug found\n");    /* multiple labels */
```

but not

```
333:  a = b + c;          /* 333 is not an identifier */
a:  a += b * c;           /* a is not a unique identifier */
```

By executing a goto statement of the form

```
goto label;
```

control is unconditionally transferred to a labeled statement. An example would be

```
if (d == 0.0)
   goto error;
else
   ratio = n / d;
   .   .   .   .   .
error:  printf("ERROR:  division by zero\n");
```

Both the goto statement and its corresponding labeled statement must be in the body of the same function.

In general the goto should be avoided. The goto is a primitive method of altering flow of control and, in a richly structured language, is unnecessary. Labeled statements and goto's are the hallmark of incremental patchwork program design. A programmer who modifies a program by adding goto's to additional code fragments soon makes the program incomprehensible.

One conceptual use of the goto is to give a technical explanation of the effect of a continue statement in a for loop; see exercise 10.

7.7 SCOPE RULES

A compound statement is a series of declarations followed by a series of statements all surrounded by the braces { and }. Its chief use is to group statements into an executable unit. When declarations are present, a compound statement is also called a *block*. Here is a simple example of a block.

```
{
    int   a = 2;

    printf("%d\n", a);        /* 2 is printed */
    {
        int b = 3;
        printf("%d\n", b);    /* 3 is printed */
    }
}
```

The chief reason for blocks is to allow memory for variables to be created where needed. If memory is a scarce resource, then block exit will release the storage allocated locally to the block, allowing the memory to be used for some other purpose. Also, blocks associate names in their neighborhood of use, making the code more readable. Functions can be viewed as named blocks with parameters and return statements allowed.

The basic rule of scoping is that identifiers are accessible only within the block in which they are declared. They are unknown outside the boundaries of that block. This would be an easy rule to follow, except that programmers for a variety of reasons choose to use the same identifier in different declarations. We then have the question of which object the identifier refers to. Let us give a simple example of this state of affairs.

```
{
    int   a = 2;              /* outer block a */

    printf("%d\n", a);        /* 2 is printed */
    {
        int   a = 3;          /* inner block a */
        printf("%d\n", a);    /* 3 is printed */
    }                         /* back to the outer block */
    printf("%d\n", a);        /* 2 is printed */
}
```

Each block introduces its own nomenclature. An outer block name is valid unless an inner block redefines it. If redefined, the outer block name is hidden, or masked, from the inner block.

Inner blocks may be nested to arbitrary depths which are determined by system limitations.

7.8 THE STORAGE CLASS auto

Every variable and function in C has two attributes: *type* and *storage class*. The four storage classes are automatic, external, static, and register, with corresponding keywords

```
auto          extern          static          register
```

Variables declared inside of function bodies are automatic by default. Thus automatic is the most common of the four storage classes. Although it is usually not done, the storage class of automatic variables can be made explicit by use of the keyword auto. The code

```
{
    char    c;
    int     i, j, k;
        .  .  .  .  .
}
```

is equivalent to

```
{
    auto char    c;
    auto int     i, j, k;
        .  .  .  .  .
}
```

When a block is entered, the system sets aside adequate memory for the automatically declared variables. Within that block those variables are defined, and they are considered to be "local" to the block. When the block is exited, the system no longer reserves the memory set aside for the automatic variables. Thus the values of these variables are lost. If the block is reentered, the storage once again is appropriately allocated, but previous values are unknown. Each invocation of a function sets up a new environment.

7.9 THE STORAGE CLASS extern

All functions and all variables declared outside of function bodies have external storage class. One method of transmitting information across blocks and functions is to use external variables. When a variable is declared outside a function, storage is permanently assigned to it, and its storage class is external. A declaration for an external variable looks just the same as a variable declaration occurring inside a function or block. Such a variable is considered to be global to all functions declared after it, and upon function exit, the external variable remains in existence.

```
int   a = 7;

main()
{
   printf("%d\n", a);     /* 7 is printed */
   f();
}

f()
{
   printf("%d\n", a);     /* 7 is printed */
}
```

In the above program it would be wrong to code

```
extern int   a = 7;
```

The keyword extern is used to tell the system to look for a variable externally, perhaps even in another file that is used to make up the program. Here is an example.

In file1.c

```
int   v = 33;     /* an external variable is globally defined */

main()
{
   double   x = 1.11;

   printf("%d\n", v);
   f(x);
}
```

In file2.c

```
f(x)
double   x;
{
   extern int   v;
   /*****
      The system will look for v externally,
      either in this file or in another file
      that will be combined into the final program.
   *****/

   printf("v = %d\nx = %f\n", v, x);
}
```

The use of extern to avoid undefined variable names makes possible the separate compilation of functions in different files. The functions main() and f() written in *file1.c* and *file2.c*, respectively, can be compiled separately. The extern declaration of the variable v in *file2.c* tells the system that it will be declared externally, either in this file or some other. The executable program obtained by compiling these two functions separately will act no differently than a program obtained by compiling a single file containing both functions and the external variable defined at the beginning of the file.

External variables never disappear. Since they exist throughout the execution life of the program, they can be used to transmit values across functions. Of course, a variable may be hidden if it is redefined in an inner block. Thus information can be passed into a function in two ways: by use of external variables and by use of the parameter mechanism. Although there are exceptions, the use of the parameter mechanism is the preferred method to pass information into a function. This tends to improve the modularity of the code, and the possibility of undesirable side effects is reduced.

One form of "side effect" occurs when a function changes a global variable within its body rather than through its parameter list. Such a construction is error prone. Correct practice is to effect changes to global variables through the parameter and return mechanisms. However, to do this requires the use of pointers and the address operator, material which will be covered in Chapter 8. Adhering to this practice improves the modularity and readability of programs.

7.10 THE STORAGE CLASS register

The storage class `register`, used in a declaration, indicates that, if physically and semantically possible, the associated variables will be stored in high-speed memory registers. Since resource limitations and semantic constraints sometimes make this impossible, this storage class defaults to automatic whenever the compiler cannot allocate an appropriate physical register.

Basically, the use of storage class `register` is an attempt to improve execution speed. When speed is of concern, the programmer may choose a few variables that are most frequently accessed and declare them to be of storage class `register`. Common candidates for such treatment include loop variables and function parameters. An example might be

```
{
    register int   i;

    for (i = 0; i < LIMIT; ++i) {
        .  .  .  .  .
    }
}      /* block exit will free the register */
```

Note that the register variable i was declared as close to its place of use as possible. This is to allow maximum availability of the physical registers, using them only when needed.

Always remember that a register declaration is taken only as *advice* to a compiler.

7.11   THE STORAGE CLASS static

Static declarations have two important and distinct uses. The more elementary use is to allow a local variable to retain its previous value upon reentry into a block. This is in contrast to ordinary automatic variables which lose their value upon block exit. As an example of this use, we can use a static variable to find out how many times a function is called during execution of a program.

```
f()
{
   char       a, b, c;
   static int   cnt = 0;

   printf("cnt = %d\n", ++cnt);
   .  .  .  .  .
}
```

The variable cnt in f() is initialized to 0 only once. Whenever the function is called, the old value is retained, then it is indexed and printed out.

7.12   STATIC EXTERNAL VARIABLES

The second and more subtle use of static is in connection with external declarations. With external constructs it provides a "privacy" mechanism very important for program modularity. By privacy, we mean visibility or scope restrictions on otherwise accessible variables or functions.

As an example of this privacy mechanism and the value-retention use of static, we will write a family of two pseudo random number generators. The function random() produces an apparently random sequence of integer values. (It is based on linear congruential methods that will not be explained here.)

```
/* Two pseudo random number generators. */

#define   INITIAL_SEED       17
#define   MULTIPLIER         25173
#define   INCREMENT          13849
#define   MODULUS            65536
#define   FLOATING_MODULUS   65536.0

static int   seed = INITIAL_SEED;   /* external,
                                       but private to this file */
random()       /* a value between 0 and MODULUS is returned */
{
   seed = (MULTIPLIER * seed + INCREMENT) % MODULUS;
   return (seed);
}

probability()       /* a value between 0.0 and 1.0 is returned */
{
   seed = (MULTIPLIER * seed + INCREMENT) % MODULUS;
   return (seed / FLOATING_MODULUS);
}
```

The static external variable seed is first initialized. Each call to random() or probability() will produce a new value for seed. Since seed has the storage class static, it will retain its value upon function exit. Had we declared seed externally, but not static, all of this would still be true. External variables already retain their values across block and function exit. The difference is that static external variables are scope-restricted external variables. The scope is the remainder of the source file in which they are declared. Thus they are unavailable to functions defined earlier in the file or to functions defined in other files, even if these functions attempt to use the keyword extern.

A last use of static is as a storage class specifier for function identifiers. This is used to restrict scope. Static function declarations are visible only within the file in which they are declared. Thus unlike ordinary functions, which can be accessed from other files, a static function is available throughout its own file, but no other. Again, this facility is useful in developing private modules of function definitions.

7.13 STYLE

A main principle of structured programming is that exceptional interruption of the ordinary flow of control should be minimized. The goto statement is the worst culprit, because it permits arbitrary transfer of control. The return statement should be used in a disciplined fashion. Ideally, at most one return statement should occur in a function, and when it occurs, it should be the last statement in the function. The use of break and continue statements should be minimized, except in a switch, where the use of break is essential. Ideally, the use of break and continue statements should simplify a program.

Except where control is meant to fall through, a break is used just before the next case label in a switch. However, after the last case or default label a break statement is not needed since after that, program control falls off the end. Nonetheless, many programmers put a break statement there too, partly out of force of habit, and partly to minimize difficulties that may arise later when more cases are added. This is an example of defensive programming; if you can forsee potential trouble, try to avoid it.

Although a default label is not required in a switch, to detect errors, programmers frequently include a default even when all the expected cases have been accounted for. When present, the default typically is placed at the end of the switch, although it is not required to be there.

It is considered good programming style to use parentheses in a conditional expression, even if the parentheses are not required. They make the expression more readable. A typical example is

```
max = (a > b) ? a : b;
```

If one were to be consistent with the style of indentation that we have used in previous chapters, then one would write nested if-else statements in the form

```
if (a == 1)
   printf("a is 1\n");
else
   if (a == 2)
      printf("a is 2\n");
   else
      if (a == 3)
         printf("a is 3\n");
      else
         .   .   .   .   .
```

However, it is generally agreed among programmers that this is *not* desirable. This style marches the code off to the right, so that in situations where the construct is long, the programmer may end up with little or no room left on the screen. Since this is unacceptable, the preferred style is

```
if (a == 1)
   printf("a is 1\n");
else if (a == 2)
   printf("a is 2\n");
else if (a == 3)
   printf("a is 3\n");
else
   .   .   .   .
```

In situations where program control can be accomplished by use of either a for or a while statement, which gets used is often a matter of taste. One major advantage of a for loop is that control and indexing both can be kept right at the top. When loops are nested, this facilitates the reading of the code.

7.14 COMMON PROGRAMMING ERRORS

A number of common programming errors occur with use of a switch. For example, if x is a floating type, then

```
switch (x) {

   .   .   .   .
```

is an error. Only integral expressions are allowed in a switch. Another error is the use of a variable expression, or an expression of the wrong type, in a case label. The rule is that only constant integral expressions may be used. Also, missing break statements are a frequent cause of error in switch statements. It is easy to leave one out, especially when adding new cases to the switch at a later time.

7.15 OPERATING SYSTEM CONSIDERATIONS

There is some ambiguity on what is allowed in a switch expression. Some systems allow floating expressions, but implicitly convert the value to an int before passing control to the appropriate case or default label. Since this feature is not universal, however, it is best not to rely on it.

Some compilers use the keyword extern in the sense of "look for it elsewhere" (with "elsewhere" meaning "either in this file or in some other file"), whereas other compilers use extern to indicate that the storage class of a variable is external. Consider the following program:

```
extern int   a = 1;

main() {}   /* do nothing */
```

Some compilers will accept this code as correct, others will not. Even though the storage class of a is external, our system will not compile this code unless the word extern is removed.

7.16 SUMMARY

1   The four statement types

    return   break   continue   goto

    cause an unconditional transfer of program control. Except
    for the use of break statements in a switch, their use should be
    minimized.
2   The switch statement provides a multi-way conditional branch.
    It is useful when dealing with a large number of special cases.
3   The iterative statements for, while, and do can be nested. In
    such a case the inner loop is executed for each iteration of the
    outer loop. Since nested iterative statements can result in the
    use of a lot of machine resources, care should be exercised.
4   Avoid the use of goto's. They are considered harmful to good
    programming.
5   The principal storage class is automatic. Automatic variables
    appear and disappear with block entry and exit. They can be
    hidden when an inner block redeclares an outer block
    identifier.
6   The external storage class is the default class for all functions
    and all variables declared outside of functions. These
    identifiers may be used throughout the program. Such
    identifiers can be hidden by redeclaration but their values can-
    not be destroyed. The storage class register is of use for
    speeding up programs, but is semantically equivalent to auto-
    matic.
7   The storage class static is used to preserve exit values of varia-
    bles. It is also used to restrict the scope of external identifiers.
    This latter use enhances modularization and program security
    by providing a form of privacy to functions and variables.

7.17 EXERCISES

1   Test the *count_abc_C* program so that you understand its
    effects. Then modify the program so that the letters a, A,
    . . . , e, E are counted, with the letters a and A counted
    together, the letters b and B counted together, and so forth.

2   If you are ambitious, modify the program in the previous exercise so that all the letters in the alphabet are counted. In
Chapter 9 we will show how an array can be used to accomplish this task.

3   Recall that if the action following a case label in a switch does
not end with a break statement, then control "falls through" to
the next case. In this exercise we want to illustrate this. Write
a program that incorporates the following switch. What gets
counted? Run some tests that illustrate how the switch works.

```
switch (c) {
case 'a':
   ++a_cnt;
case 'b':
   ++ab_cnt;
case 'c':
   ++abc_cnt;
   break;
default:
   ++other_cnt;
}
```

4   Rewrite the following code to avoid using break:

```
while ((c = getchar()) != EOF) {
   if (c == 'E')
      break;
   ++count;
   if (c >= '0' && c <= '9')
      ++digit_count;
}
```

5   Rewrite the following code to avoid using continue:

```
i = -5;
n = 50;
while (i < n) {
   ++i;
   if (i == 0)
     continue;
   total += i;
   printf("i = %d\ntotal = %d\n", i, total);
}
```

6   Show how a while statement can be rewritten as a goto statement and an if statement. Which is the better construct and
why?

7   In the cnt_char program replace the nested if-else construct by
a switch statement. Test your modified program to see that it
produces the same results as the original program. In this particular exercise the use of a switch is somewhat contrived, but
there is another point to be made. Read on. In the while loop
in the original program we need to replace the nested if-else
construct by a switch statement. It would begin like this.

```
switch (c) {
case '0':
case '1':

.  .  .  .  .

case '9':
   ++digit_cnt;
   break;
case 'a':
case 'b':

.  .  .  .  .
```

As you can see, the general idea of what has to be done is simple, yet to carry it out requires the tedious coding of 10 case
labels to handle the digit count, and 52 case labels to handle
the letter count. Well, even though this is tedious, with a text
editor it can be done in less than 10 minutes. However, one
has to be careful not to make a trivial typing mistake, such as
repeating case 'a' twice and leaving out case 'b'. Although
this exercise is contrived, there are many situations where

repetitive, tedious code is needed. In such situations experienced programmers use code to write code. A side benefit of doing this is that typing mistakes can be eliminated. For this exercise write a small program containing

```
for (c = 'a'; c <= 'z'; ++c) {
   printf("case '%c':\n", c);
   printf("case '%c':\n", toupper(c));
}
```

The purpose of your small program is to write the most tedious part of the code required for this exercise. Since your small program prints to the screen, you will need to use redirection to write into a file. Suppose that the executable code for your short program is in the file *prn_case_labels*. Then the command

prn_case_labels > temp

will redirect the output and write in the file *temp*.

8   How many 3-letter words are there if only the lowercase letters a to z are used and no letter is repeated in a word? For example, abc is allowed, but aab is not. *Hint:* There are more than you care to look at. To count them, make use of the code

```
for (c1 = 'a'; c1 <= 'z'; ++c1)
   for (c2 = 'a'; c2 <= 'z'; ++c2)
      for (c3 = 'a'; c3 <= 'z'; ++c3) {
         ++cnt;
         if (c1 != c2 && c1 != c3 && c2 != c3)
            ++distinct_cnt;
      }
```

9   Modify the program that you wrote for the last exercise to count all 4-letter words that contain no repeated letters. *Hint:* There are more than one-third of a million of them. If you are on a small machine, you should use variables of type long to count with.

10   In Chapter 3 we showed how the action of a for loop can be explained in terms of a while loop. But if the for loop contains a continue statement, then the syntax is not yet clear. There are two plausible ways the syntax could work. A construct of the form

```
for (exp1; exp2; exp3) {
    statement1;
    continue;
    statement2;
}
```

might be equivalent to

```
exp1;
while (exp2) {
    statement1;
    goto next;
    statement2;
    exp3;
next:
}
```

or it might be equivalent to a similar construct, but with next: and exp3; interchanged. Which one is correct? *Hint:* Find out what gets printed by the following code:

```
for (putchar('1'); putchar('2'); putchar('3')) {
    putchar('4');
    continue;
    putchar('5');
}
```

11   The following line of code is dense. Use parentheses to write an equivalent statement. If the values of x, y, and z are known, can you tell what value u will take on? If not, write a test program and experiment.

```
u = x < y ? x < z ? x : z : y < z ? y : z;
```

12   What is the effect of the following code? Explain its effect on digits, letters, and other characters. If the effect of the code is not obvious to you, write a test program and experiment. After you understand its effect, rewrite the code, making use of if and if-else statements.

```
while ((c = getchar()) != EOF) {
   if (isalpha(c))
      c = (c == 'z') ? 'a' : (c == 'Z') ? 'A' : c + 1;
   putchar(c);
}
```

13   There is a pattern generated by the output of the *boolean* program. To find the pattern, execute the program and look at the values printed for b5, then b4, and so forth. This pattern comes from cycling through all values for 5 boolean variables. Suppose you were to cycle through 6 boolean variables and print a table of values. Can you describe the entries in the new table in terms of those of the old table?

14   Of the 32 majority values in the table generated by the *boolean* program, how many have value 1? Make a table of values for 7 boolean variables and the majority function. Of the n majority values in your new table, how many have value 1? Do you know what the value of n is before you run your program?

15   Make a new version of the program in the previous exercise to test for the efficiency achieved by the use of the storage class register. Change all of the loop index variables to storage class register. Compare the running times for both versions of the program.

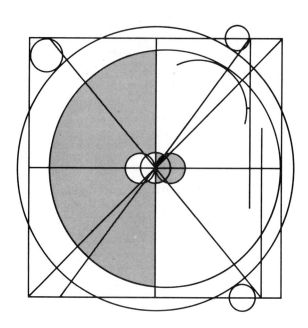

8

FUNCTIONS
AND POINTERS:
CALL-BY-REFERENCE

When an expression is passed as an argument to a function, a copy of the value of the expression is made, and it is this copy that is passed to the function. This mechanism is known as *call-by-value* and is strictly adhered to in C. Suppose that v is a variable and f() is a function. Then a function call such as f(v) cannot change the value of v in the calling environment, because only a copy of the value of v is passed to f(). In other programming languages, however, such a function call *can* change the value of v in the calling environment. The mechanism that accomplishes this is known as *call-by-reference*.

It is often convenient to have functions modify the values of the variables referred to in the argument list. To get the effect of call-by-reference in C, we must use pointers in the parameter list in the function definition, and pass addresses of variables as arguments in the function call. Before we explain this in detail, however, we need to understand how pointers work.

In C pointers have many uses. In this chapter we explain how they are used as arguments to functions. In the two chapters that follow we will explain their use with arrays and strings. In Chapter 13 we will show how pointers are used with structures, and in

Chapter 14 we will see that pointers are used when dealing with files.

8.1 POINTER DECLARATION AND ASSIGNMENT

Pointers are used in programs to access memory and manipulate addresses. We have already seen the use of addresses as arguments to scanf(). A function call such as scanf("%d", &v) causes an appropriate value to be stored at a particular address in memory.

If v is a variable, then &v is the address, or location, in memory of its stored value. The address operator & is unary and has the same precedence and "right to left" associativity as the other unary operators. Pointer variables can be declared in programs and then used to take addresses as values. The declaration

```
int   *p;
```

declares p to be of type "pointer to int." The legal range of values for any pointer always includes the special address 0, also defined as NULL in <stdio.h>, and a set of positive integers that are interpreted as machine addresses on a particular C system. Some examples of assignment to the pointer p are

```
p = &i;
p = 0;
p = NULL;              /* equivalent to  p = 0; */
p = (int *) 1507;      /* an absolute address in memory */
```

In the first example we think of p as "referring to i" or "pointing to i" or "containing the address of i." The compiler decides what address to assign the variable i. This will vary from machine to machine and may even be different for different executions on the same machine. The second and third example are assignments of the special value 0 to the pointer p. In the fourth example the cast is necessary to avoid a compiler warning. In this example an actual memory address is used. This is not typical in most programming. Code like this may be necessary for system programs, but rarely for user programs.

8.2 ADDRESSING AND DEREFERENCING

We have already seen that addresses are passed as arguments to
scanf(). We want to show how a pointer can be used instead. Suppose we declare

```
int   i, *p;
```

Then the statements

```
p = &i;
scanf("%d", p);
```

cause the next value from the standard input stream to be stored at
p. But since p points to i, this is equivalent to storing the value at
the address of i.

The dereferencing or indirection operator * is unary and has the
same precedence and "right to left" associativity as the other unary
operators. If p is a pointer, then *p is the value of the variable that
p points to. The name "indirection" is taken from machine language programming. The direct value of p is a memory location,
whereas *p is the indirect value of p, namely the value at the memory location stored in p. In a certain sense * is the inverse operator
to &. Suppose we declare

```
float   x, y, *p;
```

Then the two statements

```
p = &x;
y = *p;
```

first assign to p the address of x, and then assign to y the value of
what is pointed to by p. The two statements are equivalent to

```
y = *&x;
```

which in turn is equivalent to

```
y = x;
```

Now consider

```
char   c1, c2 = 'A', *p, *q;

p = &c1;
q = &c2;
*p = *q;
```

First the addresses of c1 and c2 are assigned to the variables p and q, respectively. The last statement assigns the value of what is pointed to by q to what is pointed to by p. The three statements are equivalent to

```
c1 = c2;
```

Let us write a short program that illustrates the distinction between a pointer value and its dereferenced value.

```
main()
{
    int   i = 777, *p;

    p = &i;
    printf(" Value of i:  %d\n", *p);
    printf("Address of i:  %d\n", p);
}
```

The output of this program on our system is the following:

```
  Value of i:  777
Address of i:  2147479212
```

The actual location of a variable in memory is system dependent. The operator * takes the value of p to be a memory location and returns the value stored in this location, appropriately interpreted according to the type declaration of p.

In the above program, if we had wanted to initialize p rather than assign its value in an assignment statement, we would have written

```
int    i = 777, *p = &i;
```

Note carefully that this is an initialization of p, not *p. The variable p is declared to be of type "int *" and its initial value is &i.

Declarations and initializations		
int i = 3, j = 5, *p = &i, *q = &j;		
Expression	Equivalent expression	Value
p == & i	p == (& i)	1
* p - * q	(* p) - (* q)	-2
* * & p	* (* (& p))	3
3 * - * p / * q + 7	(((3 * (- (* p)))) / (* q)) + 7	6

8.3 CALL-BY-REFERENCE

Whenever variables are passed as arguments to a function, their values are copied to the corresponding function parameters, and the variables themselves are not changed in the calling environment. This call-by-value mechanism is strictly adhered to in C. In this section we will describe how the *addresses* of variables can be used as arguments to functions so as to be able to modify the stored values of the variables in the calling environment.

For a function to effect call-by-reference, pointers must be used in the parameter list in the function definition. Then, when the function is called, addresses of variables must be passed as arguments. As an example of this, let us write a simple program that orders the values of two variables.

```
main()
{
    int    i = 7, j = 3;
    int Order();
    printf("%d  %d\n", i, j);       /* 7  3 is printed */
    order(&i, &j);
    printf("%d  %d\n", i, j);       /* 3  7 is printed */
}
```

Most of the work of this program is carried out by the function call
to order(). Notice that the addresses of i and j are passed as arguments. As we shall see, this allows the function call to change the
values of i and j in the calling environment.

```
order(p, q)
int   *p, *q;
{
    int   temp;

    if (*p > *q) {
        temp = *p;
        *p = *q;
        *q = temp;
    }
}
```

■ DISSECTION OF THE order() FUNCTION

```
order(p, q)
int   *p, *q;
{
    int   temp;
```

■ The parameters p and q are both of type pointer to int. The
variable temp is local to this function and is of type int. As
the name indicates, we think of this as temporary storage.

```
if (*p > *q) {
    temp = *p;
    *p = *q;
    *q = temp;
}
```

■ If the value of what is pointed to by p is greater than the value of what is pointed to by q, then the following is done. First, temp is assigned the value of what is pointed to by p; second, what is pointed to by p is assigned the value of what is pointed to by q; and third, what is pointed to by q is assigned the value of temp. This has the effect of interchanging in the calling environment the stored values of whatever p and q are pointing to.

Call-by-reference is accomplished by

1 declaring a function parameter to be a pointer
2 using the dereferenced pointer in the function body
3 passing an address as an argument when the function is called

8.4 AN EXAMPLE: PROCESSING CHARACTERS

A function that uses a return statement can pass back to the calling environment a single value. If more than one value is needed in the calling environment, then addresses must be passed as arguments to the function. To illustrate this idea let us write a program that processes characters in a particular way. Here is what we want to accomplish:

Read characters from the input stream until EOF is encountered.

Change any lowercase letter to an uppercase letter.

Print three words to a line with a single space between each word.

Count the number of characters and the number of letters printed.

For this program we will consider a word to be a maximal sequence of characters containing no white space characters. Here is main().

```
#include    <stdio.h>
#include    <ctype.h>

#define    NWORDS    3    /* number of words per line */

main()
{
    int    c, nchars = 0, nletters = 0;

    while ((c = getchar()) != EOF)
        if (process(&c, &nchars, &nletters) == 1)
            putchar(c);
    printf("\n%s%5d\n%s%5d\n\n",
        "Number of characters:", nchars,
        "Number of letters:   ", nletters);
}
```

The processing of each character takes place in the function process(). Since the values of the variables c, nchars, and nletters are to be changed in the calling environment, addresses of these variables are passed as arguments to process(). Notice that c is an int rather than a char. This is because c must eventually take on the special value EOF, which is not a character. Notice also that a character gets written to the screen only if process() returns the value 1. In this context we think of 1 as signaling that the character has been appropriately processed and that it is ready to print. We will use the value 0 to signal that the character is not to be printed. This case will occur when contiguous white space characters occur. Let us now see how process() does its work.

```
process(p, nchars_ptr, nletters_ptr)
int   *p, *nchars_ptr, *nletters_ptr;
{
   static int   cnt = 0, last_char = ' ';

   if (isspace(last_char) && isspace(*p))
      return (0);
   if (isalpha(*p)) {
      ++*nletters_ptr;
      if (islower(*p))
         *p = toupper(*p);
   }
   else if (isspace(*p))
      if (++cnt % NWORDS == 0)
         *p = '\n';
      else
         *p = ' ';
   ++*nchars_ptr;
   last_char = *p;
   return (1);
}
```

Before we dissect this function, we want to show some output from the program. Suppose we create a file called *data* with the following lines in it:

```
   she sells sea shells
by      the      seashore
```

Notice that we have deliberately put contiguous blanks into the file. Now, if we give the command

process < data

here is what appears on the screen:

```
SHE SELLS SEA
SHELLS BY THE
SEASHORE
Number of characters:   37
Number of letters:      30
```

■ DISSECTION OF THE process() FUNCTION

```
process(p, nchars_ptr, nletters_ptr)
int   *p, *nchars_ptr, *nletters_ptr;
{
    static int   cnt = 0, last_char = ' ';
```

■ The parameters of the function are three pointers to int. Although we think of p as a pointer to a character, its declaration here must be consistent with its use in main(). The local variables cnt and last_char are of storage class static so that they will only be initialized once. If they were of storage class auto, they would be reinitialized every time the function is called.

```
if (isspace(last_char) && isspace(*p))
    return (0);
```

■ If the last character seen was a white space character and the character pointed to by p is also a white space character, the value 0 is returned to the calling environment. Back in the calling environment, that is, back in main(), when this value is received, the current character is not printed.

```
if (isalpha(*p)) {
    ++*nletters_ptr;
    if (islower(*p))
        *p = toupper(*p);
}
```

■ If the character pointed to by `p` is a letter, then we increment the value pointed to by `nletters_ptr`. If, moreover, the value pointed to by `p` is a lowercase letter, then we assign to the value pointed to by `p` the corresponding uppercase letter.

```
+++*nletters_ptr;
```

■ Let us consider this statement in some detail. The increment operator `++` and the indirection operator `*` are both unary and associate "right to left." Thus

```
++(*nletters_ptr);
```

is an equivalent statement. What is being incremented is the dereferenced value in the calling environment. Note carefully that the expression

  `+++*nletters_ptr`   is not equivalent to   `*nletters_ptr++`

The latter expression is equivalent to

```
*(nletters_ptr++)
```

which causes the current pointer value to be dereferenced and then the pointer itself to be incremented. This is an instance of pointer arithmetic; see the next chapter.

```
else if (isspace(*p))
   if (++cnt % NWORDS == 0)
      *p = '\n';
   else
      *p = ' ';
```

■ If the character pointed to by `p` is a white space character, then `last_char` cannot also be a white space character; we already have handled that case. No matter what this character is, we want to print a newline or a blank, depending on the incremented value of `cnt`. Since the symbolic constant `N` has the value 3, every third time we print a newline, and the other two

times we print a blank. The effect of this is to print at most
three words to a line with a single blank between them.

```
++*nchars_ptr;
last_char = *p;
return (1);
```

■ First we increment the value pointed to by nchars_ptr. Then
  we assign to last_char the value pointed to by p. Finally, we
  return the value 1 to the calling environment to indicate that a
  character is to be printed.

8.5 STYLE

One often finds p, q, and r used as identifiers for pointer variables
in a program. This is a natural convention, with p standing for
"pointer," and q and r being the next letters in the alphabet. In a
similar fashion p1, p2, . . . are also used as identifiers for pointer
variables. Other common ways to designate that an identifier is a
pointer is to prepend p_ to a name, as in p_hi and p_lo, or to
append _ptr, as in nchars_ptr.

An alternative declaration style for a pointer is

```
    char*   p;
```
            which is equivalent to   `char   *p;`

Some programmers prefer this style because the * is now more
closely associated with the type being pointed to. One must be
careful, however, because

```
    char*   p, q, r;
```
            is not equivalent to   `char   *p, *q, *r;`

Our last concern in this section deals with how one writes functions. It is considered bad programming style to write functions
that change the stored values of variables in the calling environment
without making use of the return mechanism or the parameter
mechanism. A call to such a function is said to have a *side effect*.
To illustrate these ideas, let us rewrite the *order* program presented
at the beginning of this chapter.

```
int   i = 7, j = 3;

main()
{
    printf("%d   %d\n", i, j);      /* 7   3 is printed */
    order();
    printf("%d   %d\n", i, j);      /* 3   7 is printed */
}
```

We have moved the declaration of i and j from inside the body of main() to the very top of the file. This makes these variables global to the program. Now we rewrite the order() function.

```
order()        /* very bad programming style */
{
    int   temp;

    if (i > j) {
        temp = i;
        i = j;
        j = temp;
    }
}
```

The modification of the global int variables i and j is a side effect of the function call order(). With this programming style large programs can be very difficult to read and maintain. Ideally, one writes code that is locally intelligible.

8.6   COMMON PROGRAMMING ERRORS

Beginning programmers often make conceptual mistakes when learning to use pointers. A typical example of this is

```
int   *p = 3;
```

Here an attempt is being made to initialize the value of what is pointed to by p. But this is an initialization of p itself, and most likely not what was intended. All right, let us try to fix this by writing

```
int   *p = &i, i = 3;
```

Now there is a more subtle error. C does not provide look ahead capability. At the point where p is initialized to the address of i, space for the variable i has yet not been allocated. To correct this situation we can write

```
int   i = 3, *p = &i;
```

When dealing with pointers, the programmer must learn to distinguish carefully between a pointer p and its dereferenced value *p. To minimize any chance for confusion, one should use names for pointer variables that indicate pointer usage. Here is an example of what *not* to do. Suppose that v1 and v2 are floating variables and that we want to interchange their values in the calling environment by the function call swap(&v1, &v2). To code swap() one could write

```
swap(v1, v1)
float   *v1, *v2;
{
      .  .  .
```

But now there is confusion. In main() the identifiers v1 and v2 are used as names of variables of type float, but in swap() the same identifiers are used as names of variables of type pointer to float. It would be much better to use p_v1 and p_v2. Using names that clearly indicate pointer usage helps the programmer minimize mistakes, and helps others who read the code to understand its intent.

Of course, not every value is stored in an accessible memory location. It is useful to keep in mind the following prohibitions.

Constructs *not* to be pointed at

Do not point at constants.

```
&3              /* illegal */
```

Do not point at ordinary expressions.

```
&(k + 99)       /* illegal */
```

Do not point at register variables.

```
register  v;
&v              /* illegal */
```

8.7   OPERATING SYSTEM CONSIDERATIONS

Programs that make explicit use of absolute addresses are frequently nonportable. Different systems have different address spaces, and they may use their address spaces in noncompatible ways. If you must write programs that make use of absolute addresses, it is best to use the #define facility to localize any possible system-dependent code.

Pointer expressions should not be of mixed type. Although such expressions are considered illegal, some compilers will only issue a warning. For example, if p is of type pointer to int and q is of type pointer to double, then the assignment expression p = q will result in a compiler warning on our system. C is still an evolving language, and it is expected that, in the future, compilers will treat this as an error. For portable code intended to run on different operating systems, it is essential that all compiler warnings be heeded. What is a warning on one system may be prohibited on another.

8.8   SUMMARY

1   A pointer variable typically takes as values either NULL or addresses of other variables.

2   The address operator & and the indirection or dereferencing operator * are unary operators with the same precedence and "right to left" associativity as the other unary operators. If v is a variable, then the expression

*&v   is equivalent to   v

3   In C the call-by-value mechanism is strictly adhered to. This means that when an expression occurs as an argument to a function, a copy of the value of the expression is made, and it is this copy that is passed to the function. Thus a function call such as f(v) cannot change the stored value of v in the calling environment.

4   Call-by-reference can be effected in C by making proper use of pointers and the address operator & and the dereferencing operator *.

5   To effect call-by-reference a pointer is used as a formal parameter in the header of the function definition. In the function body the dereferenced pointer can be used to change the value of a variable in the calling environment. When such a function is called, an address is passed as an actual argument.

8.9 EXERCISES

1   What gets printed by the following code?

```
int   i = 5, *p = &i;

printf("%d %d %d %d %d\n", p, *p + 2, **&p, 3**p, **& p+4);
```

2   If i and j are int's and p and q are pointers to int, which of the following assignment expressions are illegal?

```
p = &i          p = &*&i          i = (int) p          q = &p
*q = &j         i = (*&)j          i = *&*&j            i = (*p)++ + *q
```

3   Write a program with the declaration

```
char   a, b, c, *p, *q, *r;
```

that prints out the locations assigned to all these variables by your compiler. From the values that are printed out, can you tell how many bytes are allocated for each of the variables?

4 Write a function that shifts the stored value of five character variables in a circular fashion. Your function should work in the following way. Suppose that c1, c2, . . ., c5 are variables of type char, and suppose that the values of these variables are 'A', 'B', . . ., 'E', respectively. The function call shift(&c1, &c2, &c3, &c4, &c5) should cause the variables c1, c2, . . ., c5 to have the values 'B', 'C', 'D', 'E', 'A', respectively. Your function definition should start as follows:

```
shift(p_c1, p_c2, p_c3, p_c4, p_c5)
char   *p_c1, *p_c2, *p_c3, *p_c4, *p_c5;
{
    .  .  .  .  .
```

Test your function by calling it five times and printing out in turn BCDEA, CDEAB, DEABC, EABCD, and ABCDE.

5 Write a function that orders the stored values of three characters. Suppose, for example, that c1, c2, and c3 are character variables having the values 'C', 'B', and 'D', respectively. Then the function call order_chars(&c1, &c2, &c3) should cause the stored values of c1, c2, and c3 to be 'B', 'C', and 'D', respectively. Write a program that thoroughly tests your function.

6 The program that we wrote to process characters in Section 8.4 is short enough so that one could do away with the function process() and write all the code in main(). Of course, we did the work in process() to illustrate how pointers can be used. Rewrite the program, making no use of pointers.

7 In the previous exercise we went from pointers to no pointers. In this exercise we want to do the reverse. Take the *cnt_char* program presented in Chapter 7 and rewrite it so that the majority of the work is done by calling a function. *Hint:* Write a function definition that begins

```
cnt_char(c, p_digit_cnt, p_letter_cnt, . . . )
int   c, *p_digit_cnt, *p_letter_cnt, . . .
```

8   How many bytes are used by your system to store pointer variables? Does it take less space to store a pointer to a char than to store a pointer to a double? Use the sizeof operator to find out. Print a table of values that shows the number of bytes needed to store a pointer to each of the fundamental types.

9   Since the symbol * represents both the indirection operator and the multiplication operator, it is not always immediately clear what is intended. What gets printed by the following code and why? Rewrite the expressions in the printf() statements in two ways. First, remove all the blanks in the two expressions. Does the compiler get confused when you do this? Second, leave a blank around each binary operator, but remove the blanks between any unary operator and whatever it is operating on. After you have done this, is the code more readable?

```
main()
{
    int     i = 2, j = 4, k = 6;
    int     *p = &i, *q = &j, *r = &k;

    printf("%d\n",  *  p  *  *  q  *  *  r);
    printf("%d\n",  ++  *  p  *  --  *  q  *  ++  *  r);
}
```

10   The following program has a conceptual mistake. See if you can spot the mistake and correct it, with your code still making use of a pointer.

```
#define   LUCKY_NUMBER   777

main()
{
    int   *p = LUCKY_NUMBER;

    printf("Is this my lucky number?  %d\n", *p);
}
```

As presented, this program may or may not run on your system. On our system the program produces the following output:

```
Is this my lucky number?  11665668
```

Can you explain this output?

11 With the following code, what gets printed and why?

```
int   v = 7, *p = &v;

printf("%d  %d  %d\n", &v, *&v, &p, *&p, **&p);
```

Notice that we have used the combination *&, but not &*. Are there situations where &* is semantically correct?

12 Just as there are pointers to int, there are pointers to pointers to int. We do not wish to make serious use of this concept here, but we can easily illustrate the idea in a simple way. Write a test program with the declaration

```
int   v = 7, *p = &v, **q = &p;
```

The identifier q is a pointer to pointer to int, and its initial value is the address of p. To test this concept try

```
printf("%d  %d  %d\n", q, *q, **q);
```

Does an expression such as q == &p make sense? Include this expression in your test program.

13 Extend the ideas presented in the previous exercise by writing a test program where r is declared to be a pointer to pointer to pointer to int.

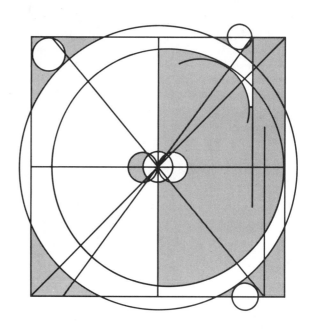

9

ARRAYS
AND POINTERS

Arrays are a data type that is used to represent a large number of homogeneous values. The elements of an array are accessed by the use of subscripts. Arrays of all types are possible, including arrays of arrays. Strings are just arrays of characters, but they are sufficiently important to be treated separately in the next chapter.

A typical array declaration allocates memory starting from a base address. The array name is in effect a pointer constant to this base address. In this chapter this relationship of array to address will be carefully explained. Another key point is how to pass arrays as parameters to functions. A number of carefully worked examples will illustrate these points.

9.1 ONE-DIMENSIONAL ARRAYS

Programs often use homogeneous data. For example, if we want to manipulate some grades, we might declare

```
int    grade0, grade1, grade2;
```

However, if the number of grades is large, it will be cumbersome to represent and manipulate the data by means of unique identifiers. Instead, an array, which is a derived type, can be used. Individual elements of the array are accessed using a subscript, also called an index. The brackets [ ] are used to contain the subscripts of an array. To use grade[0], grade[1], and grade[2] in a program, we would declare

```
int    grade[3];
```

where the integer 3 in the declaration represents the size of the array, or the number of elements in the array. The indexing of array elements always starts at 0. This is one of the characteristic features of the C language.

A one-dimensional array declaration is a type followed by an identifier with a bracketed constant integral expression. The value of the constant expression, which must be positive, is the size of the array; it specifies the number of elements in the array. To store the elements of the array, the compiler assigns an appropriate amount of memory starting from a base address.

To illustrate some of these ideas, let us write a small program that fills an array, prints out values, and sums the elements of the array.

```
#define    SIZE    5

main()
{
    int    a[SIZE];        /* space for a[0], ..., a[4] is allocated */
    int    i, sum = 0;

    for (i = 0; i < SIZE; ++i)                /* fill the array */
        a[i] = i * i;
    for (i = 0; i < SIZE; ++i)                /* print values */
        printf("a[%d] = %d    ", i, a[i]);
    for (i = 0; i < SIZE; ++i)                /* sum the elements */
        sum += a[i];
    printf("\nsum = %d\n", sum);
}
```

The output of this program is

```
a[0] = 0    a[1] = 1    a[2] = 4    a[3] = 9    a[4] = 16
sum = 30
```

The above array required memory to store five integer values. Thus if a[0] is stored at location 1000, then on a system needing 4 bytes for an int, the remaining array elements are successively stored at locations 1004, 1008, 1012, and 1016. It is considered good programming practice to define the size of an array as a symbolic constant. Since much of the code may depend on this value, it is convenient to be able to change a single #define line to process different size arrays. Notice how the various parts of the for statement are neatly tailored to provide a terse notation for dealing with array computations.

INITIALIZATION

Arrays may be of storage class automatic, external, or static, but not register. External and static arrays can be initialized using an array initializer. An example is

```
static float    x[7] = {-1.1, 0.2, 33.0, 4.4, 5.05, 0.0, 7.7};
```

This initializes x[0] to -1.1, x[1] to 0.2, and so forth. When a list of initializers is shorter than the number of array elements to be initialized, the remaining elements are initialized to zero. If an external or static array is not initialized, then the system initializes all elements to zero automatically. In contrast, automatic arrays cannot be initialized. The elements of an automatic array always start with "garbage" values, that is, with the arbitrary values that happen to be in memory when the array is allocated.

If an external or static array is declared without a size and is initialized to a series of values, it is implicitly given the size of the number of initializers. Thus

```
int a[] = {3, 4, 5, 6};        and        int a[4] = {3, 4, 5, 6};
```

are equivalent external declarations.

SUBSCRIPTING

Assume that a declaration of the form

```
int    i, a[size];
```

has been made. Then we can write a[i] to access an element of the
array. More generally, we may write a[*expr*], where *expr* is an integral expression, to access an element of the array. We call *expr* a
subscript, or index, of a. The value of a subscript must lie in the
range 0 to *size* − 1. An array subscript value outside this range
will cause a run-time error. When this happens, the condition is
called "overrunning the bounds of the array" or "subscript out of
bounds." It is a common programming error. The effect of the
error is system dependent and can be quite confusing. One frequent
result is that the value of some unrelated variable will be returned
or modified. Thus the programmer must ensure that all subscripts
stay within bounds.

9.2 AN EXAMPLE: COUNTING EACH LETTER SEPARATELY

In previous chapters we showed how to count digits, letters, etc. By
using an array, we can easily count the occurrence of each uppercase letter separately. Here is the program that does this.

```
/* Count each uppercase letter separately. */

#include    <stdio.h>
#include    <ctype.h>

main()
{
   int   c, i, letter[26];

   for (i = 0; i < 26; ++i)          /* initialize array to zero */
      letter[i] = 0;
   while ((c = getchar()) != EOF)   /* count the letters */
      if (isupper(c))
         ++letter[c - 'A'];
   for (i = 0; i < 26; ++i) {        /* print the results */
      if (i % 6 == 0)
         printf("\n");
      printf("%5c:%4d", 'A' + i, letter[i]);
   }
   printf("\n\n");
}
```

Among our files is one that contains the current version of this chapter. If we compile the program into *cnt_letters* and then give the command

   cnt_letters < chapter9

the following appears on the screen:

```
A:  75   B:  52   C: 219   D:  14   E: 121   F:  13
G:   9   H:  13   I: 121   J:   1   K:   1   L:  39
M:  25   N:  44   O:  38   P: 243   Q:   1   R:  37
S:  73   T:  96   U:   7   V:   3   W:  17   X:   9
Y:  11   Z:  27
```

■ DISSECTION OF THE *cnt_letters* PROGRAM

```
int   c, i, letter[26];
```

- The count for each of the 26 capital letters will be stored in the array letter. It is important to remember that the elements of the array are letter[0], letter[1], ..., letter[25]. Forgetting that array subscripting starts at 0 causes many errors. The variable i will be used as a subscript.

```
for (i = 0; i < 26; ++i)          /* initialize array to zero */
   letter[i] = 0;
```

- Automatic arrays must be explicitly initialized. This for loop follows a standard pattern for processing all the elements of an array. It is a C programming cliché. The subscripting variable is initialized to 0. The termination test is to see if the upper bound is exceeded.

```
while ((c = getchar()) != EOF)   /* count the letters */
   if (isupper(c))
      ++letter[c - 'A'];
```

- The library function getchar() is used repeatedly to read a character in the input stream and assign its value to c. The while loop is exited when the end-of-file sentinel is detected. The macro isupper() from <ctype.h> is used to test whether c is an uppercase letter. If it is, then an appropriate element of the array letter is incremented.

```
++letter[c - 'A'];
```

- This line of code is machine dependent. On ASCII machines the expression c - 'A' has the value 0 if c has the value 'A', the value 1 if c has the value 'B', and so forth. Thus the uppercase letter value of c is mapped into the range of values 0 to 25. Because brackets have higher precedence than ++, an equivalent statement is

```
++(letter[c - 'A']);
```

Thus we see that letter[0] is incremented if c has the value 'A', letter[1] is incremented if c has the value 'B', and so forth.

```
for (i = 0; i < 26; ++i) {        /* print the results */
   if (i % 6 == 0)
      printf("\n");
   printf("%5c:%4d", 'A' + i, letter[i]);
}
```

■ Once again the same for loop cliché is used to process the array letter. Every sixth time through the loop a newline is printed. As i runs from 0 to 25 the expression 'A' + i is used to print A through Z with each letter followed by a colon and the appropriate count.

9.3 THE RELATIONSHIP BETWEEN ARRAYS AND POINTERS

An array name by itself is an address, or pointer value, and pointers and arrays are almost identical in terms of how they are used to access memory. However, there are differences, and these differences are subtle and important. A pointer is a variable that takes addresses as values. An array name is a particular fixed address that can be thought of as a constant pointer. When an array is declared, the compiler must allocate a base address and a sufficient amount of storage to contain all the elements of the array. The base address of the array is the initial location in memory where the array is stored; it is the address of the first element (index 0) of the array. Suppose that we make the declaration

```
#define  N  100
```

```
int  a[N], *p;
```

and that the system causes memory bytes numbered 300, 304, 308,
..., 696 to be the addresses of a[0], a[1], a[2], ..., a[99], respectively, with location 300 being the base address of a. We are
assuming that each byte is addressable and that 4 bytes are used to
store an int. This is system dependent. The two statements

```
p = a;        and        p = &a[0];
```

are equivalent and would assign 300 to p. Pointer arithmetic provides an alternative to array indexing. The two statements

```
p = a + 1;        and        p = &a[1];
```

are equivalent and would assign 304 to p. Assuming that the
elements of a have been assigned values, we can use the following
code to sum the array.

```
sum = 0;
for (p = a; p < &a[N]; ++p)
    sum += *p;
```

In this loop the pointer variable p is initialized to the base address
of the array a. Then the successive values of p are equivalent to
&a[0], &a[1], . . ., &a[N-1]. In general, if i is a variable of type
int, then p + i is the ith offset from the address p. In a similar
manner a + i is the ith offset from the base address of the array a.
Here is another way of summing the array.

```
sum = 0;
for (i = 0; i < N; ++i)
    sum += *(a + i);
```

Just as the expression *(a + i) is equivalent to a[i], so is the expression *(p + i) equivalent to p[i]. Here is yet another way of summing the array.

```
p = a;
sum = 0;
for (i = 0; i < N; ++i)
    sum += p[i];
```

Although in many ways arrays and pointers can be treated alike, there is one essential difference. Because the array a is a constant pointer and not a variable, expressions such as

```
a = p          ++a          a += 2
```

are illegal. We cannot change the address of a.

9.4 POINTER ARITHMETIC AND ELEMENT SIZE

Pointer arithmetic is one of the powerful features of C. If the variable p is a pointer to a particular type, then the expression p + 1 yields the correct machine address for storing or accessing the next variable of that type. In a similar fashion pointer expressions such as p + i and ++p and p += i all make sense. If p and q are both pointing to elements of an array, then p − q yields the int value representing the number of array elements between p and q. Even though pointer expressions and arithmetic expressions have a similar appearance, there is a critical difference in interpretation between the two types of expressions. The following code illustrates the difference:

```
double   a[2], *p, *q;

p = &a[0];
q = p + 1;                      /* equivalent to q = &a[1]; */
printf("%d\n", q - p);          /* 1 is printed */
printf("%d\n", (int) q - (int) p);    /* 8 is printed */
```

What is printed by the last statement is machine dependent. On a VAX a double is stored in 8 bytes. Hence the difference of the two machine addresses interpreted as integers is 8.

9.5 PASSING ARRAYS TO FUNCTIONS

In a function definition a formal parameter that is declared as an array is actually a pointer. When an array is being passed, its base address is passed call-by-value. The array elements themselves are not copied. As a notational convenience, the compiler allows array bracket notation to be used in declaring pointers as parameters. This notation reminds the programmer and other readers of the code that the function should be called with an array. To illustrate this we write a function that sums the elements of an array of type int.

```
sum(a, n)
int   a[], n;      /* n is the size of the array */
{
   int   i, s = 0;

   for(i = 0; i < n; ++i)
      s += a[i];
   return (s);
}
```

As part of the header of a function definition the declaration

```
int a[];          is equivalent to            int *a;
```

On the other hand, as declarations within the body of a function they are *not* equivalent. The first will create a constant pointer (and no storage), whereas the second will create a pointer variable.

Suppose that v has been declared to be an array with 100 elements of type int. After the elements have been assigned values, we can use the above function sum() to add various of the elements of v. The following table illustrates some of the possibilities.

Various ways that sum() might be called

Invocation	What gets computed and returned
sum(v, 100)	v[0] + v[1] + · · · + v[99]
sum(v, 88)	v[0] + v[1] + · · · + v[87]
sum(v + 7, k)	v[7] + v[8] + · · · + v[k+6]

The last function call illustrates again the use of pointer arithmetic. The base address of v is offset by 7, and sum() initializes the local pointer variable a to this address. This causes all address calculations inside the function call to be similarly offset.

9.6 AN EXAMPLE: BUBBLE SORT

Efficient sorting algorithms typically require on the order of $n \log n$ comparisons to sort an array with n elements. A bubble sort is inefficient because it requires n^2 comparisons. Nonetheless, for small arrays its performance is usually acceptable. After we present the code for bubble(), we will illustrate in detail how the function works on a particular array of integers. We will use the function order(), written in Chapter 8.

```
bubble(a, n)
int   a[], n;      /* n is the size of a[] */
{
    int   i, j;

    for (i = 0; i < n - 1; ++i)
        for (j = n - 1; i < j; --j)
            order(&a[j-1], &a[j]);
}
```

Suppose we declare

```
static int   a[] = {7, 3, 66, 3, -5, 22, -77, 2};
```

and then invoke bubble(a, 8). The following table shows the elements of the array a[] after each pass of the outer loop:

Unordered data:	7	3	66	3	−5	22	−77	2
First pass:	−77	7	3	66	3	−5	22	2
Second pass:	−77	−5	7	3	66	3	2	22
Third pass:	−77	−5	2	7	3	66	3	22
Fourth pass:	−77	−5	2	3	7	3	66	22
Fifth pass:	−77	−5	2	3	3	7	22	66
Sixth pass:	−77	−5	2	3	3	7	22	66
Seventh pass:	−77	−5	2	3	3	7	22	66

At the start of the first pass a[6] is compared with a[7]. Since the values are in order they are not exchanged. Then a[5] is compared with a[6], and since these values are out of order they are exchanged. Then a[4] is compared with a[5], etc. Adjacent out-of-order values are exchanged. The effect of the first pass is to "bubble" the smallest value in the array into the element a[0]. In the second pass a[0] is left unchanged and a[6] is compared first with a[7], etc. After the second pass the next to the smallest value is in a[1]. Since each pass bubbles the next smallest element to its appropriate array position, the algorithm after n − 1 passes will have put all the elements in order. Notice that in this example all the elements have been ordered after the fifth pass. It is possible to modify the algorithm to terminate earlier by adding a variable that detects if no exchanges are made in a given pass. We leave this as an exercise.

9.7 MULTI-DIMENSIONAL ARRAYS

The C language allows arrays of any type, including arrays of arrays. With two bracket pairs we obtain a two-dimensional array. This idea can be iterated to obtain arrays of higher dimension. With each bracket pair we add another array dimension.

Examples of declarations of arrays	Remarks
int a[100];	a one-dimensional array
int b[3][5];	a two-dimensional array
int c[7][9][2];	a three-dimensional array

A k-dimensional array has a size for each of its k dimensions. If we let s_i represent the size of its ith dimension, then the declaration of the array will allocate space for $s_1 \times s_2 \times \cdots \times s_k$ elements. In the above table, b has 3×5 elements, and c has $7 \times 9 \times 2$ elements. Starting at the base address of the array, all the array elements are stored contiguously in memory.

Even though array elements are stored one after the other, it is often convenient to think of a two-dimensional array as a rectangular collection of elements with rows and columns. For example, suppose we declare

```
int   b[3][5];
```

Then we can think of the array elements arranged as

	col 1	col 2	col 3	col 4	col 5
row 1	b[0][0]	b[0][1]	b[0][2]	b[0][3]	b[0][4]
row 2	b[1][0]	b[1][1]	b[1][2]	b[1][3]	b[1][4]
row 3	b[2][0]	b[2][1]	b[2][2]	b[2][3]	b[2][4]

To illustrate these ideas, let us write a program that fills a two-dimensional array, prints out values, and sums the elements of the array.

```
#define   M   3      /* number of rows */
#define   N   4      /* number of columns */

main()
{
    int   a[M][N], i, j, sum = 0;

    for (i = 0; i < M; ++i)          /* fill the array */
        for (j = 0; j < N; ++j)
            a[i][j] = i + j;
    for (i = 0; i < M; ++i) {         /* print array values */
        for (j = 0; j < N; ++j)
            printf("a[%d][%d] = %d    ", i, j, a[i][j]);
        printf("\n");
    }
    for (i = 0; i < M; ++i)          /* sum the array */
        for (j = 0; j < N; ++j)
            sum += a[i][j];
    printf("\nsum = %d\n\n", sum);
}
```

The output of this program is

```
a[0][0] = 0    a[0][1] = 1    a[0][2] = 2    a[0][3] = 3
a[1][0] = 1    a[1][1] = 2    a[1][2] = 3    a[1][3] = 4
a[2][0] = 2    a[2][1] = 3    a[2][2] = 4    a[2][3] = 5

sum = 30
```

In processing every element of a multi-dimensional array, a single for loop is required for each dimension.

9.8 STYLE

As the examples of this chapter have shown, it is often desirable to use a symbolic constant to define the size of an array. This constant allows the programmer to make a single modification if code is needed to process a different size array.

A `for` loop that is to be used to do 10 things repetitively can be written

```
for (i = 1; i <= 10; ++i)
    .  .  .  .  .
```

or it can be written

```
for (i = 0; i < 10; ++i)
    .  .  .  .  .
```

Which form gets used depends on just what is in the body of the loop. However, in cases where either form can be used, C programmers generally favor the second form. The reason for this is clear: When dealing with arrays, the second form is the correct programming idiom. Because arrays are used extensively in programming tasks, most experienced C programmers begin counting from 0 rather than 1.

A generally important style consideration is to structure a program so that each elementary task is accomplished by its own function. This is at the heart of structured programming. However, this can lead to inefficient code when processing arrays. Let us look at a specific example.

```
/* Compute various statistics. */

#define    SIZE    10

main()
{
    int      i;
    double   a[SIZE], average(), maximum(), sum();

    printf("Input %d numbers:  ", SIZE);
    for (i = 0; i < SIZE; ++i)
        scanf("%lf", &a[i]);
    printf("\n%s%5d\n%s%7.1f\n%s%7.1f\n%s%7.1f\n\n",
        "       Array size:", SIZE,
        "Maximum element:", maximum(a, SIZE),
        "         Average:", average(a, SIZE),
        "             Sum:", sum(a, SIZE));
}
```

We have written main() so that it calls three other functions, each one computing a desired value. Let us write these functions next.

```
double maximum(a, n)
double    a[];
int       n;
{
    int      i;
    double   max = a[0];

    for(i = 0; i < n; ++i)
        if (max < a[i])
            max = a[i];
    return (max);
}
```

```
double average(a, n)
double    a[];
int       n;
{
    double   sum();

    return (sum(a, n) / (double) n);
}


double sum(a, n)
double    a[];
int       n;
{
    int       i;
    double    s = 0.0;

    for(i = 0; i < n; ++i)
        s += a[i];
    return (s);
}
```

Two of these three functions use a for loop to process the elements
of an array. And average() calls sum() to do its work. For the sake
of efficiency we could restructure our program as follows. First we
rewrite main().

```
#define   SIZE   10

main()
{
   int      i;
   double   a[SIZE], average, max, sum;

   printf("Input %d numbers:  ", SIZE);
   for (i = 0; i < SIZE; ++i)
      scanf("%lf", &a[i]);
   stats(a, SIZE, &average, &max, &sum);
   printf("\n%s%5d\n%s%7.1f\n%s%7.1f\n%s%7.1f\n\n",
      "     Array size:", SIZE,
      "Maximum element:", max,
      "        Average:", average,
      "            Sum:", sum);
}
```

Now we write the function stats(), using a single for loop to compute all the desired values.

```
stats(a, n, p_average, p_max, p_sum)
double   a[], *p_average, *p_max, *p_sum;
int      n;
{
   int   i;

   *p_max = *p_sum = a[0];
   for (i = 1; i < n; ++i) {
      *p_sum += a[i];
      if (*p_max < a[i])
         *p_max = a[i];
   }
   *p_average = *p_sum / (double) n;
}
```

This example is so small that efficiency is not really an issue. However, when code is to be used in a serious working environment, the ideas that we have presented are often relevant. In general, along with clarity and correctness, efficiency is an important consideration in programming.

9.9 COMMON PROGRAMMING ERRORS

The most common programming error with arrays is using a subscript value that is out of bounds. Suppose that 10 is the size of an array a[] of integers. If we were to write

```
sum = 0;
for (i = 1; i <= 10; ++i)
   sum += a[i];
```

we would get a system-dependent error. The value at the address corresponding to a[10] would be used, but the value in memory at this address would be unpredictable.

In many programming languages, when an array of size n is declared, the corresponding subscript range is from 1 to n. It is very important to remember that C uses 0 as a lower bound and $n - 1$ as an upper bound. Bounds checking is an important programming skill to cultivate. It is often useful to hand simulate programs on small size arrays before processing very large arrays.

9.10 OPERATING SYSTEM CONSIDERATIONS

On many systems the function calloc() is provided in the standard library to allocate space in memory dynamically for arrays. Rather than having an array size given by a specific constant in a program, it may be desirable to allow the user to input the array size. A function call of the form calloc(n, object_size) returns a pointer to enough space in memory to store n objects, each of object_size bytes. Both n and object_size should be of type unsigned. The pointer value returned by calloc() is of type pointer to char. Often it must by appropriately cast. The storage set aside by calloc() is automatically initialized to all zeros. The name calloc comes from "contiguous allocation."

To illustrate these ideas, let us write a small program that prompts the user to input the desired array size.

```
main()
{
    char   *calloc();
    int    *a, i, n, sum = 0;

    printf("\nEnter your array size: ");
    scanf("%d", &n);
    a = (int *) calloc((unsigned) n, sizeof(int));
    printf("\nTo fill your array, input %d integers: ", n);
    for (i = 0; i < n; ++i)
        scanf("%d", &a[i]);
    for (i = 0; i < n; ++i)
        sum += a[i];
    printf("\n%s%7d\n%s%7d\n\n",
        "Number of elements:", n,
        "             Sum:", sum);
}
```

Notice that we declared calloc() to be a function that returns a pointer to char. Even though the executable code for this function is provided by the system, we still must declare the function appropriately. Let us consider in some detail the assignment statement

```
a = (int *) calloc((unsigned) n, sizeof(int));
```

The first argument to calloc() is cast to be of type unsigned so as to prevent a warning by *lint*. If we had declared the variable n to be of type unsigned instead of int, this cast would not have been necessary. The second argument to calloc() uses the sizeof operator. This makes the code more readable, and at the same time makes the code portable. Since sizeof returns a value of type unsigned, no cast is needed for the second argument. Finally, we use (int *) to cast the value returned by calloc(), which is of type pointer to char, to the desired pointer type. After memory has been allocated for a, we can proceed with our array-processing chores.

9.11 SUMMARY

1   Arrays can be used to deal with a large number of homogeneous values. A declaration such as

```
int   a[100];
```

makes a an array of int's. The compiler allocates contiguous space in memory for 100 int's and numbers the elements of a from 0 to 99.

2   Elements of the array are accessed by expressions such as a[i]. More generally, we can use a[expr], where the subscript, or index, *expr* is an integral expression having a nonnegative value that does not overrun the upper bound of a. It is the programmer's responsibility to make sure that an array index stays within bounds.

3   When an array name is passed as an argument to a function, only a copy of the base address of the array is actually passed. In the header to a function definition the declaration

```
int   a[];        is equivalent to        int   *a;
```

In the header to a function definition the declaration of a multi-dimensional array must have all sizes specified except the first; see exercise 9.

4   An external or static array can be initialized by assigning an appropriate length list of values within braces. If an external or static array is declared but not initialized, then all the elements of the array are automatically initialized to zero. Automatic arrays cannot be initialized. They start with "garbage" values.

5   Arrays of any type can be created, including arrays of arrays. For example,

```
double   b[30][50];
```

declares b to be an array of "array of 50 double's." The elements of b are accessed by expressions such as b[i][j].

9.12 EXERCISES

1   Explain the following terms:

(a) lower bound
(b) subscript
(c) out of bounds

2   The following array declarations have several errors. Identify each of them.

```
#define    SIZE    4

main()
{
    int    a[SIZE] = {0, 2, 2, 3, 4};
    int    b[SIZE - 5];
    int    c[3.0];
    .  .  .  .  .
```

3   Write a function that sums the even and odd indexed elements of an array of double's separately. Each element of the array contributes to one of the two sums, depending on whether the index of the element is even or odd. Your function definition should look something like

```
sum(a, n, even_index_sum_ptr, odd_index_sum_ptr)
double    a[], *even_index_sum_ptr, *odd_index_sum_ptr;
int       n;    /* n is the size of a[] */
{
    .  .  .  .  .
```

4   Write a function that computes two sums from the elements of an array of integers. Each element of the array contributes to one of the two sums, depending on whether the element itself is even or odd. Your function definition should look something like

```
sum(a, n, even_element_sum_ptr, odd_element_sum_ptr)
int    a[], n, *even_element_sum_ptr, *odd_element_sum_ptr;
{
      .   .   .   .   .
```

5   Modify the *cnt_letters* program to also count each lowercase letter separately.

6   This exercise is designed to test your understanding of pointer arithmetic. Suppose that SIZE is a symbolic constant with value 100. If we make the declaration

```
char    a[SIZE], *p = a;
int     i;
```

then the compiler allocates 100 bytes of contiguous storage in memory with the array name a pointing to the base address of this storage. We are deliberately using an array of char's, because each char is stored in 1 byte. The pointer p is initialized to have the same value as a. Now we want to fill the array in a very simple way.

```
for (i = 0; i < SIZE; ++i)
   a[i] = i;
```

The elements of the array have been assigned the consecutive values 0, 1, 2, . . . , 99. Now consider

```
printf("%d\n", *(p + 3));
printf("%d\n", *(char *)((int *) p + 3));
printf("%d\n", *(char *)((double *) p + 3));
```

What gets printed? The answer to this question is machine dependent. Explain why this is so, and explain what would get printed on a machine different from your own. *Hint:* Consider the expression

```
(int *) p + 3
```

Of the two operators that are acting, which has the higher precedence? Use this information to help you determine which element of the array this pointer expression is pointing to. Now consider

(char *) *pointer_expression*

This casts the pointer expression to be a pointer to char. Now consider

*(char *) *pointer_expression*

Of the two unary operators that are acting, how do they associate?

7   Modify bubble() so that it terminates after the first pass in which no two elements are interchanged.

8   Write a program that finds the maximum and minimum element of a two-dimensional array. Do all of this within main(). See the next exercise.

9   Rewrite the program that you wrote for exercise 8, using a function that has a two-dimensional array in its parameter list. *Hint:* When a multi-dimensional array occurs as a parameter in a header to a function definition, the size for each dimension, except the first dimension, must be specified. The effect of this is to hard-wire the function so that it can be used only for certain arrays. Consider

```
double sum(b, m)
int   m;          /* m is the number of rows */
double   b[][5];
{
    . . . . .
```

In this example we specified 5 as the column size of b. This information is needed by the compiler to handle expressions of the form b[i][j] within the function. To call this function we could write sum(b, 3) if b is a 3 by 5 array in the calling environment. We could also invoke sum(c, 7) if c is a 7 by 5 array in the calling environment. We can pass any array to sum() as long as it is an *n* by 5 array. From all of this you may gather that C does not handle multi-dimensional arrays gracefully. That is not true. There is more to the story, but since it involves a more sophisticated use of pointers, we will not tell the story here.

10   Write a program that keeps sales data for 10 years by month. The array should have a month index of size 12. Given this data, compute by sorted order the months of the year for which sales are best.

11   There are many known sorting methods. Here is the heart of a simple transposition sort.

```
for (i = 0; i < SIZE; ++i)
   for (j = i + 1; j < SIZE; ++j)
      order(&a[i], &a[j]);
```

Write a program that implements this sort. After your program is working, modify it so that all the elements of the array are printed after each pass of the outer loop. Suppose, for example, that the size of your array is 8 and that its starting values are

7   3   66   3   −5   22   −77   2

Your program should print the following on the screen:

Unordered data:	7	3	66	3	−5	22	−77	2
After pass 1:	−77	7	66	3	3	22	−5	2
After pass 2:	−77	−5	66	7	3	22	3	2

.   .   .   .   .

12   The output of the program that you wrote for exercise 11 illustrated the effects of a particular sorting method acting on a particular array. In this exercise we want to dig a little deeper. Modify the program that you wrote for exercise 11 so that every time two elements are interchanged, the array is written out with the interchanges underlined. With the array of size 8 previously suggested, your program should print on the screen:

```
3    7   66   3   -5   22   -77   2
--   --

-5   7   66   3    3   22   -77   2
--                --
```

.   .   .   .   .

13   Write a program that reads *n* integers into an array, and then prints the value of each distinct element along with the number of times that it occurs on a separate line. The values should be printed in descending order. Suppose, for example, that you input the values

```
-7  3  3  -7  5  5  3
```

as the elements of your array. Then your program should print

```
5 occurs 2 times
3 occurs 3 times
-7 occurs 2 times
```

Use your program to investigate the output of random(). First use random() to create a file, say *random_data*, containing 100 random integers in the range 1 to 10. Recall that this can be done with a for loop of the form

```
for (i = 1; i <= 100; ++i) {
   printf("%7d", random() % 10 + 1);
   if (i % 10 == 0)
      printf("\n");
}
```

Do not forget to declare random() as a function returning a long. Since we have not yet explained how one writes to a file (see Chapter 14), you will have to write a small program, call it *make_random*, and then give the command

make_random > random_data

to redirect the output of the program.

14 Rewrite the previous program to make use of calloc(). Suppose that the file *random_data* has as its first entry the number of random numbers contained in that file. Write your program to read that first entry into a variable named size. Suppose that the variable rand_array has been declared as a pointer to int. You can dynamically allocate storage by making use of calloc() as follows:

```
rand_array = (int *) calloc((unsigned) size, sizeof(int));
```

The cast (int *) is necessary because the standard library function calloc() returns a value of type pointer to char. The cast (unsigned) is necessary because calloc() expects both of its arguments to be of type unsigned. The pointer rand_array can be treated as an array after space has been allocated. For example, to fill the array, you can write

```
for (i = 0; i < size; ++i)
   scanf("%d", &rand_array[i]);
```

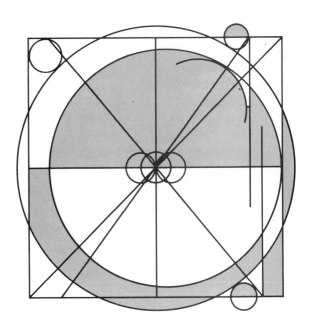

10

STRINGS
AND POINTERS

In C a string is a one-dimensional array of type `char`. A character in a string can be accessed either as an element in an array or by making use of a pointer to `char`. The flexibility this provides makes C especially useful in writing string processing programs. The standard library provides many useful string handling functions.

While string processing can be viewed as a special case of array processing, it has characteristics that give it a unique flavor. Important to this is the use of the character value \0 to terminate a string. This chapter includes a number of example programs that illustrate string processing ideas. Again, as in the previous chapter, the important relationship between pointer and array is shown. The type pointer to `char` is conceptually a string. Our examples will illustrate the pointer arithmetic and dereferencing needed to properly process string data.

10.1 THE END-OF-STRING SENTINEL \0

By convention a string is terminated by the end-of-string sentinel \0, or null character. A constant string such as "abc" is stored in memory as four characters, the last one being \0. Thus the length of the string "abc" is 3, but the size of the string is 4. To allocate storage in memory for a string, we could write

```
#define   MAXWORD   100

main()
{
    char   w[MAXWORD];
    .  .  .  .  .
```

After storage has been allocated, there are a number of ways of getting character values into the string w. First, we can do it character by character as follows:

```
w[0] = 'A';
w[1] = 'B';
w[2] = 'C';
w[3] = '\0';
```

Notice that we ended the string with the null character.

Another way to get character values into w is to make use of scanf(). The format %s is used to read in a string. The statement

```
scanf("%s", w);
```

causes any white space characters in the input stream to be skipped. Then nonwhite space characters are read in and placed in memory beginning at the base address of w. The process stops when a white space character or EOF is encountered. At that point a null character is placed in memory to end the string. Notice that we did not use &w as the second argument to scanf(). To do so would be an error. Since an array name is a pointer to the base address of the array, the expression w is equivalent to &w[0]. Because the size of w is 100, we can enter up to 99 characters on the keyboard. If more are entered, we will overrun the bounds of w.

There are other ways of getting values into the string w. Later in this chapter we discuss the use of functions in the standard library.

The sentinel \0, also called a delimiter, allows a simple test to detect the end of a string. It is useful to think of strings as having a variable length delimited by the null character, but with a maximum length determined by the size of the string. The size of a string must include the storage needed for the null character. As with all arrays it is the job of the programmer to make sure that string bounds are not overrun.

Note carefully that 'a' and "a" are different. The first is a character constant, and the second is a string constant. The string "a" is an array of characters with two elements, the first with value 'a' and the second with value '\0'.

10.2   INITIALIZATION OF STRINGS

Recall that external and static arrays can be initialized. This feature works with character arrays as well. However, the compiler allows for an initialization of the form

```
static char   s[] = "abc";
```

which is taken to be equivalent to

```
static char   s[] = {'a', 'b', 'c', '\0'};
```

Automatic arrays, including character arrays, cannot be initialized. However, it is possible to initialize a pointer to char of any storage class to a constant string. Consider, for example,

```
char   *p = "abc";
```

The effect of this is for the string "abc" to be placed in memory and for the pointer p to be initialized with the base address of the string.

10.3   AN EXAMPLE: HAVE A NICE DAY

Since a string is an array of characters, one way to process a string is to use array notation with subscripts. We want to write an interactive program to illustrate this. Our program will read a line of characters typed by the user into a string, print the string in reverse order, and then sum the elements of the string.

```c
/* Have a nice day! */

#define   MAXLINE   100

main()
{
    char   c, line[MAXLINE];
    int    i, sum = 0;

    printf("\nHi!  What is your name?  ");
    for (i = 0; (c = getchar()) != '\n'; ++i)
        line[i] = c;
    line[i] = '\0';
    printf("\n%s%s%s\n",
        "Nice to meet you ", line, ".");
    printf("Your name spelled backwards is ");
    while (i > 0)
        putchar(line[--i]);
    putchar('.');
    for (i = 0; line[i] != '\0'; ++i)
        sum += line[i];
    printf("\n%s%d%s\n\n%s\n\n",
        "Your character sum is ", sum, ".",
        "Have a nice day!");
}
```

Suppose that we execute this program and enter C. B. Diligent when prompted. Here is what appears on the screen:

```
Hi!  What is your name?  C. B. Diligent

Nice to meet you C. B. Diligent.
Your name spelled backwards is tnegiliD .B .C.
Your character sum is 1105.


Have a nice day!
```

■ DISSECTION OF THE *nice_day* PROGRAM

```
#define   MAXLINE   100

main()
{
    char   c, line[MAXLINE];
    int    i, sum = 0;
```

■ The character array line has size 100. Since the null character is always used to delimit a string, this means that the array can hold strings of length up to 99. The length of a string is a count of all characters up to, but not including, the null character. In this program we are making the assumption that the user will not type in more than 99 characters.

```
printf("\nHi!  What is your name?  ");
```

■ This is a prompt to the user. The program now expects a name to be typed in, followed by a carriage return.

```
for (i = 0; (c = getchar()) != '\n'; ++i)
    line[i] = c;
```

■ In this for loop the variable i is initialized to 0. The function getchar() gets a character and assigns it to c. If c is not a newline character, then it is assigned to the array element line[i] and i is incremented. The loop is repeatedly executed until a newline character is received.

```
line[i] = '\0';
```

- After the for loop is finished, the null character '\0' is assigned to the element line[i]. By convention, all strings end with a null character. Functions that process strings, such as printf(), use the null character as an end-of-string sentinel. We now can think of the array line stored in memory as

C	.	\0	B	.	\0	D	i	l	i	g	e	n	t	\0	*	...	*

```
0   1   2   3   4   5   6   7   8   9  10  11  12  13  14  15        99
```

Notice that * has been used to indicate that the contents of all the characters beyond \0 in the array are not known.

```
printf("\n%s%s%s\n",
    "Nice to meet you ", line, ".");
```

- The format %s is used to print a string. Here, the array line is one of three string arguments that are being printed. The effect of this statement is to print

```
    Nice to meet you C. B. Diligent.
```

on the screen.

```
printf("Your name spelled backwards is ");
while (i > 0)
    putchar(line[--i]);
putchar('.');
```

- At the start of this while loop the value of i is 14 and the value of line[i] is a null character. The expression --i first causes the stored value of i to be decremented by 1, and then the expression takes on this value. The effect of this loop is to print backwards the characters stored in the array. After the loop is finished, a period is printed to end the sentence.

```
for (i = 0; line[i] != '\n'; ++i)
   sum += line[i];
```

- Characters in C have integer value, namely the value of their ASCII code representation. This for loop is summing the values of the characters in the array. The loop stops when a newline character is reached.

```
printf("\n%s%d%s\n\n%s\n\n",
   "Your character sum is ", sum, ".",
   "Have a nice day!");
```

- The control string "\n%s%d%s\n\n%s\n\n" is telling printf() to print its remaining arguments in turn as a string, a decimal integer, a string, and a string interspersed with newline characters.

10.4 USING POINTERS TO PROCESS A STRING

In the last section we illustrated string processing with the use of subscripts. In this section we want to use pointers to process a string. Also, we want to show how strings can be used as arguments to functions.

Let us write a small interactive program that reads into a string a line of characters input by the user. Then the program will use this to create a new string and print it.

```
/* Character processing:  change a line. */

#define    MAXLINE    100

#include    <stdio.h>

main()
{
    char    line[MAXLINE], *change();

    printf("\nWhat is your favorite line?  ");
    read_in(line);
    printf("\n%s\n\n%s\n\n",
       "Here it is after being changed:", change(line));
}
```

After prompting the user, this program uses read_in() to put characters into line. Then line is passed as an argument to change(), which returns a pointer to char. The returned pointer value is printed by printf() in the format of a string. Here is the function read_in().

```
read_in(s)
char    s[];
{
    int    c, i = 0;

    while ((c = getchar()) != EOF && c != '\n')
       s[i++] = c;
    s[i] = '\0';
}
```

The parameter s is of type pointer to char. It could just as well have been declared as

```
char    *s;
```

In the while loop successive characters are gotten from the input stream and placed one after another into the array with base address s. When a newline character is received, the loop is exited and a null character is put into the array to act as the end-of-string sentinel. Notice that this function allocates no space. In main() space is allocated with the declaration of line. We are making the assumption that the user will not type in more than MAXLINE − 1 characters. When line is passed as an argument to read_in(), a copy of the base address of the array is made, and this value is taken on by the parameter s. The array elements themselves are not copied, but they are accessible in read_in() via this base address.

```c
char *change(s)
char   *s;
{
    static char   new_string[MAXLINE];
    char          *p = new_string;

    *p++ = '\t';
    for ( ; *s != '\0'; ++s)
      if (*s == 'e')
         *p++ = 'E';
      else if (*s == ' ') {
         *p++ = '\n';
         *p++ = '\t';
      }
      else
         *p++ = *s;
    *p = '\0';
    return (new_string);
}
```

This function takes a string and copies it, changing every e to E and replacing every blank by a newline and a tab. Suppose we run the program and type in the line

```
she sells sea shells
```

after receiving the prompt. Here is what appears on the screen:

What is your favorite line? she sells sea shells

Here it is after being changed:

```
    shE
    sElls
    sEa
    shElls
```

We want to explain in some detail how the function `change()` works.

■ DISSECTION OF THE change() FUNCTION

```
char *change(s)
char    *s;
{
    static char    new_string[MAXLINE];
    char           *p = new_string;
```

■ The first `char *` tells the compiler that this function returns a value of type pointer to `char`. The parameter `s` and the local variable `p` are both declared to be of type pointer to `char`. Since `s` is a parameter in a function header, it could just as well have been declared as

```
char    s[];
```

However, since `p` is a local variable and not a parameter, a similar declaration for `p` would be wrong. The array `new_string` is declared to have static storage class, and space is allocated for `MAXLINE` characters. The reason for static rather than automatic is explained below. The pointer `p` is initialized to the base address of `new_string`.

```
*p++ = '\t';
```

■ This one line of code is equivalent to

```
*p = '\t';
++p;
```

The situation is analyzed as follows. Since the operators * and ++ are both unary and associate "right to left," the expression *p++ is equivalent to *(p++). Thus the ++ operator is causing p to be indexed. In contrast, the expression (*p)++ would cause the value of what is pointed to by p to be indexed, which is something quite different. Since the ++ operator occurs on the right side of p rather than the left, the indexing of p occurs after the total expression *p++ = '\t' has been evaluated. Assignment is part of the evaluation process, and this causes a tab character to be assigned to what is pointed to by p. Since p points to the base address of new_string, a tab character is assigned to new_string[0]. After the indexing of p occurs, p points to new_string[1].

```
for ( ; *s != '\0'; ++s)
```

- Each time through the for loop a test is made to see if the value of what is pointed to by s is the end-of-string sentinel. If not, then the body of the for loop is executed and s is indexed. The effect of indexing a pointer to char is to cause it to point at the next character in the string.

```
if (*s == 'e')
    *p++ = 'E';
```

- In the body of the for loop a test is made to see if s is pointing to the character e. If it is, then the character E is assigned to what p is pointing at, and then p is indexed.

```
else if (*s == ' ') {
    *p++ = '\n';
    *p++ = '\t';
}
```

- Otherwise, a test is made to see if s is pointing to a blank character. If it is, then a newline character is assigned to what p is pointing at, followed by the indexing of p, followed by the assignment of a tab character to what p is pointing at, followed by the indexing of p.

```
else
    *p++ = *s;
```

- Finally, if the character to which s is pointing is neither an e nor a blank, then what p is pointing at is assigned the value of what s is pointing at, followed by the indexing of p. The effect of this for loop is to copy the string passed as an argument to change() into the string with base address &new_string[1], except that each e is replaced by an E and each blank is replaced by a newline and a tab.

```
*p = '\0';
```

- When the for loop is exited, what p is pointing at is assigned an end-of-string sentinel.

```
return (new_string);
```

- The array name new_string is a pointer to char, and this value is returned. If the storage class for new_string were automatic instead of static, then the memory allocated to new_string would not need to be preserved on exit from change(). If the memory is overwritten, then the final printf() statement in main() will not work properly.

10.5 AN EXAMPLE: COUNTING WORDS

The example in the last section illustrated the use of pointers and pointer arithmetic to process a string. In this section we want to give another illustration of this. We will write a function that counts the number of words in a string. For the purposes of this function a maximal sequence of nonwhite space characters will constitute a word.

```
/* Count the number of words in a string. */

#include    <ctype.h>

word_cnt(s)
char    *s;
{
    int    cnt = 0;

    while (*s != '\0') {
        while (isspace(*s))     /* skip white space */
            ++s;
        if (*s != '\0') {      /* found a word */
            ++cnt;
            while (!isspace(*s) && *s != '\0') /* skip the word */
                ++s;
        }
    }
    return (cnt);
}
```

This is a typical string processing function. Pointer arithmetic and dereferencing are used to search for various patterns or characters.

10.6 PASSING ARGUMENTS TO main()

C provides for arrays of any type, including arrays of pointers. Although this is an advanced topic that we do not wish to treat in detail, we need to use arrays of pointers to char to write programs that use command line arguments. Two arguments, conventionally called argc and argv, can be used with main() to communicate with the operating system. Here is a program that prints its command line arguments. It is a variant of the *echo* command in UNIX.

```
/* Echo the command line arguments. */

main(argc, argv)
int     argc;
char    *argv[];
{
    int   i;

    printf("argc = %d\n", argc);
    for (i = 0; i < argc; ++i)
        printf("argv[%d] = %s\n", i, argv[i]);
}
```

The variable argc provides a count of the command line arguments. The array argv is an array of pointers to char, and can be thought of as an array of strings. Since the element argv[0] always contains the name of the command itself, the value of argc is always 1 or more. Suppose that the above program is in the file *my_echo.c*. If we compile the program with the command

  cc my_echo.c

and then give the command *a.out*, the following is printed on the screen:

```
argc = 1
argv[0] = a.out
```

Now suppose that we give the command

  a.out try this

Here is what appears on the screen:

```
argc = 3
argv[0] = a.out
argv[1] = try
argv[2] = this
```

Finally, suppose that we move *a.out* to *my_echo*, and then give the command

   my_echo big sky country

The following is printed on the screen:

```
argc = 4
argv[0] = my_echo
argv[1] = big
argv[2] = sky
argv[3] = country
```

The parameter argv could just as well have been declared

```
char    **argv;
```

It is a pointer to pointer to char that can be thought of as an array of pointers to char, which in turn can be thought of as an array of strings. Notice that we have not allocated any space for the strings. The system does this for us and passes information to main() via the two arguments argc and argv.

In Chapter 14 we will see that file names are often passed as arguments to main().

10.7 STRING HANDLING FUNCTIONS IN THE STANDARD LIBRARY

The standard library contains many useful string handling functions. Although these functions are not part of the C language, they are available on most systems. There is nothing special about these functions. They are all written in C and are quite short. Variables in them are often declared with storage class register in an attempt to make them execute more quickly. They all require that strings passed as arguments be null terminated, and they all return either an int or a pointer to char. The following table describes some of the available functions. The reader should consult a manual to learn about others.

Some string handling functions in the standard library

```
strlen(s)
char   *s;
```

- A count of the number of characters that occur before \0 is returned.

```
strcmp(s1, s2)
char   *s1, *s2;
```

- An integer is returned that is less than, equal to, or greater than zero depending on whether s1 is lexicographically less than, equal to, or greater than s2.

```
strncmp(s1, s2, n)
char   *s1, *s2;
```

- Similar to strcmp() except that at most n characters are compared.

```
char *strcat(s1, s2)
char   *s1, *s2;
```

- The two strings s1 and s2 are concatenated and the resulting string is placed in s1. The pointer value s1 is returned. The programmer must ensure that enough memory has been allocated so that s1 can hold the result.

```
char *strcpy(s1, s2)
char   *s1, *s2;
```

- The string s2 is copied into memory beginning at the base address pointed to by s1. Whatever might have been in the string s1 is lost. The pointer value s1 is returned. The programmer is responsible for ensuring that array bounds are not overrun.

```
char *index(s, c)
char   *s, c;
```

■ A pointer to the first occurrence of c in the string s is
  returned, or NULL is returned if c is not in the string.

To demonstrate that there is nothing special about these functions, let us consider strlen(). Here is one way the function
strlen() could be written.

```
strlen(s)
register char   *s;
{
    register int   n;

    for (n = 0; *s != '\0'; ++s)
        ++n;
    return (n);
}
```

In the following table we illustrate the use of some of the string
handling functions in the standard library. Note carefully that it is
the programmer's responsibility to allocate sufficient space for
strings passed to these functions. Overrunning the bounds of a
string is a common programming error.

Declarations and statements
`char    s1[100], s2[100], t[100], *strcat(), *strcpy();`
`strcpy(s1, "she sells sea shells");` `strcpy(s2, "beautiful");`

Expression	Value
`strlen(s1)`	20
`strlen(s1 + 19)`	1
`strcmp(s1, s2)`	*positive integer*

Statements	What gets printed
`strcpy(t, s1 + 10);` `printf("%s", t);`	sea shells
`printf("%s", index(s2, 'a'));`	autiful

`strcpy(t, s2);`
`strcat(t, " ");`
`strcat(t, s1 + 10);`
`strcat(t, "!");`
`printf("%s", t);`
	beautiful sea shells!

Before making use of string functions in the standard library, the programmer must properly declare the functions in the program. Even though the code for the functions is provided by the system, the compiler needs to know the type of the value returned by these functions. The programmer can provide explicit declarations as illustrated in the above table, or use the control line

```
#include   <strings.h>
```

to include the header file `<strings.h>`. This header file contains all the declarations needed to use the string functions in the standard library.

10.8 STYLE

There are two styles of programming that can be used to process strings. Namely, one can use array notation with subscripts, or one can use pointers and pointer arithmetic. Although both styles are common, there is a tendency for experienced programmers to favor the use of pointers. In some C systems the pointer versions may execute faster.

Since the null character is always used to delimit a string, it is a common programming style to explicitly test for \0 when processing a string. However, it is not necessary to do so. The alternative is to use the length of the string. As an example of this we could write

```
n = strlen(s);
for (i = 0; i <= n; ++i)
   if (islower(s[i]))
      s[i] = toupper(s[i]);
```

to capitalize all the letters in the string s. This style of string processing is certainly acceptable. Notice, however, that a for loop of the form

```
for (i = 0; i <= strlen(s); ++i)
   .  .  .  .  .
```

is inefficient. This code causes the length of s to be recomputed every time through the loop.

It is sometimes convenient to use a pointer to char to point at a constant string. As an example of this consider

```
char   *p;

p = " RICH";
printf("C. B. DeMogul is%s%s%s%s%s!", p, p, p, p, p);
```

In this example the repetitive use of p saves a little space. The compiler allocates separate storage for each constant string, even if one is the same as another. However, pointers should not be used to change the characters in a constant string; see exercise 8. To do so is considered a bad programming style.

Where possible the programmer should use a function in the standard library rather than code an equivalent routine, even when the specially coded routine would have a marginal gain in efficiency. Most of the functions in the standard library are portable across systems.

10.9 COMMON PROGRAMMING ERRORS

A common programming error is overrunning the bounds of a
string. As with other arrays, it is the programmer's responsibility
to make sure that enough space is allocated for a string. Consider

```
char    s[17], *strcpy();

strcpy(s, "Have a nice day!\n");
```

Here the programmer made a careful count of the characters in the
string to be copied into s, but forgot to allocate space for the null
character too. Overrunning the bounds of a string can easily occur
with a function call such as strcat(s1, s2). The concatenation of
the two strings must fit within the space allocated for s1.

Another common programming error is to forget to terminate a
string with the null character. On most systems this type of error
cannot be caught by the compiler or by *lint*. The effect of the error
can be sporadic; sometimes the program may run correctly and
other times not. This kind of error can be very difficult to find.

Other common errors include writing 'a' for "a", or vice versa.
Usually the compiler will find this kind of mistake. Also, using a
function call such as scanf("%s", &w) to read a string into the character array w is an error. Since w is itself a pointer, one should use
the expression w rather than &w as the second argument to scanf().
Usually the compiler will find this kind of mistake, too.

10.10 OPERATING SYSTEM CONSIDERATIONS

C systems vary from one operating system to another, even from
one UNIX operating system to another. Here we want to give an
example of this. For string processing the header file to be used in
4.2 Berkeley UNIX is <strings.h>, whereas in AT&T's System V
UNIX it is <string.h>. Moreover, there is disagreement in the nam-
ing of certain functions in the standard library. For example, the
string handling function index() in 4.2 Berkeley UNIX is named
strchr() in AT&T's System V UNIX. Also, there are some other
System V string handling functions that are not available in 4.2

Berkeley UNIX. These minor differences can cause portability difficulties. Of course, things change with time. In 4.3 Berkeley UNIX the header file <string.h> is available and all the new System V string handling functions have been added to the standard library.

10.11 SUMMARY

1 Strings are one-dimensional arrays of type char. The null character \0 is used to delimit a string. Systems functions such as printf() will work properly only on null terminated strings.

2 A function call such as scanf("%s", w) can be used to read a sequence of nonwhite space characters into the string w. After all the characters have been read in, scanf() automatically ends the string with the null character.

3 External and static strings may be initialized. An initialization of the form

```
char    *s[] = "cbd";
```

is taken by the compiler to be equivalent to

```
char    *s[] = {'c', 'b', 'd', '\0'};
```

4 String processing can be done by making use of array notation with subscripts and by making use of pointers and pointer arithmetic. Because of this flexibility, C is used extensively for string processing.

5 C provides access to the command line arguments. This is done by making use of the two parameters argc and argv in the function definition of main(). The parameter argc is an int and its value is the number of command line arguments. The parameter argv is an array of pointers to char that can be thought of as an array of strings. The arguments on the command line are placed in memory as strings and are pointed to by the elements of the array argv. The value of argc is always 1 or more, and the string pointed to by argv[0] is always the name of the command.

6   The standard library contains many useful string handling functions. For example, a function call such as strcmp(s1, s2) can be used to lexicographically compare the strings s1 and s2.

1   Rewrite the *nice_day* program using pointers and pointer arithmetic throughout.

2   Rewrite the function word_cnt() using array notation with subscripts. Write an interactive program that reads in lines typed by the user, and then reports to the user the number of words in the line. Your program should allow for very long lines. Experiment to see what happens when you type in a line that is so long it runs off the screen.

3   Write a function search() that searches the alphabetic characters in a string. From among the letters that occur in the string the function is to find the letter that occurs least, but at least once, and the letter that occurs most. Report this information back to the calling environment along with the count of the occurrences of the two letters. Your function definition should start as follows:

```
search(s, p_least, p_most, p_least_cnt, p_most_cnt)
char    s[], *p_least, *p_most;
int     *p_least_cnt, *p_most_cnt;
{
      .   .   .   .   .
```

Treat lower- and uppercase letters separately. Make sure that you handle gracefully the case when there are no letters in the string. Write a program to test your function.

4   Write a function that when invoked as bubble_string(s) causes the characters in the string s to be bubble sorted. If s contains the string "xylophone", then the statement

```
printf("%s\n", bubble_string(s));
```

should cause `ehlnoopxy` to be printed.

5 Modify the *my_echo* program so that it has the following effect. If the command line

my_echo pacific sea

is typed, then the following should be printed:

```
pacific
sea
```

Make a further modification so that if the option −*c* is present, the arguments are printed with capital letters. Do not print out the argument that contains the option.

6 If UNIX is available to you, read about the *echo* command in the on-line manual, and then write your own program that will accomplish the same thing.

7 In this exercise we use a multi-dimensional array of pointers to `char`. To initialize the array we use the storage class `static`. Is this really necessary? Complete the following table.

Declarations and initializations		

`static char  *p[2][3] = {`
`  "abc", "defg", "hi", "jklmno",`
`  "pqrstuvw", "xyz"`
`};`		

Expression	**Equivalent expression**	**Value**
`***p`	`p[0][0][0]`	`'a'`
`**p[1]`		
`**(p[1] + 2)`		
`*(*(p + 1) + 1)[7]`		`/* error */`
`(*(*(p + 1) + 1))[7]`		
`*(p[1][2] + 2)`		

8 Although constant strings are not really constant, they should be treated as such. Here is an example of what *not* to do. Explain what gets printed and why.

```
char   *p, *q;

p = q = " RICH";
printf("C. B. DeMogul is%s%s%s!\n", p, p, p);
*++q = 'p';
*++q = 'o';
*++q = 'o';
*q = 'r';
printf("C. B. DeMogul is%s%s%s!\n", p, p, p);
```

9   Write an interactive program that makes use of scanf() to read
    in 7 strings input by the user. The program should print the 7
    strings as a list, and then sort the strings alphabetically and
    print a new list. Use the function strcmp() to assist in the sort-
    ing of the strings. Also, use the control line

```
#define   N_STRINGS   7
```

    to write your program in such a way that it can sort a different
    number of strings by changing only this line.

10 (Advanced) Write a program similar to the one you wrote in
    exercise 9 that sorts and prints command line arguments.

11 Does the standard library on your system provide index() or
    strchr() or both? Which header file do you have on your sys-
    tem, <string.h> or <strings.h>? Find out where it is and read
    it. While you are at it, read <math.h>, too. *Hint:* On most
    UNIX systems the header files are in the directory */usr/include*.

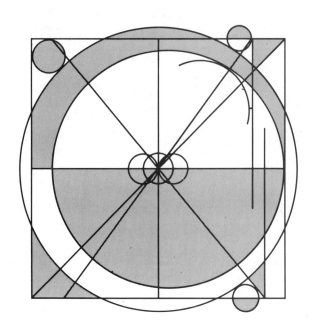

11

THE PREPROCESSOR
AND SOFTWARE
METHODOLOGY

The C language uses the preprocessor to extend its power and notation. In this chapter we present a detailed discussion of the preprocessor. First we explain the use of the #include facility. Then we thoroughly discuss the use of the #define macro facility. Macros can be used to generate in-line code in place of function calls, and their use can reduce code execution time.

The chapter ends with a discussion of software methodology. A fundamental concept of software methodology is modularity, and this issue is discussed in relation to C. The use of #include allows the programmer to create a header file consisting of common information to be shared among functions written in separate files.

11.1 THE USE OF #include

Lines that begin with a # in column one are called *control lines*. These lines communicate with the preprocessor. The syntax for control lines is independent of the rest of the C language. A control line has an effect from its place in a file until the end of that file.

We have already made use of control lines such as

```
#include    <stdio.h>
#include    <ctype.h>
```

Another form of the #include facility is given by

```
#include    "filename"
```

This causes the preprocessor to replace the line with a copy of the contents of the named file. A search for the file is made first in the current directory and then in other system dependent places. With a control line of the form

```
#include    <filename>
```

the preprocessor looks for the file only in the other places and not in the current directory. In many systems these files are looked for in the directory */usr/include*, but other places can be searched as well. Where the standard #include files are stored is system dependent. There is no restriction on what an included file can contain. In particular, it can contain other control lines that will be expanded by the preprocessor in turn.

11.2 THE USE OF #define

Control lines with #define occur in two forms:

> #define   *identifier*   *token_string*$_{opt}$

> #define   *identifier*(*identifier*, ... , *identifier*)   *token_string*$_{opt}$

A long definition of either form can be continued to the next line by placing a backslash \ at the end of the current line. If a simple #define of the first form occurs in a file, the preprocessor replaces every occurrence of *identifier* by *token_string* in the remainder of the file, except in quoted strings. Consider the example

```
#define    SECONDS_PER_DAY    (60 * 60 * 24)
```

In this example the token string is (60 * 60 * 24) and the preprocessor will replace every occurrence of the symbolic constant SECONDS_PER_DAY by that string in the remainder of the file.

There are many important uses of simple #define's that improve program clarity and portability. For example, if special constants such as π or the speed of light c are used in a program, they should be defined.

```
#define   PI   3.14159
#define   C    299792.4562       /* speed of light in km/sec */
```

Other special constants that are used in programs are also best coded as symbolic constants.

```
#define   EOF      (-1)          /* typical end-of-file value */
#define   MAXINT   2147483647     /* largest 4 byte integer */
```

Program limits that are programmer decisions can also be specified symbolically.

```
#define   ITERS   50       /* number of iterations */
#define   SIZE    250      /* array size */
#define   EPS     1.0e-9   /* a numerical limit */
```

In general, symbolic constants aid documentation by replacing what might otherwise be a mysterious constant with a mnemonic identifier. They aid portability by allowing constants that may be system dependent to be altered once. They aid reliability by restricting to one place the check on the actual representation of the constant.

11.3 SYNTACTIC SUGAR

It is possible to alter the syntax of C towards some user preference. A frequent programming error is to use the token = in place of the token == in logical expressions. A programmer could use

```
#define   EQ   ==
```

to defend against such a mistake. This superficial alteration of the programming syntax is called *syntactic sugar*. Another example of this is to change the form of the `while` statement by introducing "do," which is an ALGOL style construction.

```
#define   do   /* blank */
```

With these two `#define` lines at the top of the file, the code

```
while (i EQ 1) do {
    .   .   .   .   .
```

will become, after the preprocessor pass,

```
while (i == 1) {
    .   .   .   .   .
```

One must keep in mind that since `do` will disappear from anywhere in the file, the do-while statement cannot be used.

11.4 THE USE OF MACROS WITH ARGUMENTS

So far, we have considered only simple `#define` control lines. We now want to discuss how one can use the `#define` facility to write macro definitions with parameters. The form is given by

$$\text{\#define}\quad identifier(\ identifier,\ \dots\ ,\ identifier\ )\quad token\_string_{opt}$$

There can be no space between the first identifier and the left parenthesis. Zero or more identifiers can occur in the parameter list. An example of a macro definition with a parameter is

```
#define   SQ(x)   ((x) * (x))
```

The identifier `x` in the `#define` is a parameter that is substituted for in later text. The substitution is one of string replacement without consideration of syntactic correctness. For example, with the argument 7 + w the macro call

SQ(7 + w)   expands to   ((7 + w) * (7 + w))

In a similar fashion

SQ(SQ(*p))   expands to   ((((*p) * (*p))) * (((*p) * (*p))))

The seemingly extravagant use of parentheses is to protect against the macro expanding an expression that would then lead to an unanticipated order of evaluation; see Section 11.9, Common Programming Errors.

Macros are frequently used to replace function calls by in-line code, which is more efficient. For example, instead of a function min() a programmer could use the macro MIN() given by

```
#define  MIN(x, y)  (((x) < (y)) ? (x) : (y))
```

After this definition an expression such as

```
m = MIN(u, v)
```

gets expanded by the preprocessor to

```
m = (((u) < (v)) ? (u) : (v))
```

The arguments of MIN() can be arbitrary expressions of compatible type.

A macro can be defined using another macro. A simple example is

```
#define  SQ(x)      ((x) * (x))
#define  CUBE(x)    (SQ(x) * (x))
#define  FIFTH(x)   (CUBE(x) * SQ(x))      /* x to the fifth power */
```

11.5 AN EXAMPLE: USING MACROS

In this section we want to illustrate the use of macros with arguments. There are a number of pitfalls, which we will explain in the dissection that follows. In general, the use of macros is not robust, and the programmer who uses them must be prepared for trouble. Debugging code with macros can be quite difficult.

Suppose that we want to fill an array with randomly distributed integers and then print all the elements of the array followed by the maximum element. The following program makes use of macros to accomplish this task repeatedly.

```c
#define    ITERS      2        /* number of iterations */
#define    N         12        /* array size */

#define    FILL(array, size)    for (i = 0; i < size; ++i)    \
                                    array[i] = rand() % 1000

#define    PRN(array, size)     printf("\n");                 \
                                for (i = 0; i < size; ++i)    \
                                   printf("%5d", array[i])

#define    FIND_MAX(array, size, max)    max = array[0];                \
                                         for (i = 1; i < size; ++i)    \
                                            max = MAX(array[i], max)

#define    MAX(x, y)    (((x) > (y)) ? (x) : (y))

main()
{
    int    a[N], i, j, max;

    for (j = 0; j < ITERS; ++j) {
        FILL(a, N);
        PRN(a, N);
        FIND_MAX(a, N, max);
        printf("\nMaximum value: %d\n", max);
    }
}
```

Here is the output from this program.

```
 590  575   84  781  474  899  952  185  886  847  308  821
Maximum value: 952

 866  851  288  321  366  519   52   29  722  115   72  521
Maximum value: 866
```

■ DISSECTION OF THE *fill_and_find* PROGRAM

```
#define   ITERS    2       /* number of iterations */
#define   N       12       /* array size */
```

- We use ITERS as the symbolic constant that controls the number of iterations performed in main(). The symbolic constant N is used for the size of the array a[] in main().

```
#define   FILL(array, size)   for (i = 0; i < size; ++i)   \
                                 array[i] = rand() % 1000
```

- In this macro definition the identifiers array and size are parameters. They will be substituted for when the macro is expanded in main(). We are using a for loop to fill an array with randomly distributed integers between 0 and 1000. A backslash is used to continue a line. Notice the absence of a semicolon on what appears to be the statement controlled by the for loop. When the macro is used in main(), it is followed by a semicolon, making the expanded code correct.

```
#define   PRN(array, size)    printf("\n");                \
                                 for (i = 0; i < size; ++i)   \
                                    printf("%5d", array[i])
```

- This macro is used in main() to print out the elements of the array. Like the previous macro, it is not particularly robust. There is an assumption that an int variable i is available for use in the for loop. Also, if p is a pointer to int, then the expanded code for a statement such as

```
  PRN(p + 2, 3);
```

will not be syntactically correct. The last line of the expanded code will become

```
  printf("%5d", p + 2[i]);
```

causing a syntax error. If instead we rewrite the macro definition as

```
  #define   PRN(array, size)    printf("\n");                    \
                                for (i = 0; i < (size); ++i)  \
                                    printf("%5d", (array)[i])
```

then the macro will be more robust. However, the intended use of this macro is limited. For this simple program we did not bother to make the macro robust.

```
#define   FIND_MAX(array, size, max)   max = array[0];                \
                                       for (i = 1; i < size; ++i)  \
                                           max = MAX(array[i], max)
```

- The macro FIND_MAX() is used to find the maximum element of an array. It makes use of the macro MAX().

```
#define   MAX(x, y)   (((x) > (y)) ? (x) : (y))
```

- This macro uses the conditional operator to find the larger of two values. Notice that we have written it to be robust. It could be safely used in a large programming project. Note that the definition of MAX() can occur after its use in a previous macro.

```
main()
{
   int   a[N], i, j, max;

   for (j = 0; j < ITERS; ++j) {
      FILL(a, N);
      PRN(a, N);
      FIND_MAX(a, N, max);
      printf("\nMaximum value: %d\n", max);
   }
}
```

■ The first three statements in the body of the for loop look like
  function calls. However, they are macros that get expanded by
  the preprocessor. Notice that i is declared because the macros
  use it. See exercise 11 for further discussion.

11.6 CONDITIONAL COMPILATION

The preprocessor provides control lines for conditional compilation.
These facilities can be used for program development and for writing code that is more easily portable from one machine to another.
There are three types of conditional statements. Each control line
of the form

> #if   *constant_expression*
> #ifdef   *identifier*
> #ifndef   *identifier*

provides for conditional compilation of the code that follows until
the control line

> #endif

is reached. For the intervening code to be compiled, after #if the
constant expression must be nonzero (*true*). After #ifdef the named
identifier must be currently defined in a #define line. After #ifndef
the named identifier must be currently undefined.

As an example of these ideas, suppose that at the top of the file we write

```
#define   DEBUG   1
```

and then throughout the rest of the code we write lines such as

```
#if DEBUG
printf("debug:  a = %d\n", a);
#endif
```

Since the symbolic constant DEBUG has value 1, the printf() statements will be compiled. Later, these lines can be omitted from compilation by changing the value of the symbolic constant DEBUG to 0.

An alternative scheme is to define a symbolic constant having no value, as in the example

```
#define   DEBUG
```

and then use the #ifdef form of conditional compilation, as in the example

```
#ifdef    DEBUG
   .   .   .   .   .
#endif
```

A symbolic constant can be undefined by a control line of the form

```
#undef    DEBUG
```

Here is a common use of conditional compilation. Imagine that you are in the testing phase of program development and that your code has the form

statements
more statements
and still more statements

For debugging or testing purposes, you may wish to temporarily disregard, or block out, some of your code. To do this, you can try to put the code into a comment.

> *statements*
> /*
> *more statements*
> */
> *and still more statements*

However, if the code to be blocked contains comments within it, this method will result in a syntax error; see exercise 13. The use of conditional compilation solves this problem.

> *statements*
> #if 0
> *more statements*
> #endif
> *and still more statements*

Just as C has an if-else statement, so does the preprocessor. Each of the three forms of #if can be followed by any number of lines, possibly containing control lines of the form

> #elif   *constant_expression*

possibly followed by the control line

> #else

and finally followed by the control line

> #endif

Note that #elif is a contraction for "else-if." The flow of control for conditional compilation is analogous to that of the if-else statement in C.

11.7 SOFTWARE METHODOLOGY

Some of the concerns of software methodology for writing code are correctness, readability, portability, maintainability, and ease of code development. These issues become more important as program size grows. For all of these issues, modularity is a key idea. C provides the function facility to write modular code. This facility allows the programmer to break the code into manageable pieces. Most C compilers provide for the separate compilation of functions.

Modularity is a fundamental concept of software methodology. It is the grouping together of logically related units of code and data in such a way that the details of implementation are hidden from other sections of the program. Each of these groups is called a *module*. Ideally, a module should present only the simplest interface to the rest of the program. This is important since critical errors can occur in the interactions between sections of a program. Another important effect of this isolation is to greatly enhance reusability, the ability to reuse a module in the same or subsequent programs. In C a module corresponds to a file.

When a program consists of multiple files, each of the files can be compiled separately, as necessary. Separate compilation can facilitate the edit-compile-test cycle of code development. That is, when a new function is added to the program, or an old function is corrected or redesigned, all the other functions do not have to be recompiled. In developing a large program, this can save a lot of time. In Section 11.10, Operating System Considerations, we will explain how separate compilation of functions is accomplished in a UNIX environment. In Chapter 15 we will discuss the UNIX utility *make*, which automatically keeps track of the files that need to be recompiled.

When a program consists of multiple files, there usually is a need to share common information among the files. This information can be put into a header file, which is then included with the other files as necessary. Typically, the header file for the program as a whole contains the #include's for system header files, the definitions of symbolic constants, the definitions of macros with parameters, and declarations of functions. In Chapter 13 we will see that this is also an appropriate place for declaring the templates of structures.

As an illustration of these ideas let us write a program composed of functions written in separate files that does some text processing. The program will read words from the standard input file and write the words in columns in the standard output file. Let us use *make_columns* as the name of the program. If we want the words in *infile* printed in 7 columns, then an appropriate command would be

> *make_columns   −n7   −u   <   infile   >   outfile*

We are using the UNIX convention that command line options are flagged with a minus sign; see exercise 19. The option *−n7* is used to indicate that 7 columns are desired, the *n* being mnemonic for "number of columns." If present, the command line option *−u* causes all letters to be printed uppercase. As an example of how *make_columns* is to be used, let us suppose that *infile* contains the line

```
she sells sea shells by the seashore
```

If we were to give the command

> *make_columns   −n3   −u   <   infile*

then we would expect to see on the screen

```
SHE                     SELLS                   SEA
SHELLS                  BY                      THE
SEASHORE
```

The algorithm for computing the widths of the columns is as simple as possible. Since our screen width is 80 characters, and we want to print our words in 3 columns, all we did was divide 80 by 3, discarding any fractional part. The output shown above is printed in 3 columns, each column being 26 characters wide.

We are now ready to describe our program. Each function definition making up the program will be in a separate file. Let us begin by showing the contents of the header file *make_columns.h* that is to be included with most of the function definitions.

In file make_columns.h:

```
#include    <stdio.h>
#include    <ctype.h>
#include    <strings.h>

#define    MAXWORD       100
#define    SCREEN_WIDTH   80

char    *get_word();
void    capitalize(), make_columns(), prn_info();
```

We have declared all the functions other than main() here, even those that return nothing. As we build our program we add to or change this header file as necessary. What we see here is the final product. Let us look at main() next. For this particular program, this is where we started program development, simultaneously building the header file *make_columns.h* as we went along.

```
/* Print words in columns. */

#include   "make_columns.h"

main(argc, argv)
int     argc;
char    *argv[];
{
    int   i, number_of_columns = 0, uppercase_option = 0;

    for (i = 1; i < argc; ++i)
        if (strncmp(argv[i], "-n", 2) == 0 && isdigit(argv[i][2]))
            sscanf(argv[i] + 2, "%d", &number_of_columns);
        else if (strcmp(argv[i], "-u") == 0)
            uppercase_option = 1;
        else {
            printf("\nUnknown option\n\n");
            prn_info(argv);
            exit(1);
        }
    if (number_of_columns == 0) {
        printf("\nNumber of columns not specified\n\n");
        prn_info(argv);
        exit(1);
    }
    make_columns(number_of_columns, uppercase_option);
}
```

The parameters argc and argv are used so that command line
options can be read. Recall that argv can be thought of as an array
of strings, each string containing a word from the command line.
Thus argv[i] is the ith string (counting from zero) and argv[i][j]
refers to the jth character (counting from zero) in the string. Notice
that we called sscanf(), the string version of scanf(). This function
is in the standard library. The general form of its use is given by

   sscanf(*string*, *control_string*, *other_arguments*)

It is similar to scanf() except that instead of reading characters
from the standard input file, it reads characters in the string passed
as its first argument. Consider the statement

```
sscanf(argv[i] + 2, "%d", &number_of_columns);
```

If we think of the pointer argv[i] as pointing to the string "-n3", then the pointer expression argv[i] + 2 points to the character 3 in "-n3". Thus the effect of the expression is to skip the -n in the string. From the string pointed to by argv[i] + 2, digits are read in, converted to an int, and stored at an appropriate address in memory.

The program expects command line options such as −*n3* and −*u* to occur on the command line. The options can appear in reverse order, and −*u* is optional. If an option such as −*n3* is not present, or an unknown option exists, the two functions prn_info() and exit() are invoked. The function prn_info() is used to explain to the user the proper use of the program. The standard library function exit() provides an immediate exit from the program. By convention, exit(1) is called if something has gone wrong. The value of the argument passed to exit() is used to communicate with the operating system. We will explain this further in Chapter 14.

Let us look at the function definition for prn_info() next. Since this function does not make use of anything in the header file make_columns.h, we have not included it.

```
void prn_info(argv)
char    *argv[];
{
   printf("%s%s%s\n\n%s\n%s%s\n%s%s\n\n",
      "Usage: ", argv[0], " -nN -u < in_file > out_file",
      "This program reads from stdin and writes to stdout.",
      "The words in stdin are printed in N columns, ",
      "where N is a positive integer.",
      "If present, the command line option -u ",
      "causes letters to be printed uppercase.");
}
```

Notice the use of the pointer argv[0], which points to the name of the program. Even if we rename the program, this function will still provide correct information to the user; see exercise 14.

After main() has processed the command line arguments, and no errors have occurred, the function make_columns() is invoked. This is where most of the work of the program is accomplished. Notice that the header file *make_columns.h* has been included at the top of the file.

```
#include   "make_columns.h"

void make_columns(number_of_columns, uppercase_option)
int    number_of_columns, uppercase_option;
{
    char    s[MAXWORD];
    int     col_cnt = 0, col_width, i, nblanks = 0;

    col_width = SCREEN_WIDTH / number_of_columns;
    while (get_word(s) != NULL) {
        if (uppercase_option == 1)
            capitalize(s);
        for (i = 0; i < nblanks; ++i)    /* pad with blanks */
            putchar(' ');
        printf("%s", s);                 /* print the word */
        if (++col_cnt >= number_of_columns) {
            putchar('\n');
            col_cnt = nblanks = 0;
        }
        else
            nblanks = col_width - strlen(s);
    }
    if (col_cnt != 0)
        putchar('\n');
}
```

After a column width is computed, the function get_word() is used to repeatedly read a word into the character array s[]. It is assumed that the length of each word is less than the column width. If it is not, then the columns will not be aligned properly.

Here is the function get_word(). Notice that once again the header file *make_columns.h* is included at the top of the file.

```
#include   "make_columns.h"

char *get_word(s)
char   *s;
{
   int   c;

   while (!isalpha(c = getchar()) && c != EOF)
      ;   /* find the first letter, if there is one */
   if (c == EOF)
      return (NULL);
   else {
      *s++ = c;
      while (isalpha(c = getchar()) && c != EOF)
         *s++ =c;
      *s = '\0';
      return (s);
   }
}
```

For the purpose of this program, we have defined a word to be a maximal string of alphabetic characters. Other characters, such as digits and punctuation, are disregarded. See exercises 16 and 17 at the end of this chapter for other suggestions.

Finally, we present the function capitalize(). Since it makes use of some of the macros in *ctype.h*, this file is included in *make_columns.h*, which in turn is included here.

```
#include   "make_columns.h"

void capitalize(s)
char   *s;
{
   for ( ; *s != '\0'; ++s)
      if (islower(*s))
         *s = toupper(*s);
}
```

11.8 STYLE

A common programming style is to use names ending in .*h* for header files. Of course, the #include facility can be used to include any file, not just those ending in .*h*. There are no restrictions on what can be put into a header file, but it is not considered good programming style to put function definitions there. If functions exist in separate files, they should be in .*c* files that can be compiled separately.

By convention, capital letters are used for the names of symbolic constants and macros. Although any identifier can be used, the use of capitals allows the reader of a program to readily identify text that will be expanded by the preprocessor.

Another common programming style is to use the #define facility to indicate type specifiers that are used for special purposes. In the following code UPPERCASE is defined as char to convey the programmer's intention of using only uppercase letters as values.

```
#define    UPPERCASE    char
#define    MAXLINE      1000

main()
{
    UPPERCASE   c, line[MAXLINE];
    .  .  .  .  .
```

11.9 COMMON PROGRAMMING ERRORS

Recall that in Section 11.4 we gave a fully parenthesized macro definition of SQ(). In this section we want to explain fully why all the parentheses are necessary. First, suppose that we had defined the macro as

```
#define    SQ(x)    x * x
```

With this definition

```
SQ(a + b)              expands to           a + b * a + b
```

which, because of operator precedence, is not the same as

```
((a + b) * (a + b))
```

Now suppose that we had defined the macro as

```
#define  SQ(x)   (x) * (x)
```

With this definition

```
4 / SQ(2)            expands to            4 / (2) * (2)
```

which, because of operator precedence, is not the same as

```
4 / ((2) * (2))
```

Finally, let us suppose that we had defined the macro as

```
#define  SQ (x)   ((x) * (x))
```

With this definition

```
SQ(7)            expands to            (x)   ((x) * (x)) (7)
```

which is not even close to what was intended. In a macro definition with parameters there can be no space between the first identifier and the following left parenthesis.

Another common mistake is to end a #define line with a semicolon, making it part of the replacement string when it is not wanted. As an example of this, consider

```
#define  SQ(x)   ((x) * (x));
```

The semicolon here was typed by mistake; it is a mistake that is easily made since programmers often end a line of code with a semicolon. When used in the body of a function, the line

```
x = SQ(y);        gets expanded to        x = ((y) * (y));;
```

The last semicolon creates an unwanted null statement. If we were to write

```
if (x == 2)
    x = SQ(y);
else
    ++x;
```

we would get a syntax error caused by the unwanted null statement. The extra semicolon does not allow the else to be attached to the if statement.

As a final common programming error let us discuss an error that arises easily when using a macro consisting of many lines. Consider the macro PRN(), which we used in the *fill_and_find* program in Section 11.5.

```
#define   PRN(array, size)   printf("\n");                    \
                             for (i = 0; i < size; ++i)   \
                                 printf("%5d", array[i])
```

Suppose that we want to use this macro to print an array five times. To accomplish this, we might write

```
for (j = 0; j < 5; ++j)
    PRN(a, n);
```

This, however, will not produce the desired results. The preprocessor will expand these two lines of code into new code that is equivalent to

```
for (j = 0; j < 5; ++j)
    printf("\n");
for (i = 0; i < n; ++i)
    printf("%5d", a[i]);
```

We will get five newlines and a single printout of the array. If an error such as this occurs, it can be quite mystifying. To guard against this type of error, one can use braces in the macro definition; see exercise 12.

11.10 OPERATING SYSTEM CONSIDERATIONS

Most C compilers provide for the separate compilation of functions. We will work with the functions making up our program *make_columns* to show how this is done in a UNIX environment. The −*c* option to the *cc* command causes object files to be produced, the letter *c* in the option being mnemonic for "compile only." Consider the command

> *cc   −c   main.c   prn_info.c*

This will create the object files *main.o* and *prn_info.o*. The compiler creates a corresponding *.o* file for each *.c* file. After all the object files for our program have been produced, we can give the command

> *cc   main.o   prn_info.o   make_columns.o   get_word.o   capitalize.o*

to create an executable file in *a.out*. Typically, we would have all the *.c* and *.o* files making up one program in a separate directory. If this is the case, then to link the *.o* files and create an executable file in *make_columns*, we would give the command

> *cc   −o   make_columns   *.o*

Now suppose that we make a change in one of our functions, say main(). All that is necessary to recompile our program is to give the command

> *cc   −o   make_columns   main.c   *.o*

Only *main.c* will be recompiled. After the new *main.o* is created, all the *.o* files will be used to create executable code that is placed in *make_columns*. The use of *.o* files where possible will speed the work of the compiler.

Most C compilers provide the programmer with an option that allows for the viewing of code after the preprocessor pass, just prior to compilation. In UNIX this is accomplished by using *cc* along with the −*E* command line option. Thus the command *cc −E function.c*

causes the preprocessor to expand *function.c* and print on the screen. No compilation takes place. This allows the programmer to check the results of the preprocessor. It is always helpful to keep in mind that the preprocessor does not "know C."

Under certain conditions some system functions are implemented as macros. In UNIX, for example, when *stdio.h* is included, both getchar() and putchar() are implemented as macros. Normally, the user is not aware of this. The macros work just as well as the functions. From an operating system viewpoint, however, the macros have the advantage of not requiring the overhead of a function call. Because of this, character processing programs require less execution time.

On most UNIX systems the header files provided by the system for use in C programs, such as *stdio.h* and *ctype.h*, are found in the directory */usr/include*. If UNIX is available to you, you can see what is in the file *stdio.h* by giving the command

cat /usr/include/stdio.h

11.11 SUMMARY

1   The preprocessor provides facilities for file inclusion and for macros. Files may be included with source text passed to the compiler by use of control lines of the form

```
#include   "filename"
#include   <filename>
```

2   A #define control line can be used to give a symbolic name to a token string. The preprocessor substitutes the string for the symbolic name in the source text before compilation.

3   The use of the #define facility to define symbolic constants enhances readability and portability of programs.

4   The preprocessor provides a general macro facility with argument substitution. A macro with parameters is defined by a control line of the form

```
#define   identifier( identifier, ... , identifier )   token_string_opt
```

For example,

```
#define   SWAP(x, y)   {int t; t = x; x = y; y = t;}
```

allows for in-line code to perform the swap of two values. It is not a function call.

5 A common programming methodology for creating a large program is to write the functions in modules. An essential part of this methodology is to create appropriate header files that can be included at the top of the modules. These header files provide a central place to include system header files, to define symbolic constants and macros, and to declare functions and templates of structures.

11.12 EXERCISES

1 Make use of the operators && and || to write a macro definition for XOR(), called "exclusive or." A macro call such as XOR(a, b) should be true if a is true and b is false, or if a is false and b is true. In all other cases the macro call should be false. For example, XOR(0, 1) should be true and XOR(1, 1) should be false. In contrast to this, the expression 1 || 1 is true. Write a program that tests your XOR() macro.

2 Write macro definitions for XOR_3() and XOR_4() that can be considered extended versions of "exclusive or." In general, the macro XOR_n() would have n parameters in its macro definition. The macro call XOR_3(a, b, c) should be true if and only if one of the three arguments a, b, and c is true and all the others are false. Similarly, the macro call XOR_4(a, b, c, d) should be true if and only if one of the four arguments a, b, c, and d is true and all the others are false. Write a program that tests your macros. *Hint:* To write your test program, use nested for loops, as illustrated in Sections 7.4 and 7.5.

3 Can XOR be defined as a macro so that one could write a XOR b instead of XOR(a, b)? That is, can XOR be defined to be a binary operator in the same sense as && and ||?

4 Write a macro definition PRN_STRING(x) that prints the string x followed by an integer representing the length of the string and

a newline character. There should be three spaces between the end of the string and the number. Write a program to test your macro.

5   This exercise assumes that you are working in a UNIX environment. Rewrite the macro of exercise 4 so that the definition of PRN_STRING(s) uses the parameter s instead of x. Now, when you try to compile your test program, most likely you will get a syntax error. However, the difficulty may not be obvious to you. To find out what is wrong, try the command

   cc −E prn_string.c

where *prn_string.c* is the name of the file containing your test program.

6   Suppose in a program that x, y, and z have the values 1.1, 2.2, and 3.3, respectively. The statement

```
PRN3(x, y, z);
```

should cause the line

```
x has value 1.1 and y has value 2.2 and z has value 3.3
```

to be printed. Write the macro definition for PRN3().

7   Macro definitions are not always as safe as function definitions, even when all the arguments are enclosed in parentheses. Write the macro definition for MAX(x, y, z) so that it produces a value corresponding to the largest of its three arguments. Construct some expressions to use in MAX() that produce unanticipated results.

8   What is the largest floating point constant available on your system? *Hint:* If UNIX is available to you, create a file called *look.c* with the line

```
#include   <math.h>
```

in it and then give the command

cc −E look.c

9   The following program makes use of macros. What gets printed? Rewrite the program, converting each macro into a function. Test your program to see that the same printout is obtained.

```
#define   PRN(name, x) \
          printf("%s%s%s%d\n", "Value of ", name, ": ", x)

#define   PRN2(name1, x1, name2, x2) \
          PRN(name1, x1);   PRN(name2, x2)

#define   PRN4(n1, x1, n2, x2, n3, x3, n4, x4) \
          PRN2(n1, x1, n2, x2);   PRN2(n3, x3, n4, x4)

main()
{
   int   a = 1, b = 2, c = 3, d = 4,
         e = 5, f = 6, g = 7, h = 8;

   PRN4("a", a, "b", b, "c", c, "d", d);
   PRN4("e", e, "f", f, "g", g, "h", h);
}
```

10 Consider exercise 9. Instead of variables of type int in main(), try a mixture of short's and long's. The macro version of the program should still work. Does the function version still work? Explain.

11 It is very easy to make mistakes when using macros with parameters. In the *fill_and_find* program, experiment to see what happens if i is used instead of j in main(). Rewrite the program so that main() begins as

```
main()
{
   int   a[N], i, max;

   for (i = 0; i < ITERS; ++i) {      /* use i instead of j */
      FILL(a, N);
         .  .  .  .  .
```

This is a simple error that a programmer might make. Run the program twice. First the symbolic constant ITERS should have the value 5, and then it should have the value 15. In each case explain what happens.

12 Exercise 11 points out one of the difficulties that can occur if a variable other than a parameter is used in a macro definition. Consider the following scheme:

```
#define   FILL(array, size)   {  \
   int   i;                       \
   for (i = 0; i < size; ++i)     \
      array[i] = rand() % 1000;   \
}
```

In a similar fashion rewrite the macro definitions for PRN() and FIND_MAX() and then test the program. Explain why the use of i instead of j in the for loop in main() will no longer cause trouble. The new program has null statements. Can you find them?

13 Most C compilers do not allow for the nesting of comments, although a few do. Thus

```
/* is this /* really */ a comment? */
```

will cause a syntax error on most systems. Even if your compiler does allow for the nesting of comments, you should not use this feature if you want your code to be portable to other systems. Write a test program to see if your C compiler allows for the nesting of comments. Also, check to see that the construct

```
#if   0
   .   .   .   .
#endif
```

can be used on your system to block out code, including code
that is commented.

14   Experiment with the *make_columns* program. Execute it without command line options, causing prn_info() to be called.
Rename the program and do it again. Explain why the use of
argv[0] is better than hard-wiring the name of the program into
the program itself.

15   Rewrite the *make_columns* program to allow the command line
option −*l* to indicate that all letters are to be printed lowercase. Both of the command line options −*u* and −*l* should be
optional, but at most one of them should appear.

16   In the program *make_columns* a word is defined as a maximal
string of alphabetic characters. Thus a hyphenated word such
as "end-of-file" will be treated as three separate words.
Rewrite the program so that a hyphenated word will be treated
as a single word.

17   Redesign the *make_columns* program to use the function
get_number() instead of get_word(). The function should pick
out numbers such as 1.23 and −55 and 77 from the input file,
disregarding all other characters. *Hint:* In a UNIX environment a programmer typically creates a directory and then writes
all the functions making up a program in separate files within
that directory. Suppose that this has been done. If the programmer wants to replace the function get_word() with the
function get_number(), then the UNIX command

   grep get_word ∗.h ∗.c

can be used to find all occurrences of the name get_word in the
program. In dealing with a large program *grep* is a powerful
tool.

18   We did not explain the purpose of the last two lines of code in
the function definition of make_columns(). Remove the lines

```
if (col_cnt != 0)
    putchar('\n');
```

from the function and experiment with the program to see what the effect is.

19   In UNIX the command to get a long listing of files is

ls −l

In MS-DOS the comparable command is

dir /w

By convention, command line options are flagged with a minus sign in UNIX and with a slash in MS-DOS. By making use of the strings "−n" and "−u", we hard-wired the flag character − into the function main(). Redesign the *make_columns* program so that it can be moved easily from a UNIX environment to an MS-DOS environment. Add the line

```
#define   FLAG    '-'
```

to the header file *make_columns.h* and rewrite main() so that the flag character is used only via the symbolic constant FLAG. If the program is to be moved to an MS-DOS environment, the only change necessary should be to redefine the symbolic constant FLAG as

```
#define   FLAG    '/'
```

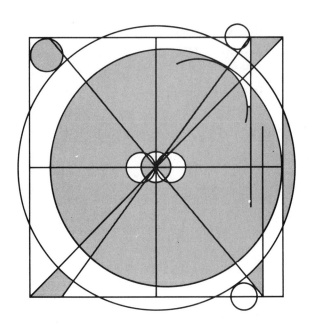

12

RECURSION

Recursion is a function invoking an instance of itself, either directly or indirectly. Some programming tasks are naturally solved with the use of recursion, which can be considered an advanced form of flow of control. Recursion is an alternative to iteration.

Recursion will be explained using some simple example programs. One particularly nice example is a function that draws different patterns on the screen. Another example is the recursive calculation of string length. Recursion is a programming technique that naturally implements the "divide and conquer" problem solving methodology, a powerful strategy that will be explained along with an example taken from sorting algorithms.

12.1 ANY FUNCTION CAN CALL ITSELF

A function is said to be recursive if it calls itself, either directly or indirectly. In C all functions can be used recursively. In its simplest form the idea of recursion is straightforward. The following program does not halt of its own accord, but it illustrates recursion in a straightforward way.

```
main()
{
    printf(" The universe is ever expanding! ");
    main();
}
```

This function prints The universe is ever expanding! continually across the screen until interrupted. This could have been accomplished by using a nonterminating iterative statement enclosing the printf(). What is new here is that main() invokes itself.

Another simple example of a recursive function is the following. It computes the sum of the first *n* positive integers.

```
sum(n)
int   n;
{
    if (n <= 1)
        return (n);
    else
        return (n + sum(n - 1));
}
```

The recursive function sum() is analyzed as illustrated in the following table. First the base case is considered. Then working out from the base case, the other cases are considered.

Function call	Value returned		
sum(1)	1		
sum(2)	2 + sum(1)	is	2 + 1
sum(3)	3 + sum(2)	is	3 + 2 + 1
sum(4)	4 + sum(3)	is	4 + 3 + 2 + 1
sum(5)	5 + sum(4)	is	5 + 4 + 3 + 2 + 1

Simple recursive routines follow a standard pattern. Typically there is a base case that is tested for on entry to the function. Then there is a general recursive case in which one of the variables, often an integer, is passed as an argument in such a way as to ultimately lead to the base case. In sum() the variable n was reduced by 1 each time until the base case with n equal to 1 was reached.

When an integer *n* is passed to sum(), the recursion activates *n* nested copies of the function before returning level by level to the original call. This means that *n* function calls are used in the computation. Most simple recursive functions can be rewritten in an equivalent iterative form. Since function calls usually require more computation than iteration, why use recursion at all? The answer is that if the code for a job is easier to write and maintain using recursion, and the cost of doing so is slight, then the use of recursion is justified.

In the remainder of this chapter we will present examples that illustrate the ideas and power of recursion. The following program first prompts the user to type in a line, and then by means of a recursive function reprints the line backwards.

```
/* Write a line backwards. */

main()
{
    printf("Input a line: ");
    prn_it();
    printf("\n\n");
}


prn_it()
{
    char    c;

    if ((c = getchar()) != '\n')
        prn_it();
    putchar(c);
}
```

If the user types in the line sing a song of sixpence when prompted, then the following appears on the screen:

```
Input a line:  sing a song of sixpence

ecnepxis fo gnos a gnis
```

■ DISSECTION OF THE *write_backwards* PROGRAM

```
printf("Input a line: ");
prn_it();
```

- The invocation of the recursive function prn_it() occurs after a prompt to the user. The user writes a line and terminates it by hitting a carriage return, which is the character \n.

```
if ((c = getchar()) != '\n')
   prn_it();
```

- As each character is read in it initiates a new call to prn_it(). Each call has its own local storage for the variable c. This local c, local to a particular invocation of the function prn_it(), is where the individual characters of the input line will be stored. Each call is stacked until the newline character is read.

```
putchar(c);
```

- Only after the newline character is read does anything get written. Each invocation of prn_it() now prints the value stored in its local variable c. First the newline character is outputted, then the character just before it, and so on, until the first character is outputted. Thus the input line is reversed.

An interesting variation on this theme is to read in a line of words and print the line back out with the order of the words reversed. Here is a program that does this.

```
#include    <stdio.h>

#define    MAXWORD    100

main()
{
    printf("Input a line:  ");
    prn_it_by_word();
    printf("\n\n");
}



prn_it_by_word()
{
    char    w[MAXWORD];

    get_word(w);
    if (w[0] != '\n')
        prn_it_by_word();
    printf("%s ", w);
}



get_word(s)
char    *s;
{
    static char    c = '\0';

    if (c == '\n')
        *s++ = c;
    else
        while ((c = getchar()) != ' ' && c != '\t' && c != '\n')
            *s++ = c;
    *s = '\0';
}
```

If the user types in the line deep in the heart of texas when prompted, then the following appears on the screen:

```
Input a line:  deep in the heart of texas

texas of heart the in deep
```

Notice that the variable c has storage class static so that when a newline character is read in and assigned to c, that sentinel value will not be lost on exit from the function. The initialization of c occurs only when the function get_word() is invoked for the first time. This is because the storage class of c is static. On subsequent function calls, the value of c is whatever was there when the previous call exited. Since static storage is guaranteed to be initialized to zero, the explicit initialization of c is not really necessary. Nonetheless, it reminds the reader of the code that the initial value of the variable c is the null character. This program can be written without the use of recursion, but it is difficult to do so.

The next example illustrates a recursive function that manipulates characters in a string. It can easily be rewritten as an equivalent iterative function.

```
/* Reverse the characters between s[j] and s[k] recursively. */

reverse(s, j, k)
char    *s;
int     j, k;
{
   if (j < k) {
      swap(&s[j], &s[k]);
      reverse(s, ++j, --k);
   }
}
```

```
swap(p, q)
char   *p, *q;
{
    char   temp;

    temp = *p;
    *p = *q;
    *q = temp;
}
```

12.2 AN EXAMPLE: DRAWING PATTERNS ON THE SCREEN

Elaborate patterns can be drawn on the screen with the use of recursive functions. We will illustrate this with a simple example.

```
#define   SYMBOL   '*'
#define   OFFSET   0
#define   LENGTH  19

main()
{
    display(SYMBOL, OFFSET, LENGTH);
}


display(c, m, n)
char   c;
int    m, n;
{
    if (n > 0) {
        draw(' ', m);
        draw(c, n);
        putchar('\n');
        display(c, m + 2, n - 4);
    }
}
```

```
draw(c, k)
char    c;
int     k;
{
   if (k > 0) {
      putchar(c);
      draw(c, k - 1);
   }
}
```

The function main() calls display(), which in turn calls draw() and display(). Thus display() is recursive. The function draw() prints k copies of a character c. We have written this function to be recursive as well. Here is what appears on the screen when we execute this program:

12.3 STRING HANDLING USING RECURSION

A string consists of contiguous characters in memory, ending with the null character \0. Conceptually, we can think of a string as either the null string, consisting of just the null character, or as a character followed by a string. This definition of a string describes it as a recursive data structure. We can use this to code some basic string handling functions recursively.

In Chapter 10 we showed how the standard library function strlen() could be coded as an iteration. Here we will show how it can be coded as a recursion.

```
/* Recursive string length. */

r_strlen(s)
char    *s;
{
    if (*s == '\0')
        return (0);
    else
        return (1 + r_strlen(s + 1));
}
```

The base case tests for the empty string. The recursion is invoked as r_strlen(s + 1), where s + 1 is a pointer expression. The expression points one character further down the string.

String comparison is somewhat more complicated. We will write a recursive version of the standard library function strncmp(). It lexicographically compares at most the first *n* characters of two strings.

```
/* Recursive string n compare. */

r_strncmp(s1, s2, n)
char    *s1, *s2;
int     n;
{
    if (*s1 != *s2 || *s1 == '\0' || n == 1)
        return (*s1 - *s2);
    else
        return (r_strncmp(++s1, ++s2, --n));
}
```

This function looks at the first character of the two strings pointed at by s1 and s2. If the two characters are different, or both of them are the null character, or the value of n is 1, then the value returned is the difference of the two characters. Otherwise the function recurs, incrementing both string pointers and decrementing n. The recursion will terminate at the first position where the two strings differ, or at the position where both of the characters are null, or after at most n - 1 recursions.

12.4 THE DIVIDE AND CONQUER METHODOLOGY

A typical place where recursion is used is in coding a "divide and conquer" algorithm. Such an algorithm divides the problem into smaller pieces, solves each piece either directly or by recursion, and recombines the solution of the parts into the solution of the whole.

Let us use the "divide and conquer" method to find both the maximum and minimum element in an array of integers. In 1972 in the article "A Sorting Problem and Its Complexity" (*Communications of the ACM, Vol. 15, No. 6*), one of the authors, Ira Pohl, published the best possible algorithm for this problem. The criterion for "best" is the least number of comparisons needed. For simplicity, we will treat here only the case where the number of elements in the array is a power of 2. In the exercises at the end of the chapter we will continue our discussion of the algorithm and modify it to remove the power of 2 restriction.

```
/* The best possible minmax algorithm - Pohl, 1972 */

minmax(a, n, min_ptr, max_ptr)          /* n is the size of a[] */
int    a[], n, *min_ptr, *max_ptr;      /* n must be a power of 2 */
{
    int    min1, max1, min2, max2;

    if (n == 2)
        if (a[0] < a[1]) {
            *min_ptr = a[0];
            *max_ptr = a[1];
        }
        else {
            *min_ptr = a[1];
            *max_ptr = a[0];
        }
    else {
        minmax(a, n/2, &min1, &max1);
        minmax(a + n/2, n/2, &min2, &max2);
        if (min1 < min2)
            *min_ptr = min1;
        else
            *min_ptr = min2;
        if (max1 < max2)
            *max_ptr = max2;
        else
            *max_ptr = max1;
    }
}
```

■ DISSECTION OF THE minmax() FUNCTION

```
if (n == 2)
   if (a[0] < a[1]) {
      *min_ptr = a[0];
      *max_ptr = a[1];
   }
   else {
      *min_ptr = a[1];
      *max_ptr = a[0];
   }
```

■ This is the base case. The smaller of the two elements a[0] and a[1] will be assigned to the value pointed to by min_ptr, and the larger of the two elements will be assigned to the value pointed to by max_ptr.

```
else {
   minmax(a, n/2, &min1, &max1);
   minmax(a + n/2, n/2, &min2, &max2);
```

■ This is the divide and conquer step. The array a is divided into two halves. The first invocation finds the minimum and maximum among the elements a[0], . . . , a[n/2 - 1]. The second invocation looks for the minimum and maximum among the second half of the elements a[n/2], . . . , a[n - 1]. Note that a is a pointer expression having the value &a[0] and that a + n/2 is a pointer expression having the value &a[n/2].

```
if (min1 < min2)
   *min_ptr = min1;
else
   *min_ptr = min2;
```

■ The minimum values from the two halves are compared, and the smaller of the two values is assigned to whatever is pointed to by min_ptr, the overall minimum.

```
if (max1 < max2)
    *max_ptr = max2;
else
    *max_ptr = max1;
```

■ Similarly the overall maximum value is assigned to whatever is pointed to by max_ptr.

This algorithm has theoretical, as well as practical, implications. Further ideas are discussed in exercises 11 and 12 at the end of this chapter. In particular, exercise 12 concerns the removal of the power of 2 restriction on the size of the array a[].

Many algorithms for sorting use the divide and conquer technique. An especially important one is the sorting algorithm "quicksort"; see *A Book on C* by Al Kelley and Ira Pohl (Menlo Park, California: Benjamin/Cummings, 1984).

12.5 STYLE

In most common uses of recursion there is a simple equivalent iterative program. Which method to code is frequently a matter of individual taste. Recursion simplifies the coding by suppressing the need for local variables that keep track of different indices. Iteration is often a more efficient method of solution.

Let us write a simple recursive program that computes the average value of an array.

```
double average(a, n)
double    a[];
int       n;              /* n is the size of a[] */
{
    if (n == 1)
        return (a[0]);
    else
        return ((a[n - 1] + (n - 1) * average(a, n - 1)) / n);
}
```

In such cases, where the recursion is elementary, there is a simple transformation to an iterative form using a `while` or `for` loop. Here is the iterative form of the function `average()`.

```
double average(a, n)
double   a[];
int      n;
{
   double   sum = 0.0;
   int      i;

   for (i = 0; i < n; ++i)
      sum += a[i];
   return (sum / n);
}
```

In this case the iterative form of the function is simpler. It also avoids $n - 1$ function calls, where n is the size of the array being averaged. A common programming style is to choose the iterative version over the recursive version of a function if both versions are simple. Nonetheless, many algorithms are commonly coded as a recursion. One such algorithm is "quicksort." Another is the greatest common divisor algorithm given in exercise 9 at the end of this chapter.

12.6 COMMON PROGRAMMING ERRORS

The most common errors in recursive functions lead to infinite loops. We shall use the recursive definition of factorial to illustrate several common pitfalls.

For a nonnegative integer n, the factorial of n, written $n!$, is defined by

$$0! = 1$$
$$n! = n(n - 1) \cdots 3 \cdot 2 \cdot 1 \quad \text{for} \quad n > 0$$

or equivalently

$$n! = n((n - 1)!) \quad \text{for} \quad n > 0$$

Thus for example, $5! = 5 \cdot 4 \cdot 3 \cdot 2 \cdot 1$ or 120. Using the recursive definition of factorial, it is easy to write a recursive version of the factorial function.

```
factorial(n)
int   n;
{
   if (n <= 1)
      return (1);
   else
      return (n * factorial(n - 1));
}
```

This code is correct and will work properly within the limits of integer precision available on a given system. However, since the numbers $n!$ grow very large very fast, the function call factorial(n) yields a valid result only for a few values of n. On our system the function call factorial(12) returns a correct value, but if the argument to the function is greater than 12, an incorrect value is returned. This type of programming error is common. Functions that are logically correct can return incorrect values if the logical operations in the body of the function are beyond the integer precision available to the system.

Now let us suppose that the programmer has incorrectly coded the factorial function, omitting the base case. This leads to an infinite loop.

```
factorial_forever(n)
int   n;
{
   return (n * factorial_forever(n - 1));
}
```

Suppose that the base case is coded, but only for n having the value 1. Now the function will work properly with argument values in the range 1 to 12, but if the function is called with an argument that is zero or negative, an infinite loop will occur.

```
factorial_positive(n)
int    n;
{
   if (n == 1)
      return (1);
   else
      return (n * factorial_positive(n - 1));
}
```

Another common error, not specifically tied to the use of recursion, is the incorrect use of the decrement operator. In many recursions there is a variable, say n, that is used to pass an argument of lower value to the function in the recursion step. For some algorithms --n is a correct argument, for others it is not. Consider

```
factorial_decrement(n)
int    n;
{
   if (n <= 1)
      return (1);
   else
      return (n * factorial_decrement(--n));
}
```

The second return statement returns the value of an expression that makes use of the variable n twice. Because the decrement operator has a side effect, when it is applied to the second n, it may also affect the value of the first n. This type of programming error is common, especially when recursive functions are coded. On our system the function call factorial_decrement(5) returns the value 24. The compiler on our system does not complain, but *lint* does.

12.7   OPERATING SYSTEM CONSIDERATIONS

Recursive function calls require memory for each invocation. Since many invocations are active at the same time, the operating system may run out of available memory. Obviously, this is more of a problem on small systems than on large ones. Of course, if you are writing code meant to run on many systems, you must know and respect all the system limitations.

Let us write a program that will show us the depth of recursion that can occur on our system. The depth varies from one system to another, and varies from one time to another on the same system, and depends on the recursive function that is being used. Nonetheless, our experiment will give us some indication of our machine limits. We will use the recursive function sum() presented at the beginning of this chapter. The function call sum(n) activates n nested copies of the function. Thus n indicates the depth of recursion.

```
/* Test the depth of recursion for sum() */

main()
{
    int    n = 0;

    for ( ; ; n += 100)
        printf("recursion test:  n = %d  sum = %d\n", n, sum(n));
}
```

Here are the last few lines printed by this program on our system:

```
.  .  .  .  .
recursion test:  n = 18500  sum = 171134250
recursion test:  n = 18600  sum = 172989300
Segmentation fault (core dumped)
```

This shows that failure occurs after the depth of the recursion exceeds 18600 calls to sum(). The system is allowing very deep recursions to occur before some system limit is reached. Note carefully that it is not the number of recursive calls per se that causes the failure. It is the depth of the recursion (18600) that causes the problem. The table on page 228 of *A Book on C* by Ira Pohl and Al Kelley (Menlo Park, California: Benjamin/Cummings, 1984) shows the number of function calls required to compute fibonacci(n) recursively for various values of n. In particular 866988873 recursive function calls are required to compute fibonacci(42) recursively. Our system is able to carry out that computation.

12.8 SUMMARY

1 A function is said to be recursive if it calls itself, either directly or indirectly. Recursion is an advanced form of flow of control.

2 Recursion typically consists of a base case or cases and a general case. It is important to make sure that the function will terminate.

3 Any recursive function can be written in an equivalent iterative form. Due to system overhead in calling functions, a recursive function may be less efficient than an equivalent iterative one. However, the difference is often very slight. When a recursive function is easier to code and maintain than an equivalent iterative one, and the penalty for using it is slight, the recursive form is preferable.

12.9 EXERCISES

1 Rewrite the "The universe is ever expanding!" recursion so that it terminates after 7 calls. The program should consist of a single `main()` function that calls itself recursively.

2 Write a recursive function that tests whether a string is a palindrome. A palindrome is a string such as `"abcba"` or `"otto"` that reads the same in both directions. For comparison write an iterative version of the function as well.

3 Consider the following recursive function. On some systems the function will return correct values, whereas on other systems it will return incorrect values. Explain why. Write a test program to see what happens on your system.

```
sum(n)
int   n;
{
   if (n <= 1)
      return (n);
   else
      return (n + sum(--n));
}
```

4   Examine the base case of the recursive function r_strncmp()
    carefully. Will the following base case also work? Which is
    more efficient? Explain.

```
if (*s1 != *s2 || *s1 == '\0' || *s2 == '\0' || n == 1)
   return (*s1 - *s2);
```

5   Write a recursive version of the standard library function
    strcmp(). If s1 and s2 are strings, then the function call
    r_strcmp(s1, s2) should return an integer value that is negative,
    zero, or positive, depending on whether s1 is lexicographically
    less than, equal to, or greater than s2. Use main() given below
    to test your function. Compile main() and r_strcmp() and put
    the executable code into the file test_r_strcmp. If *infile* is a file
    containing many words, then the command

    test_r_strcmp < infile

    can be used to test your program.

```
#include   <strings.h>

#define   MAXWORD   30    /* max number of characters in a word */
#define   N         50    /* number of words in the array */

main()
{
    int    i, j;
    char   word[N][MAXWORD],   /* an array of N words */
           temp[MAXWORD];

    for (i = 0; i < N; ++i)
      scanf("%s", word[i]);
    for (i = 0; i < N - 1; ++i)
      for (j = i + 1; j < N; ++j)
        if (r_strcmp(word[i], word[j]) > 0) {
            strcpy(temp, word[i]);
            strcpy(word[i], word[j]);
            strcpy(word[j], temp);
        }
    for (i = 0; i < N; ++i)
      printf("%s\n", word[i]);
}
```

6   Write a recursive version of the standard library function
     strcpy(). If s1 and s2 are strings, then the function call
     r_strcpy(s1, s2) should overwrite whatever is in s1 with the
     contents of s2, and the pointer value of the first argument,
     namely s1, should be returned. For further details, read the
     description of strcmp() given in Chapter 10.

7   Although it is considered bad programming style to overwrite a
     constant string, we do so in this exercise in order to emphasize
     an important point. Consider the two statements

```
printf("%s\n", strcpy("try this", "and this"));
printf("%s\n", strcpy("and", "also this"));
```

     One of these statements works correctly, whereas the other can
     be expected to cause difficulty. Why? Rewrite the function
     r_strcpy(), which you wrote for exercise 6, so that if the type

of error exhibited here occurs, an error message is printed and the program stops. Even though the function is recursive, make sure that you check for the error only once. *Hint:* Make use of a static variable.

8   A function that calls another function which in turn calls the original function is said to be *corecursive*. Note that corecursive functions occur in pairs. Write a program that counts the number of alphabetic characters in a string and sums the digits in the string. For example, the string "A0is444apple7" has 8 alphabetic characters and the digits in the string sum to 19. Write a pair of corecursive functions to help carry out the tasks. Use count_alph() to count the alphabetic characters, and use sum_digit() for summing the digits. These two functions should call each other. For comparison, write a noncorecursive function that performs the two tasks in a direct, more natural fashion. *Hint:* If necessary, use static variables.

9   The greatest common divisor of two positive integers is the largest integer that is a divisor of both of them. For example, 6 and 15 have 3 as their greatest common divisor, and 15 and 22 have 1 as their greatest common divisor. The following recursive function computes the greatest common divisor of two positive integers. First write a program to test the function, and then write and test an equivalent iterative function.

```
gcd(p, q)
int   p, q;
{
    int   r;

    if ((r = p % q) == 0)
        return (q);
    else
        return (gcd(q, r));
}
```

10   Write a recursive "look up" function to search an array in sorted order. Write a program to test your function, making use of random() to fill an array a[] of size n, and making use of bubble_sort() to sort the array. The function call

look_up(v, a, n) should be used to look for the value v in the array a[]. If just one of the elements of the array, say a[i], has the value v, then i should be returned. If two or more of the elements of the array have the value v, then the index of any one of them is an acceptable answer. If none of the elements of the array have the value v, then −1 should be returned. The base case is to look at the "middle" element a[n/2]. If this element has the value v, then n/2 is returned. Otherwise recursion is used to look for v in

a[0], . . . , a[n/2 − 1]   or   a[n/2 + 1], . . . , a[n − 1]

whichever is appropriate. For example, if the value of v is less than a[n/2], then v should be looked for in the first part of the array and the appropriate recursion would be

```
return (look_up(v, a, n/2));
```

11   The following code can be used to test the recursive function minmax() given in Section 12.4. The value of n is entered interactively; the function calloc() is used to create an array a[] of size n dynamically; the array is filled with random integer values; and finally the minimum and maximum values of the array are computed two ways: recursively, by calling minmax(), and iteratively. Since all of this occurs repeatedly inside an infinite loop, we use the standard library function free() to give the storage pointed to by a back to the system at the end of the for loop. The function free() requires a pointer to char as an argument, so we cast a accordingly.

```
main()
{
    char    *calloc();
    int     *a, i,
            n,              /* n is the size of a[] */
            r_min, r_max,   /* recursive min and max */
            i_min, i_max;   /* iterative min and max */
    long    random();

    for ( ; ; ) {
        printf("Input a power of 2:  ");
        scanf("%d", &n);
        a = (int *) calloc((unsigned) n, sizeof(int));
        for (i = 0; i < n; ++i)
            a[i] = random();
        minmax(a, n, &r_min, &r_max);
        printf("\n%s%12d%9s%12d\n",
            "recursion:  min =", r_min, "max =", r_max);
        i_min = i_max = a[0];
        for (i = 1; i < n; ++i) {
            i_min = (i_min < a[i]) ? i_min : a[i];
            i_max = (i_max > a[i]) ? i_max : a[i];
        }
        printf("%s%12d%9s%12d\n\n",
            "iteration:  min =", i_min, "max =", i_max);
        free((char *) a);
    }
}
```

The value of n is the size of the array a[]. For each value of n
that is a power of 2 the minimum and maximum values of the
array are computed two ways: recursively and iteratively. How
many comparisons are used in each of these computations?
Hint: Use hand simulation to find the answer when n takes on
values that are powers of 2 of low order.

12 It is not at all obvious that the recursive algorithm minmax() is
    "best" in the sense of requiring the least number of compari-
    sons. That there cannot exist a better algorithm is proved in
    the paper by Ira Pohl cited in Section 12.4. In this exercise we
    want to show how to modify the algorithm so that arrays of

any size can be handled. The modified function may not have the property that it is the "best" possible, but nonetheless it is still a very efficient algorithm. The interested reader can compare the minmax() function given in this exercise with the version given on page 51 of *A Book on C* by Ira Pohl and Al Kelley (Menlo Park, California: Benjamin/Cummings, 1984).

```
minmax(a, n, min_ptr, max_ptr)        /* n is the size of a[] */
int   a[], n, *min_ptr, *max_ptr;
{
   int   min1, max1, min2, max2;

   if (n == 1)
      *min_ptr = *max_ptr = a[0];
   else {
      minmax(a, n/2, &min1, &max1);
      minmax(a + n/2, n - n/2, &min2, &max2);
      if (min1 < min2)
         *min_ptr = min1;
      else
         *min_ptr = min2;
      if (max1 < max2)
         *max_ptr = max2;
      else
         *max_ptr = max1;
   }
}
```

Write a program to test this function. Notice that it is still a "divide and conquer" algorithm and that it handles arrays of all sizes correctly. The base case now occurs when n has value 1. In the "best" possible algorithm, given in Section 12.4, the base case occurs when n has the value 2. The value 2 is, of course, a power of 2. But 1 is also a power of 2. Can the original minmax() be modified so that n with value 1 is the base case and the algorithm still remains "best"? Perhaps the base case with n having value 2 was used to emphasize the "2-ness" of the algorithm. After all, when n has value 1, the algorithm is not too complicated.

There is one more minor detail that needs to be considered. The algorithm in this exercise uses the argument n - n/2 whereas the comparable argument in the original algorithm is the expression n/2. Explain why.

13   (Advanced) A knight is a chess piece that moves in the pattern of an ell (L). The chessboard has 64 squares, and the knight can make 2 legal moves if placed at a corner square of the chessboard and can make 8 legal moves if placed in the middle square of the board. Write a function that computes the number of legal moves that a knight can make when starting at a specific square on the board. Associate that number with the square. It is called the *connectivity* of the square as viewed by the knight. Write a program that finds and prints the number of legal moves associated with each square on the board. The numbers should be printed as an 8 × 8 array corresponding to the 64 squares on a chessboard, with each number representing the connectivity of its square. This array is the connectivity of the chessboard as viewed by the knight.

14   (Advanced—see "A Method for Finding Hamiltonian Paths and Knight's Tours" by Ira Pohl, in *Communications of the ACM, Vol* 10, *No* 7, *July* 1967.) A knight's tour is a path the knight takes that covers all 64 squares without revisiting any square. Warnsdorf's rule states that to find a knight's tour one starts from a corner square and goes to a square that has not yet been reached and has smallest connectivity. An "adjacent" square is one the knight can immediately move to. When a square is visited, all of the connectivity numbers of adjacent squares are decremented. Employ Warnsdorf's rule to find a knight's tour. Print out an 8 × 8 array corresponding to the chessboard, and in each position print the number of moves it took the knight to reach that square.

15   (Advanced) Pohl's improvement to Warnsdorf's rule was to suggest that ties be broken recursively. Warnsdorf's rule is called a heuristic. It is not guaranteed to work. Still, it is very efficient for a combinatorially difficult problem. Sometimes two squares have the same smallest connectivity. To break the tie, compute recursively which square leads to a further smallest connectivity and choose that square. On the ordinary 8 × 8 chessboard, from any starting square, the Pohl-Warnsdorf rule was always found to work. Implement this heuristic algorithm and run it for five different starting squares, printing each tour.

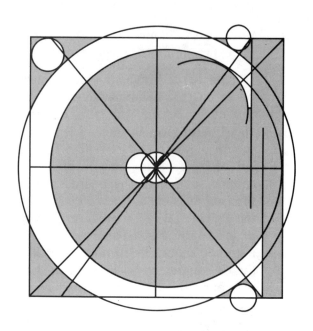

13

STRUCTURES

The structure type allows the programmer to aggregate components into a single, named variable. A structure has components that are individually named. These components are called *members*. Since the members of a structure can be of various types, the programmer can create aggregates of data that are suitable for a problem. Like arrays and pointers, structures are considered a derived type.

In this chapter we show how to declare structures and how to use them to represent a variety of familiar examples, such as a playing card or a student record. Critical to processing structures is the accessing of their members. This is done with either the member operator "." or the structure pointer operator ->. These operators, along with () and [], have the highest precedence. After these operators have been introduced, a complete table of precedence and associativity for all the operators of C is given.

Many examples are given in the chapter to show how structures are processed. An example that implements a student record system is given to show the use of structures and the accessing of its members. The use of self-referential structures to create linked lists is explained, and code necessary for the processing of linked lists is presented.

13.1 DECLARING STRUCTURES

Structures are a means of aggregating a collection of data items of possibly different types. As a simple example let us define a structure that will describe a playing card. The spots on a card that represent its numeric value are called "pips." A playing card, such as the three of spades, has a pip value, 3, and a suit value, spades. Structures allow us to group variables together. We can declare the structure type

```
struct card {
    int     pips;
    char    suit;
};
```

to capture the information needed to represent a playing card. In this declaration struct is a keyword, card is the structure tag name, and the variables pips and suit are members of the structure. The variable pips will take values from 1 to 13 representing ace to king, and the variable suit will take values from 'c', 'd', 'h', and 's', representing the suits clubs, diamonds, hearts, and spades.

This declaration creates the derived data type struct card. The declaration can be thought of as a template; it creates the type struct card, but no storage is allocated. The tag name can now be used to declare variables of this type. The declaration

```
struct card    c1, c2;
```

allocates storage for the identifiers c1 and c2, which are of type struct card. To access the members of c1 and c2 we use the structure member operator ".". Suppose that we want to assign to c1 the values representing the five of diamonds and to c2 the values representing the queen of spades. To do this we can write

```
c1.pips = 5;
c1.suit = 'd';
c2.pips = 12;
c2.suit = 's';
```

A construct of the form

structure_variable . member_name

is used as a variable in the same way a simple variable or an element of an array is used. The member name must be unique within the specified structure. Since the member must always be prefaced or accessed through a unique structure variable identifier, there is no confusion between two members having the same name in different structures. An example is

```
struct fruit {
    char    name[15];
    int     calories;
};

struct vegetable {
    char    name[15];
    int     calories;
};

struct fruit        a;
struct vegetable    b;
```

Having made these declarations, we can access `a.calories` and `b.calories` without ambiguity.

Within a single declaration it is possible to create a structure type (make the template) and declare variables of that type at the same time. An example of this is

```
struct card {
    int     pips;
    char    suit;
} c, deck[52];
```

The identifier `card` is the structure tag name. The identifier `c` is declared to be a variable of type `struct card`, and the identifier `deck` is declared to be an array of type `struct card`. Another example of this is

```
struct {
   char   *last_name;
   int    student_id;
   char   grade;
} s1, s2, s3;
```

which declares s1, s2, and s3 to represent three student records, but does not include a tag name for use in later declarations. Suppose, instead, that we had written

```
struct student {
   char   *last_name;
   int    student_id;
   char   grade;
};
```

This declaration, unlike the previous one, has student as a structure tag name, but no variables are declared of this type. It can be thought of as a template. Now we can write

```
struct student   temp, class[100];
```

This declares temp and class to be of type struct student. Only at this point will storage be allocated for these variables. The template of a structure type by itself does not cause storage to be allocated.

13.2 ACCESSING A MEMBER

We have already seen the use of the member operator ".". In this section we give further examples of its use and introduce the structure pointer operator ->.

Suppose that we are writing a program called *class_info*, which generates information about a class of 100 students. We can begin by creating a header file.

In file class_info.h:

```
#define    CLASS_SIZE    100

struct student {
    char    *last_name;
    int     student_id;
    char    grade;
};
```

This header file can now be used to share information with the modules making up the program. Suppose in another file we write

```
#include    "class_info.h"

main()
{
    struct student    temp, class[CLASS_SIZE];
    . . . . .
```

We can assign values to the members of the structure variable temp by using statements such as

```
temp.grade = 'A';
temp.last_name = "Wootten";
temp.student_id = 590017;
```

Now suppose that we want to count the number of failing students in a given class. To do this, we can write a function that accesses the grade member. Here is a function fail() that counts the number of F grades in the array class[].

```
/* Count the failing grades. */

#include   "class_info.h"

fail(class)
struct student   class[];
{
   int   i, cnt = 0;

   for (i = 0; i < CLASS_SIZE; ++i)
      cnt += class[i].grade == 'F';
   return (cnt);
}
```

■ DISSECTION OF THE fail() FUNCTION

```
fail(class)
struct student    class[];
{
   int   i, cnt = 0;
```

■ The parameter class is of type "pointer to struct student." We can think of it as a one-dimensional array of structures. Parameters of any type, including structure types, can be used in headers to function definitions.

```
for (i = 0; i < CLASS_SIZE; ++i)
```

■ We are assuming that when this function is called, an array of type struct student of size CLASS_SIZE will be passed as an argument.

```
cnt += class[i].grade == 'F';
```

■ An expression such as this demonstrates how C can be concise. C is operator rich. To be fluent in its use, the programmer must be careful about precedence and associativity. This statement is equivalent to

```
cnt += (((class[i]).grade) == 'F');
```

The member `grade` of the *i*th element (counting from zero) of the array of structures `class` is selected. A test is made to see if it is equal to `'F'`. If equality holds, then the value of the expression

```
class[i].grade == 'F'
```

is 1 and the value of `cnt` is incremented. If equality does not hold, then the value of the expression is 0 and the value of `cnt` remains unchanged.

```
return (cnt);
```

■ The number of failing grades is returned to the calling environment.

C provides the structure pointer operator `->` to access the members of a structure via a pointer. This operator is typed on the keyboard as a minus sign followed by a greater than sign. If a pointer variable is assigned the address of a structure, then a member of the structure can be accessed by a construct of the form

pointer_to_structure `->` *member_name*

An equivalent construct is given by

(**pointer_to_structure*).*member_name*

The parentheses are necessary here. The operators `->` and ".", along with () and [], have the highest precedence, and they associate "left to right." Because of this, the above construct without parentheses would be equivalent to

*(*pointer_to_structure*.*member_name*)

In complicated situations the two accessing modes can be combined in complicated ways. The following table illustrates their use in a straightforward manner.

Declarations and assignments		
struct student temp, *p = &temp;		
temp.grade = 'A'; temp.last_name = "Wootten"; temp.student_id = 590017;		
Expression	**Equivalent expression**	**Conceptual Value**
temp.grade	p -> grade	A
temp.last_name	p -> last_name	Wootten
temp.student_id	p -> student_id	590017
(*p).student_id	p -> student_id	590017

13.3 OPERATOR PRECEDENCE AND ASSOCIATIVITY: A FINAL LOOK

We now want to display the entire precedence and associativity table for all the C operators. The operators "." and -> have been introduced in this chapter. These operators, together with () and [], have the highest precedence.

Operators	Associativity
() [] -> .	left to right
++ -- ! ~ sizeof (*type*) - (unary) * (indirection) & (address)	right to left
* / %	left to right
+ -	left to right
<< >>	left to right
< <= > >=	left to right
== !=	left to right
&	left to right
^	left to right
|	left to right
&&	left to right
||	left to right
?:	right to left
= += -= *= /= *etc*	right to left
, (comma operator)	left to right

The unary operator ~ and the binary operators <<, >>, &, ^, and |
are all bitwise operators. They are used to manipulate the bits in a
machine word. We do not discuss their use in this text. The interested reader should see Chapter 6 of *A Book on C* by Al Kelley and
Ira Pohl (Menlo Park, California: Benjamin/Cummings, 1984).
The comma operator has the lowest precedence of all the operators
of C. Its use is somewhat specialized, and is not essential; see exercise 19. The commas used in declarations and in argument lists to
functions are not comma operators.

As we saw in Chapter 6, the unary operator sizeof can be used to
find the number of bytes needed to store an object in memory. For
example, the value of the expression sizeof(struct card) is the number of bytes needed by the system to store a variable of type
struct card. The type of the expression is unsigned. Later in this
chapter we will see that the sizeof operator is used extensively when
creating linked lists.

While the complete table of operators is extensive, some simple
rules apply. The primary operators are function parentheses, subscripting, and the two addressing primitives for accessing a member
of a structure. These four operators are of highest precedence.
Unary operators come next, followed by the arithmetic operators.

Arithmetic operators follow the usual convention; namely, multiplicative operators have higher precedence than additive operators. Assignments of all kinds are of lowest precedence, with the exception of the still lowlier comma operator. If a programmer does not know the rules of precedence and associativity in a particular situation, he or she should either look the rules up or use parentheses.

One further point needs to be mentioned. Expressions involving just one of the commutative binary operators

$$* \quad + \quad \& \quad \wedge \quad |$$

are subject to reordering by the compiler for its convenience, even where they are parenthesized. To guarantee order of evaluation, one must use assignment statements to evaluate intermediate results.

13.4 STRUCTURES, FUNCTIONS, AND ASSIGNMENT

All systems allow a pointer to a structure type to be passed as an argument to a function and returned as a value. In addition, on most systems, structures themselves can be passed as arguments to functions and returned as values. Our discussion will be for this unrestricted environment. In this environment if a and b are two variables of the same structure type, the assignment expression a = b is allowed. It causes each member of a to be assigned the value of the corresponding member of b. See Section 13.14, "Operating System Considerations," for further remarks.

To illustrate the use of structures with functions, we will use the structure type struct card. For the remainder of this chapter assume the header file *card.h* contains the declaration for this structure.

In file card.h:

```
struct card {
    int     pips;
    char    suit;
};
```

Let us write functions that will assign values to a card, extract the member values of a card, and print the values of a card. We will assume that the header file *card.h* has been included wherever needed.

```
assign_values(c_ptr, p, s)
struct card    *c_ptr;
int            p;
char           s;
{
    c_ptr -> pips = p;
    c_ptr -> suit = s;
}


extract_values(c_ptr, p_ptr, s_ptr)
struct card    *c_ptr;
int            *p_ptr;
char           *s_ptr;
{
    *p_ptr = c_ptr -> pips;
    *s_ptr = c_ptr -> suit;
}
```

These functions access a card by using a pointer to a variable of type struct card. The structure pointer operator -> is used throughout to access the required member. Next, let us write a card printing routine that takes a pointer to struct card and prints its values using extract_values().

```
prn_values(c_ptr)
struct card   *c_ptr;
{
    int    p;              /* pips value */
    char   s;              /* suit value */
    char   *suit_name;

    extract_values(c_ptr, &p, &s);
    suit_name = (s == 'c') ? "clubs" : (s == 'd') ? "diamonds" :
        (s == 'h') ? "hearts" : (s == 's') ? "spades" : "error";
    printf("card:  %d of %s\n", p, suit_name);
}
```

Finally, we want to illustrate how these functions can be used. First, we assign values to a deck of cards, and then as a test we print out the heart suit.

```
main()
{
    int            i;
    struct card    deck[52];

    for (i = 0; i < 13; ++i) {
        assign_values(deck + i, i + 1, 'c');
        assign_values(deck + i + 13, i + 1, 'd');
        assign_values(deck + i + 26, i + 1, 'h');
        assign_values(deck + i + 39, i + 1, 's');
    }
    for (i = 0; i < 13; ++i)          /* print out the hearts */
        prn_values(deck + i + 26);
}
```

Functions can be designed to work with structures as parameters, rather than with pointers to structures. To illustrate this, let us rewrite the functions assign_values() and extract_values().

```
struct card assign_values(p, s)
int    p;
char   s;
{
   struct card   c;

   c.pips = p;
   c.suit = s;
   return (c);
}


extract_values(c, p_ptr, s_ptr)
struct card   c;
int    *p_ptr;
char   *s_ptr;
{
   *s_ptr = c.suit;
   *p_ptr = c.pips;
}
```

In C the value of an argument that is passed to a function is copied when the function is invoked. This call-by-value mechanism was discussed in Chapter 4. Because of this, when a structure is passed as an argument to a function, the structure is copied when the function is invoked. For this reason, passing the address of the structure is more efficient than passing the structure itself.

13.5 AN EXAMPLE: STUDENT RECORDS

The variations available in C to define complicated data structures involve all meaningful combinations of structure, pointer, and array. We will start with our previous example of struct student and develop it into a more comprehensive data structure for a student record. We begin by defining the various types needed, as follows:

In file student.h:

```
#define    CLASS_SIZE    50
#define    NCOURSES      10      /* number of courses */

struct student {
    char    *last_name;
    int     student_id;
    char    grade;
};

struct date {
    short    day;
    char     month[10];
    short    year;
};

struct personal {
    char          name[20];
    struct date   birthday;
};

struct student_data {
    struct personal    p;
    int                student_id;
    char               grade[NCOURSES];
};
```

Notice that struct student_data is constructed with nested structures. One of its members is the structure p, which has as one of its members the structure birthday. After the declaration

```
struct student_data    temp;
```

has been made, the expression

```
temp.p.birthday.month[0]
```

has as its value the first letter of the month of the birthday of the student whose data is in temp. Structures such as date and personal are used in data base applications.

Let us write the function read_date() to enter data into a variable of type struct date. When the function is called, the address of the variable must be passed as an argument to the function.

```
#include   "student.h"

read_date(d)
struct date    *d;
{
    printf("Enter   day(int)   month(string)   year(int): ");
    scanf("%hd%s%hd", &d -> day, d -> month, &d -> year);
}
```

■ DISSECTION OF THE read_date() FUNCTION

```
read_date(d)
struct date    *d;
{
    printf("Enter   day(int)   month(string)   year(int): ");
```

■ The parameter d has type "pointer to struct date." The printf() statement prompts the user for information.

```
&d -> day
```

■ This is an address. Because & is of lower precedence than -> , this expression is equivalent to

```
&(d -> day)
```

First the pointer d is used to access the member day. Then the address operator & is applied to this member to obtain its address.

```
d -> month
```

- This is an address. The pointer d is being used to access a member that is an array. An array name by itself is a pointer, or address. It points to the base address of the array.

```
scanf("%hd%s%hd", &d -> day, d -> month, &d -> year);
```

- The function scanf() is used to read in three values and to store them at appropriate addresses. Recall that in the header file *student.h* the two members day and year of struct date were declared to be of type short. The format %hd is used to convert characters in the standard input stream (keyboard) to a value of type short. (The h used to modify the conversion character d in the format comes from the second letter in the word "short.")

The function read_date() can be used to read information into a variable of type struct student_data. For example, the code

```
    struct student_data   temp;

    read_date(&temp.p.birthday);
```

can be used to place information into the appropriate member of temp.

Here is a function to enter grades.

```
    read_grades(g)
    char   g[];
    {
        int   i;

        printf("Enter %d grades:  ", NCOURSES);
        for (i = 0; i < NCOURSES; ++i)
            scanf(" %c", &g[i]);
    }
```

The control string " %c" is being used to read in a single nonwhite space character. The blank just before the % matches optional white space in the input stream. This function could be called to read a list of grades into temp as follows:

```
read_grades(temp.grade);
```

The argument temp.grade is an address (pointer) because it refers to a member of a structure that is an array, and an array name by itself is the base address of the array. Thus when the function is invoked, it causes the values of temp.grade in the calling environment to be changed.

Basically, understanding structures comes down to understanding how to access their members. As a further example let us now write a function that takes data stored in the long form in struct student_data and converts it to the short form stored in struct student.

```
#include    "student.h"

extract(s_data, n, undergrad)
struct student_data    *s_data;
struct student         *undergrad;
int                    n;                /* course number */
{
    undergrad -> student_id = s_data -> student_id;
    undergrad -> last_name = s_data -> p.name;
    undergrad -> grade = s_data -> grade[n];
}
```

13.6 INITIALIZATION OF STRUCTURES

All external and static variables, including structure variables, that are not explicitly initialized are automatically initialized by the system to zero. As with arrays, external and static structures can be initialized by the programmer. The syntax is similar to that used with arrays. An external or static structure variable can be followed by an equal sign = and a list of constants contained within braces. If not enough values are used to assign all the members of the structure, the remaining members are assigned the value zero by default. Some examples are

```
struct card   c = {12, 's'};   /* the queen of spades */

static struct fruit   frt = {"plum", 150};

static struct complex {
   double   real;
   double   imaginary;
}   m[3][3] = {
   {{1.0, -0.5}, {2.5, 1.0}, { 0.7, 0.7}},
   {{7.0, -6.5}, {-0.5, 1.0}, {45.7, 8.0}},
};   /* m[2][] is assigned zeroes */
```

In the first example c must be a global variable. Its storage class cannot be automatic. As with automatic arrays, automatic structure variables cannot be initialized.

13.7 SELF-REFERENTIAL STRUCTURES

In this section we define structures with pointer members that refer to the structure type containing them. These are called *self-referential* structures. Unlike arrays or simple variables that are normally allocated at block entry, self-referential structures often require storage management routines to explicitly obtain and release memory.

Let us define a structure with a member field that points at the same structure type. We wish to do this in order to have an unspecified number of such structures linked together.

```
struct list {
   int        data;
   struct list *next;
};
```

Each variable of type struct list contains the two members data and next. The pointer variable next is called a *link*. Each structure is linked to a succeeding structure by way of the member next.

These structures are conveniently displayed pictorially, with links shown as arrows.

The structure `list`

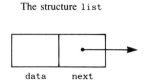

data   next

The pointer variable `next` contains an address of either the location in memory of the successor `struct list` element or the special value `NULL`, which is usually defined in *stdio.h* as a symbolic constant with value 0. The value `NULL` is used to denote the end of the list. By manipulating

```
struct list   a, b, c;
```

let us see how all this works. We begin by performing some assignments on these structures.

```
a.data = 1;
b.data = 2;
c.data = 3;
a.next = b.next = c.next = NULL;
```

The result of this code is described pictorially as follows:

Assignment

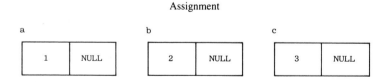

Next, let us chain the three structures together.

```
a.next = &b;
b.next = &c;
```

These pointer assignments result in linking `a` to `b` to `c`:

Chaining

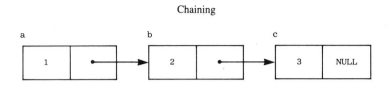

And now the links allow us to retrieve data from successive elements. For example,

```
a.next -> data          has value 2
a.next -> next -> data  has value 3
```

13.8 LINEAR LINKED LISTS

A *linear linked list* is like a clothes line on which the data structures hang sequentially. There is a head pointer addressing the first element of the list, and each element points at a successor element, with the last element having a link value NULL. Typically, a linked list is created dynamically. In this section we will show how this is done. Also, we will show how the typedef facility can be used to create a new name for a type. In practice, the typedef facility is often used to rename a structure type.

Let us begin by creating a header file that will be included with the list processing functions that we will write in the sections that follow. This header file includes the file *stdio.h* because that is where NULL is defined.

In file list.h:

```
#include   <stdio.h>

typedef   char   DATA;     /* we will use char in examples */

struct linked_list {
   DATA                d;
   struct linked_list  *next;
};

typedef   struct linked_list   ELEMENT;
typedef   ELEMENT *             LINK;
```

THE USE OF typedef

C provides a number of fundamental types, such as char and int, and other types that are derived from these, such as arrays, pointers, and structures. In addition, the language provides the typedef facility, which allows a type to be explicitly associated with an identifier. An example of this is

```
typedef   char   DATA;
```

The identifier DATA can now be used to declare variables and functions in the same way that ordinary types are used. For example,

```
DATA   a, b, c;
```

declares the variables a, b, and c to be of type DATA, which is equivalent to char.

In the header file *list.h* we used typedef to create names of types that are more suggestive of their use. Notice that although DATA is simply the type char, conceptually it could be a more complicated type, such as an array or a structure; see exercise 11.

DYNAMIC STORAGE ALLOCATION

The declaration of struct linked_list in *list.h* does not allocate storage. It acts as a template for the storage that the system will allocate later, when variables and arrays of this type are declared. We used the typedef facility to rename the type as ELEMENT, because we wish to think of it as an element in our list. What makes self-referential structure types such as ELEMENT especially useful is that utility programs exist to allocate storage dynamically. The function malloc() is provided in the standard library. A function call of the form

```
malloc(size)
```

returns a pointer to enough storage for an object of *size* bytes. The function malloc() takes a single argument of type unsigned and returns a pointer to char that points to the base address of the storage allocated by the function. If head is a variable of type LINK, then

```
head = (LINK) malloc(sizeof(ELEMENT));
```

obtains a piece of memory from the system adequate to store an ELEMENT and assigns its base address to the pointer head. As in the above example, a function call to malloc() is often used with a cast and the sizeof operator. Without the cast, a type mismatch warning would occur, because head is not a pointer to char. The sizeof operator calculates the required number of bytes for the particular data structure.

Suppose that we want to dynamically create a linear linked list to store the three characters n, e, and w. The following code will do this:

```
head = (LINK) malloc(sizeof(ELEMENT));
head -> d = 'n';
head -> next = NULL;
```

This creates a single element list.

Creating a list dynamically

A second element is added by the assignments

```
head -> next = (LINK) malloc(sizeof(ELEMENT));
head -> next -> d = 'e';
head -> next -> next = NULL;
```

Now there is a two-element list.

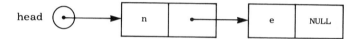

Finally we add a last element.

```
head -> next -> next = (LINK) malloc(sizeof(ELEMENT));
head -> next -> next -> d = 'w';
head -> next -> next -> next = NULL;
```

Now we have a three element list pointed at by head and ending with the sentinel value NULL.

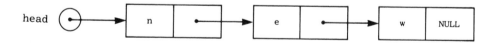

13.9 LIST OPERATIONS

Some of the basic operations on linear linked lists include:

1 creating a list
2 counting the elements
3 looking up an element
4 inserting an element
5 deleting an element

We will demonstrate the techniques for programming such operations on lists. The use of recursive functions is natural, since lists are a recursively defined construct. Each routine will require the specifications in the header file *list.h*. Observe that d in these examples could be redefined as a more complicated data structure.

As a first example we will write a function that will produce a list from a string. The function will return a pointer to the head of the resulting list. The heart of the function creates a list element by allocating storage and assigning member values.

```
/* List creation by recursion. */

#include   "list.h"

LINK string_to_list(s)
char   s[];
{
   char   *malloc();
   LINK   head;

   if (s[0] == '\0')      /* base case */
      return (NULL);
   else {
      head = (LINK) malloc(sizeof(ELEMENT));
      head -> d = s[0];
      head -> next = string_to_list(s + 1);
      return (head);
   }
}
```

Notice once more how recursion has a base case, the creation of the empty list, and a general case, the creation of the remainder of the list.

■ DISSECTION OF THE string_to_list() FUNCTION

```
LINK string_to_list(s)
char    s[];
{
    char    *malloc();
    LINK    head;
```

■ When a string is passed as an argument, a linked list of the characters in the string is created. Since a pointer to the head of the list will be returned, the type specifier in the header to this function definition is LINK. Even though the executable code for malloc() is obtained from the system, the programmer is responsible for declaring the function correctly.

```
if (s[0] == '\0')      /* base case */
    return (NULL);
```

■ When the end-of-string sentinel is detected, NULL is returned, and, as we will see, the recursion terminates. The value NULL is used to mark the end of the linked list.

```
else {
    head = (LINK) malloc(sizeof(ELEMENT));
```

■ If the string s[] is not the null string, then malloc() is used to retrieve enough bytes to store an object of type ELEMENT. The cast is necessary to avoid a type warning in the assignment. The pointer variable head now points at the block of storage provided by malloc().

```
head -> d = s[0];
```

■ The member d of the allocated ELEMENT is assigned the first character in the string s[].

```
head -> next = string_to_list(s + 1);
```

■ The pointer expression s + 1 points to the remainder of the
string. The function is called recursively with s + 1 as an argument. The pointer member next is assigned the pointer value
that is returned by string_to_list(s + 1). This recursive call
returns as its value a LINK, or, equivalently, a pointer to ELEMENT
that points to the remaining sublist.

```
return (head);
```

■ The function exits with the address of the head of the list.

13.10 COUNTING AND LOOKUP

In this section we will write two more recursive functions that perform list operations. The first function is count(). It can be used
to count the elements in a list. It involves recurring down the list
and terminating when the NULL pointer is found. If the list is empty
the value 0 is returned; otherwise the number of elements in the list
is returned.

```
/* Count a list recursively. */

#include    "list.h"

count(head)
LINK    head;
{
    if (head == NULL)
        return (0);
    else
        return (1 + count(head -> next));
}
```

The next function searches a list for a particular element. If the
element is found, a pointer to that element is returned; otherwise
the NULL pointer is returned.

```
/* Lookup c in the list pointed to by head. */

#include   "list.h"

LINK lookup(c, head)
DATA   c;
LINK   head;
{
    if (head == NULL)
        return (NULL);
    else if (c == head -> d)
        return (head);
    else
        return (lookup(c, head -> next));
}
```

13.11 INSERTION AND DELETION

One of the most useful properties of lists is that insertion takes a fixed amount of time once the position in the list is found. In contrast, if one wished to place a value in a large array, retaining all other array values in the same sequential order, the insertion would take, on average, time proportional to the length of the array. The values of all elements of the array that came after the newly inserted value would have to be moved over one element.

Let us illustrate insertion into a list by having two adjacent elements pointed at by p1 and p2, and inserting between them an element pointed at by q.

Insertion

before:

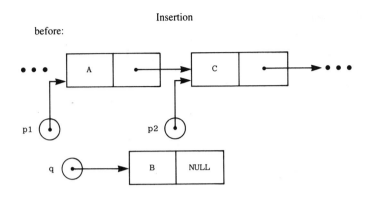

after:

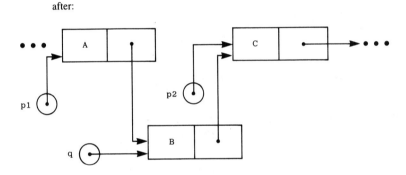

The following function insert() places the element pointed at by q between the elements pointed at by p1 and p2.

```
/* Inserting an element in a linked list. */

#include   "list.h"

insert(p1, p2, q)
LINK   p1, p2, q;
{
   p1 -> next = q;    /* insertion */
   q -> next = p2;
}
```

Deleting an element is very simple in a linear linked list. The predecessor of the element to be deleted has its link member assigned the address of the successor to the deleted element. Again, let us first illustrate graphically the delete operation. .

Deletion

before:

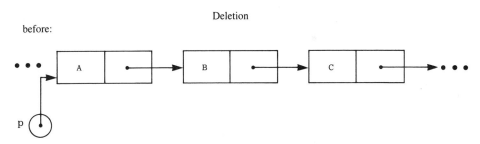

Now executing the code

```
p -> next = p -> next -> next;
```

after:

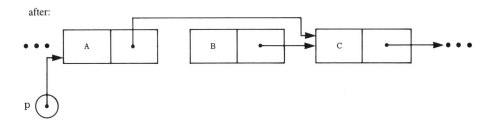

As the diagram shows, the element containing B is no longer accessible and is of no use. Such an inaccessible element is called *garbage*. Since memory is frequently a critical resource, it is desirable that this storage be returned to the system for later use. This may be done with the standard library function free(). The function call

```
free((char *) p)
```

makes again available to the system storage pointed at by p that was previously allocated dynamically by malloc() or calloc(). Since free() takes an argument of type pointer to char, the pointer p should be cast as indicated above whenever it is not a pointer to char.

Using free(), we will write a deletion routine that returns dynamically allocated list storage to the system.

```
/* Recursive deletion of a list. */

#include   "list.h"

delete_list(head)
LINK   head;
{
    if (head != NULL) {
        delete_list(head -> next);
        free((char *) head);          /* release storage */
    }
}
```

13.12 STYLE

It is good programming style to aggregate related data into a structure. By declaring a structure the programmer can create a data type suitable for a problem. The declaration should list each member on its own line, properly indented.

```
struct automobile {
    char     name[15];      /* example:  buick   */
    int      year;          /* example:  1983    */
    double   cost;          /* example:  2390.95 */
};
```

It is usually good programming practice to associate a tag name with a structure type. It is both convenient for further declarations and for documentation.

If extensive use is going to be made of a structure declaration, it is appropriate to use the typedef facility to create a new name for the type. In the case of struct automobile we could use

```
typedef   struct automobile   CAR;
```

There is no requirement for the new type name to be in capital letters. We could just as well have used `car`. What gets used depends on personal taste. Either style is acceptable.

A common programming style is to write structure declarations in header files that can then be included where needed. If the declaration of a structure type needs to be altered later, this is accomplished by changing its declaration in the header file. Perhaps later we will discover that we want `CAR` to have a member describing the horsepower of an automobile. This is easily done by adding the line

```
int    horsepower;    /* example:  225 */
```

to the structure declaration in the header file.

13.13 COMMON PROGRAMMING ERRORS

When working with self-referential structures, a common programming error is to access the wrong place in memory. For example, if a linear linked list is not properly terminated by a `NULL` pointer, some form of unexpected run-time error will occur.

Another common programming error is to mix up the order in the use of `typedef`. For example,

```
typedef  ELEMENT  struct linked_list;    /* wrong */
```

is incorrect because the identifier `ELEMENT` has to follow the type `struct linked_list`, not precede it. Notice also that a `typedef` construction is followed by a semicolon.

Our last programming error involves the comparison of two variables, say `a` and `b`, of the same structure type. Although the assignment expression

```
a = b
```

is legal, the use of the expression

```
a == b    /* wrong */
```

to test for equality of two structures is not allowed. Because the operators = and == are so visually similar, beginning programmers sometimes make this mistake.

13.14 OPERATING SYSTEM CONSIDERATIONS

C has evolved with time. All C systems allow pointers to structures to be passed as arguments to functions and returned as values. All newer compilers allow structures themselves to be passed as arguments and returned as values. In addition, the newer compilers allow structure assignment. Programmers writing code that is meant to be portable across systems must take into account restrictions that may be present in older compilers.

In data base applications structures often have tens, even hundreds, of members. If a structure is passed as an argument to a function, then a copy of the structure is made when the function is invoked. If the structure is large, and a local copy is not really needed, then for the sake of efficiency it is better to pass a pointer to the structure rather than the structure itself.

Operating systems differ on their requirements for aligning storage on boundaries. For example, some systems may require that an int be aligned on a word boundary, others may not. Because of this, when space for a structure is allocated, it can happen that the space required for the structure as a whole is more than the sum of the space required for each of its members. Moreover, the space requirement for the structure as a whole may depend on the order of the members within the structure. This is seldom of concern to the programmer, except when memory is a scarce resource. See exercise 18.

13.15 SUMMARY

1   A structure is an aggregation of subparts treated as a single variable. The subparts of the structure are called members.

2   Structure members are accessed by the member operator "." and the structure pointer operator ->. If s is a structure variable with a member named m, then s.m refers to the value of the member m within s. If p is a pointer that points at s, then

p -> m and s.m are equivalent expressions. Both "." and ->
have highest precedence among C operators.

3   Structures can be members of other structures. Considerable
    complexity is possible when nesting structures, pointers, and
    arrays within each other. Care should be taken that the proper
    variables are being accessed.

4   A self-referential structure uses a pointer member to address a
    structure of the same type. Self-referential structures can be
    used to create a linear linked list. Each element points to the
    next element, except the last element, which has the value NULL
    for its pointer member.

5   The function malloc() is used to dynamically allocate storage.
    It takes an argument of type unsigned and returns a pointer to
    char that is the base address of the allocated storage.

6   Standard algorithms for list processing are naturally imple-
    mented recursively. Frequently, the base case is the detection
    of the NULL link. The general case recurs by moving one ele-
    ment over in the linked list.

13.16 EXERCISES

1   Suppose that the following structure is used to write a dieting
    program:

```
structure food {
    char    name[15];
    int     portion_weight;
    int     calories;
};
```

What is the tag name of this structure? How would one
declare an array meal[10] of this type? Let us say an apple that
is 4 ounces contains 200 calories. How would you assign
values to the three members of meal[0] to represent such an
apple?

2   Write a program that counts the number of calories in a given
    meal. The meal would be stored in the array meal[]. The pro-
    gram should write each course of the meal.

3   The following function is supposed to assign values to a card, but does not work as expected. Describe what goes wrong.

```
#include   "card.h"

struct card *assign_values(p, s)
int    p;      /* pips value assigned */
char   s;      /* suit value assigned */
{
    card   *c_ptr;

    c_ptr -> pips = p;
    c_ptr -> suit = s;
    return (c_ptr);
}
```

4   Create a structure that can describe a restaurant. It should have members that include the name, address, average cost, and type of food. Suppose that an array of structures representing restaurants has been created. Write a function that prints out all restaurants of a given food type in order of cost, least costly first.

5   When playing poker or other card games, it is usual to arrange a hand to reflect its values. Write a program that arranges and prints out a hand of five cards in sorted order by pips value. Assume that an ace is highest in value, a king is next highest in value, and so forth.

6   Using the student record example in the text, write a function that prints the average for each student in a class. Let an A grade have value 4, a B grade have value 3, and so forth.

7   Write a function that prints out students in order of their date of birth, oldest first. The original set of student records need not be in any order.

8   Write a function prn_student_data() that prints in a nice format all the information in a variable of type struct student_data.

9   Define a structure that contains the name of a food, its calories per serving, its food type (such as meat or fruit), and its costs. Write a program that is able to produce a balanced meal. The

foods should be stored as an array of structures. The program should construct a meal so as to come from four different food types and to meet calorie and cost constraints. It should be capable of producing a large number of different menus.

10 The following declarations do not compile correctly. Explain what is wrong with the declarations and rewrite them.

```
struct husband {
    char        name[10];
    int         age;
    struct wife spouse;
} a;

struct wife {
    char            name[10];
    int             age;
    struct husband  spouse;
} b;
```

11 Modify the header file *list.h* by replacing the typedef line with

```
struct s_data {
    char    name[10];
    int     age;
    int     weight;
};

typedef    struct s_data    DATA;
```

Write a function create_list() that transforms an array of type DATA into a linear linked list. Write another function that counts the number of people above both a given age and a given weight.

12 Given a linear linked list of the type found in exercise 11, write a function sort_by_age() that sorts the list by age. Write another function sort_by_name() that sorts the list lexicographically by name.

13   Write an iterative version of the function count() that was presented in Section 13.10.

14   Write an insertion function that inserts an element at the first position in the list following an element storing a particular DATA item. You should use look_up() to find the element. If the element is not present, the insertion should occur at the end of the list.

15   Explain why the parentheses are necessary in the construct

(*pointer_to_structure).member_name

Write a test program that uses the construct. Will your program compile if the parentheses are removed? Will *lint* complain?

16   In simple situations a typedef can be replaced by a #define. Sometimes, however, this can lead to unexpected errors. Rewrite the header file *list.h* as follows:

```
#include   <stdio.h>

#define   DATA   char      /* we will use char in examples */

struct linked_list {
   DATA                 d;
   struct linked_list   *next;
};

#define   ELEMENT   struct linked_list
#define   LINK      ELEMENT *
```

After you have done this, check to see that the functions string_to_list(), count(), and lookup() can all be compiled just as before. The function insert(), however, does not compile. Explain why. Modify the function so that it does compile. *Hint:* Use *cc* with the −E option.

17   The function insert(), which we wrote in Section 13.11, assumed that p1 and p2 were pointing to adjacent elements in a

linked list. What happens if p1 and p2 are pointing to elements in the list that are not adjacent?

18 On our system, the following two structures are not stored in the same number of bytes.

```
struct s1 {
   char   c1;
   char   c2;
   int    i;
};

struct s2 {
   char   c1;
   int    i;
   char   c2;
};
```

The statement

```
printf("%d\n%d\n", sizeof(struct s1), sizeof(struct s2));
```

causes the values 8 and 12 to be printed. What are the space requirements for these structures on your system?

19 In a comma expression of the form

expr1 , expr2

expr1 is evaluated first, then *expr2*, and the comma expression as a whole has the value and type of its right operand. An example of a comma expression is

```
a = 1, b = 2
```

If b has been declared to be an int, then the value of this comma expression is 2 and its type is int. Here is a for loop that prints a column of even integers and a column of odd integers. Which commas are comma operators and which are not? Rewrite the code so that no comma operators are used.

```
int   i, j;

for (i = 0, j = 1; i < LIMIT; i += 2, j += 2)
   printf("%12d%12d\n", i, j);
```

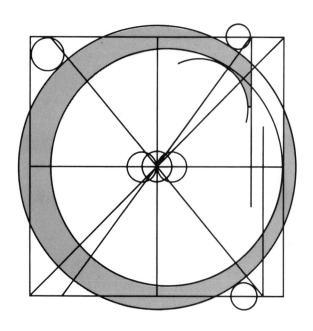

14

INPUT/OUTPUT
AND FILES

This chapter will explain in detail how to use some of the input/output functions in the standard library. These functions can be used to process user defined files. We have already made extensive use of the standard input/output functions printf() and scanf(). In this chapter we will explain their use in detail. An extensive table showing the effects of various formats is presented. The standard library provides functions related to printf() and scanf() that can be used for dealing with files and strings. The use of these functions is explained.

General file input/output is important for large-scale applications where files reside on tapes and disks. We will show how files are opened for processing and how use is made of a pointer to a file. A list of some of the more important file input/output functions is given, along with a description of their use. A program to double-space the contents of a file given as a command line argument is dissected.

14.1   THE OUTPUT FUNCTION printf()

The printf() function has two nice properties that allow flexible use at a high level. First, a list of arguments of arbitrary length can be printed, and second, the printing is controlled by simple formats. The function printf() delivers its character stream to the standard output file stdout. The argument list to printf() has two parts:

control_string   and   *other_arguments*

In the example

```
printf("she sells %d %s for $%f", 99, "sea shells", 3.77);
```

we have

control_string: "she sells %d %s for $%f"

other_arguments: 99, "sea shells", 3.77

The expressions in *other_arguments* are evaluated and converted according to the formats in the control string and then placed in the output stream. Characters in the control string that are not part of a format are placed directly in the output stream. The % symbol introduces a format, or conversion specification. A single conversion specification is a string that begins with % and ends with a conversion character.

printf()	
Conversion character	**How the corresponding argument is printed**
c	as a character
d	as a decimal integer
u	as an unsigned decimal integer
o	as an unsigned octal integer
x	as a unsigned hexadecimal integer
X	as a unsigned hexadecimal integer
e	as a floating point number; example: 7.123000e+00
E	as a floating point number; example: 7.123000E+00
f	as a floating point number; example: 7.123000
g	in the e-format or f-format, whichever is shorter
G	in the E-format or f-format, whichever is shorter
s	as a string

In the example

```
printf("she sells %d %s for $%f", 99, "sea shells", 3.77);
```

we can match the formats in the control string with their corresponding arguments in the argument list.

Format	Corresponding argument
%d	99
%s	"sea shells"
%f	3.77

Explicit formatting information may be included in a conversion specification. If it is not included, then certain defaults occur. For example, the format %f with corresponding argument 3.77 will result in 3.770000 being printed. The number is printed with 6 digits to the right of the decimal point by default. Explicit formatting information is specified as follows. Between the % sign and the conversion character there may be

■ a minus sign, which means that the converted argument is to be *left adjusted* in its field. If there is no minus sign, then the converted argument is to be *right adjusted* in its field. The place where an argument is printed is called its *field*, and the number of spaces used to print an argument is called its *field width*.

■ a plus sign, which means that a nonnegative number is to have a + prepended. This works with the conversion characters d, e, E, f, g, and G. All negative numbers automatically have a – prepended.

■ a blank instead of a plus sign, which means that a nonnegative number is to have a blank prepended. This works with the conversion characters d, e, E, f, g, and G.

■ a #, which has a meaning that depends on the conversion character. In an o-format it causes 0 to be prepended to the octal number being printed. In an x- or X-format it causes 0x or 0X to be prepended to the hexadecimal number being printed. In a g- or G-format, it causes trailing zeros to be printed. In an e-, E-, f-, g-, or G-format, it causes a decimal point to be printed, even with precision 0.

■ a positive integer, which defines the *field width* of the converted argument. If the converted argument has fewer characters than the specified field width, then it will be padded with blanks on the left or right, depending on whether the converted argument is right or left adjusted. If the converted argument has more characters than the specified field width, then the field width will be extended to "whatever is required." If the integer defining the field width begins with 0, and the argument being printed is right adjusted in its field, then 0s will be used for padding rather than blanks.

■ a period, which separates *field width* from *precision*.

■ a nonnegative integer, which defines the *precision* of the converted argument. For an e, E, f, g, or G conversion this is the number of digits to the right of the decimal point. For an s conversion it is the maximum number of characters to be printed from a string.

■ the character l or L, which specifies that the conversion character d, o, x, or u that follows corresponds to an argument of type long.

■   a *, which indicates that a value is to be obtained from the argument list. The field width or precision or both may be indicated by a * instead of a nonnegative integer.

The field width is the minimum number of spaces that must be used to print the expression. The default is whatever is required to properly display the argument. Thus the integer value 102 (decimal) will require 3 spaces for decimal conversion d or octal conversion o, but only 2 spaces for hexadecimal conversion x. These digits will appear right adjusted unless the minus sign is present. If the field width is too short to properly display the value of the corresponding argument, the field width will be increased to the default. If the entire field is not needed to display the converted argument, then the remaining part of the field is padded with blanks on the left or right, depending on whether the converted argument is right or left adjusted. The padding character on the left can be made 0 by specifying the field width with a leading zero.

The precision is specified by a nonnegative number that occurs to the right of the period. For string conversions this is the maximum number of characters to be printed from the string. For e and f conversions this is the number of digits to be printed to the right of the decimal point. Examples of formats are given in the table that follows. We use double quote characters to visually delimit the field. They are not part of what gets printed.

Declarations and initializations	
char	c = 'w';
int	i = 1, j = 29;
float	x = 333.12345678901234567890;
double	y = 333.12345678901234567890;
static char	s1[] = "she sells sea shells";
static char	s2[] = "by the seashore";

Format	Expression	How it is printed in its field	Remarks
%c	c	"w"	field length 1 by default
%2c	c	" w"	right adjusted
%-3c	c	"w "	left adjusted
%d	-j	"-29"	field length 3 by default
%010d	i	"0000000001"	padded with zeros
%-12d	j	"29 "	left adjusted
%12o	j	" 35"	octal, right adjusted
%-12x	j	"1d "	hexadecimal, left adjusted
%f	x	"333.123444"	precision 6 by default
%.1f	x	"333.1"	precision 1
%20.3f	x	" 333.123"	right adjusted
%.9f	y	"333.123456789"	precision 9
%-20.3e	y	"3.331e+02 "	left adjusted
%s	s1	"she sells sea shells"	field length 20 by default
%7s	s1	"she sells sea shells"	more space needed
%.5s	s2	"by th"	precision 5
%-15.12s	s2	"by the seash "	precision 12, left adjusted

To print the character % in the output stream one can use the conversion specification %%, which prints a single percent symbol. Of course, the conversion specification %c can be used to print the expression '%' in the argument list.

14.2 THE INPUT FUNCTION scanf()

The function scanf() has two nice properties that allow flexible use at a high level. The first is that a list of arguments of arbitrary length can be scanned, and the second is that the input is controlled by simple formats. The argument list to scanf() has two parts:

control_string   and   *other_arguments*

In the example

```
char     c, s1[100], s2[100];
int      n;
double   x;

scanf("%s%d%s%c%lf", s1, &n, s2, &c, &x);
```

we have

> *control_string*:   "%s%d%s%c%lf"
>
> *other_arguments*:   s1, &n, s2, &c, &x

The argument following the control string consists of pointer expressions, or addresses, separated by commas. The standard input file stdin provides the character stream from which scanf() receives its input. The control string may contain

- white space, which matches optional white space in the input stream.
- ordinary nonwhite space characters, other than %. Each ordinary character must match the next character in the input stream.
- conversion specifications that begin with a % and end with a conversion character. Between the % and the conversion character there may be an optional * that indicates assignment suppression, followed by an optional integer that defines a maximum scan width, followed by an optional h or l that modifies the specification character.

The characters in the input stream are converted to values according to the conversion specifications in the control string and placed at the address given by the corresponding pointer expression in the argument list. Conversion specifications begin with a % character and end with a conversion character.

scanf()	
Conversion character	**What characters in the input stream are converted to**
c	to a character
d	to a decimal integer
u	to an unsigned decimal integer
o	to an unsigned octal integer
x	to an unsigned hexadecimal integer
e	to a floating point number
f	to a floating point number, equivalent to e
g	to a floating point number, equivalent to e
s	to a string
[*string*]	to a special string

The conversion characters d, u, o, x, may be preceded by an h or an l to signify conversion to a short or long type, respectively. The conversion characters e, f, g may be preceded by an l to signify conversion to a long float, or double.

Except for character input, an input field consists of contiguous nonwhite characters that are appropriate to the specified conversion. The input field ends when a nonappropriate character is reached, or the scan width, if specified, is exhausted, whichever comes first. When a string is read in, it is presumed that enough space has been allocated in memory to hold the string and an end-of-string sentinel \0, which will be appended. The format %1s can be used to read in the next nonwhite character. It should be stored in a character array of size at least two. The format %nc can be used to read in the next *n* characters, including white space characters. When one or more characters are read in, white space is not skipped. As with strings, it is the programmer's responsibility to allocate enough space to store these characters. In this case a null character is not appended. A value of type float can be read in with an e-, f-, or g-format. The conversion characters e, f, and g are equivalent. A format such as %lf can be used to read in a long float, or double. Floating numbers are formatted in the input stream as an optional sign followed by a digit string that may contain a decimal point, followed by an optional exponent part consisting of e or E, followed by an optional sign followed by a digit string.

The conversion specification %[*string*] is used to indicate that a special string is to be read in. If the first character in *string* is not a circumflex ^, then the string is to be made up only of the characters in *string*. On the other hand, if the first character in *string* is a circumflex, then the string is to be made up of all characters other than those in *string*. Thus the format %[abc] will input a string containing only the letters a, b, c, and will stop if any other character appears in the input stream, including a blank. The format %[^abc] will input a string terminated by any of a, b, or c, but not by white space. The statement

```
scanf("%[AB \n\t]", s);
```

will read into the character array s a string containing A's, B's, and the white space characters blank, newline, and tab.

These conversion specifications interact in a predictable way. The scan width is the number of characters scanned to retrieve the argument value. The default is whatever is in the input stream. The specification %s skips white space and then reads in nonwhite space characters until a white space character is encountered or the end-of-file mark is encountered, whichever comes first. In contrast to this, the specification %5s skips white space and then reads in nonwhite characters, stopping when a white space character is encountered or an end-of-file mark is encountered or 5 characters have been read in, whichever comes first.

Characters other than % that appear in the control string are searched for in the input stream. To ignore the character % in the input stream one can use %%, which ignores a single percent character. Of course, the character % can be input to a character variable by using the conversion specification %c.

The function scanf() returns the number of successful conversions performed. The value EOF is returned when the end-of-file mark is reached. Typically this value is −1. The value 0 is returned when no successful conversions are performed, and this value is always different from EOF. An inappropriate character in the input stream can frustrate expected conversions, causing the value 0 to be returned. As long as the input stream can be matched to the control string, the input stream is scanned and values are converted and assigned. The process stops if the input is inappropriate for the next conversion specification. The value returned by scanf() can be used to test that input occurred as expected, or to test that the end of the file was reached.

An example illustrating the use of scanf() is

```
int    i;
char   c;
char   string[15];


scanf("%d , %*s %% %c %5s %s", &i, &c, string, &string[5]);
```

With the following characters in the input stream

```
45 , ignore_this % C  read_in_this**
```

the value 45 is placed in i, the comma is matched, the string "ignore_this" is ignored, the % is matched, the character C is placed in the variable c, the string "read_" is placed in string[0] through string[4], the character \0 is placed in string[5], and finally the string "in_this**" is placed in string[5] through string[14], with string[14] containing \0. Since four conversions were successfully made, the value 4 is returned by scanf().

14.3   RELATED FUNCTIONS fprintf(), sprintf(), fscanf(), AND sscanf()

The function printf() writes to the file stdout. The function fprintf() is similar to printf() and can be used to write to any file. Its first argument is a file pointer, and its remaining arguments are like those of printf(). In particular,

```
    fprintf(stdout, . . . );        and        printf( . . . );
```

are equivalent statements. We shall see in the following section that stdout is a predefined identifier of type "pointer to FILE." In addition to stdout, the user can use other file pointers. In a similar fashion the function sprintf() is used to write to a string. The function call sprintf(s, . . .) writes to the string s, whereas the function call printf(. . .) writes to stdout. The programmer must ensure that the string s is large enough to store the output.

The function fscanf() corresponds to scanf(), but has as its first argument a file pointer that indicates which file is to be read. Thus a statement of the form fscanf(*file_ptr*, *control_string*, *other_arguments*);

requires *file_ptr* to be a pointer to FILE and *control_string* and *other_arguments* to conform to the conventions required for scanf(). Similarly, sscanf() is the string version of scanf(). Its first argument is a string from which the function takes its input.

14.4 FILES

A file is accessed via a pointer to FILE. The symbolic constant FILE is defined in *stdio.h* as a particular structure. This structure contains members that describe the current state of the file. To make use of files, the user need not know the details concerning this structure. Abstractly, a file is to be thought of as a stream of characters that is processed sequentially. The system provides three standard files. They are defined in *stdio.h*.

Written in C	Name	Remark
stdin	standard input file	connected to the keyboard
stdout	standard output file	connected to the screen
stderr	standard error file	connected to the screen

Files have certain important properties. They have a name. They must be opened and closed. They can be written to, or read from, or appended to. Conceptually, until a file is opened nothing can be done to it. It is like a closed book. When it is opened, we may have access to it at its beginning or end. To prevent accidental misuse, we must tell the system which of the three activities , reading, writing, or appending, we will be performing on it. When we are finished using it, we close it.

The standard library function fopen() can be used to open a file. It returns a pointer to FILE. One could write, for example,

```
#include    <stdio.h>

main()
{
    FILE    *ifp, *fopen();

    ifp = fopen("my_file", "r");      /* open for reading */
    . . . . .
```

to open the file named *my_file* in order to read from it. The identifier ifp is mnemonic for "infile pointer." After a file has been opened, the file pointer is used exclusively in all references to the file. The function fopen() is described in some detail in the following list, which contains descriptions of some useful library functions. It is not a complete list; the reader should consult manuals to find other available functions in the standard library. There may be slight variations from system to system. In the remainder of this text, we will use the functions in the list. The reader should consult the list as necessary to understand how these functions are used.

A description of some of the functions in the standard library

fopen(file_name, file_mode)

■ Performs the necessary housekeeping to open a buffered file and returns a pointer to FILE. The pointer value NULL is returned if file_name cannot be accessed. Both file_name and file_mode are strings. The file modes are "r", "w", and "a" corresponding to read, write, and append, respectively. The file pointer is positioned at the beginning of the file if the file mode is "r" or "w", and it is positioned at the end of the file if the file mode is "a". If the file mode is "w" or "a" and the file does not exist, it is created. *Caution:* If the file mode is "w" and the file exists, its contents will be overwritten.

fclose(file_pointer)

■ Performs the necessary housekeeping to empty buffers and break all connections to the file pointed to by file_pointer. file_pointer is a pointer to FILE. The value EOF is returned if file_pointer is not associated with a file. Open files are a limited resource (20 files can be open simultaneously on the VAX); system efficiency is improved by keeping only needed files open.

getc(file_pointer)

■   Retrieves the next character from the file pointed to by file_pointer. The value of the character is returned as an int. The value EOF is returned if an end-of-file mark is encountered or if there is an error. This function may be implemented as a macro if the header file *stdio.h* is included. getchar() is equivalent to getc(stdin).

fgetc(file_pointer)

■   Acts similarly to getc(), but it is a function, not a macro.

ungetc(c, file_pointer)

■   Pushes the character value of c back onto the file pointed to by file_pointer and returns the int value of c. If the file is buffered and one or more characters have been read, then at least one character can be pushed back. The value EOF is returned if it is not possible to push back a character.

putc(c, file_pointer)

■   Places the character value of c in the output file pointed to by file_pointer. It returns the int value of the character written. It may be implemented as a macro if *stdio.h* is included.

fputc(c, file_pointer)

■   Acts similarly to putc(c, file_pointer), but it is a function, not a macro.

gets(s)

■   Reads a string into s from stdin. The argument s is a pointer to char (a string). Characters are read into s until a newline character is read, at which point the newline character is changed to a null character that is used to terminate s. The value of s (pointer to char) is returned.

fgets(s, n, file_pointer)

■   Reads a string into s from the file pointed to by file_pointer. Characters are read from the file and placed in s until n - 1 characters have been read, or a newline character is read, whichever comes first. Unlike gets(), if a newline character is read, it is placed in s. In both cases s is terminated with a null character. The int value n is the maximum number of characters, including the null character, that can be read into s. The value of s (pointer to char) is returned. If there are no characters in the file, NULL is returned.

system(command)

■ Provides a connection to the operating system. The string (pointer to char) command is passed to the operating system and executed as a command. For example, on our system the statement

```
system("date");
```

causes the current date to be printed on the screen (stdout).

exit(status)

■ Terminates a program when it is called. All buffers are flushed and all files are closed. The value of status is returned to the calling process. The function exit() takes as an argument an expression of type int. By convention, the calling process assumes that the program ran properly if status has value 0; a nonzero value indicates that it did not run properly.

14.5 AN EXAMPLE: DOUBLE-SPACE A FILE

Let us use file handling functions in the standard library to write a program to double-space a file. In main() we open files for reading and writing that are passed as command line arguments. After the files have been opened, we invoke double_space() to accomplish the task of double spacing.

```
#include    <stdio.h>

main(argc, argv)
int     argc;
char    *argv[];
{
    FILE    *fopen(), *infile_ptr, *outfile_ptr;

    if (argc != 3) {
       printf("\nUsage:  %s  infile  outfile\n\n", argv[0]);
       exit(1);
    }
    infile_ptr = fopen(argv[1], "r");      /* open for reading */
    outfile_ptr = fopen(argv[2], "w");     /* open for writing */
    double_space(infile_ptr, outfile_ptr);
    fclose(infile_ptr);
    fclose(outfile_ptr);
}


double_space(ifp, ofp)
FILE    *ifp, *ofp;
{
    int  c;

    while ((c = getc(ifp)) != EOF) {
       putc(c, ofp);
       if (c == '\n')
          putc('\n', ofp);   /* found a newline - duplicate it */
    }
}
```

Suppose that we have compiled this program and put the executable code in the file *double_space*. When we give the command

double_space file1 file2

the program will read from *file1* and write to *file2*. The contents of *file2* will be the same as *file1*, except that every newline character will have been duplicated.

■ DISSECTION OF THE *double_space* PROGRAM

```
#include   <stdio.h>

main(argc, argv)
int     argc;
char    *argv[];
{
    FILE   *fopen(), *infile_ptr, *outfile_ptr;
```

■ The symbolic constant FILE is defined in *stdio.h* as a structure
that contains information about a file. We do not need to
know system implementation details of how the file mechanism
works to make use of files. The function fopen() is provided
by the standard library. It returns a pointer to FILE. It is the
programmer's responsibility to declare it correctly. The type of
the identifiers infile_ptr and outfile_ptr is pointer to FILE.

```
if (argc != 3) {
    printf("\nUsage: %s infile outfile\n\n", argv[0]);
    exit(1);
}
```

■ The program is designed to read two file names entered as
command line arguments. If there are too few or too many
command line arguments, a message to the user is printed,
indicating how the program should be used. Instead of writing
the error message to stdout, we could have written

```
    fprintf(stderr, "\nUsage: %s infile outfile\n\n", argv[0]);
```

Now the error message will be written to stderr. In this program both ways are acceptable. See exercise 1 for further discussion. The function exit() from the standard library is
called to exit the program. By convention exit(1) is used if
something has gone wrong.

```
infile_ptr = fopen(argv[1], "r");      /* open for reading */
outfile_ptr = fopen(argv[2], "w");     /* open for writing */
```

- We can think of argv[] as an array of strings. The function fopen() is used to open the file named in argv[1] for reading. The pointer value returned by the function is assigned to infile_ptr. In a similar fashion the file named in argv[2] is opened for writing.

```
double_space(infile_ptr, outfile_ptr);
```

- The two file pointers are passed as arguments to double_space(), which then does the work of double spacing. One can see that other functions of this form could be written to perform whatever useful work on files was needed.

```
fclose(infile_ptr);
fclose(outfile_ptr);
```

- The function fclose() from the standard library is used to close the files pointed to by infile_ptr and outfile_ptr. It is good programming style to close files explicitly in the same function in which they were opened. Any files not explicitly closed by the programmer will be closed automatically by the system on program exit.

```
double_space(ifp, ofp)
FILE    *ifp, *ofp;
{
    int  c;
```

- The identifiers ifp and ofp stand for "infile pointer" and "outfile pointer," respectively. The identifier c is an int. Although it will be used to store characters obtained from a file, eventually it will be assigned the value EOF, which is not a character value.

```
while ((c = getc(ifp)) != EOF) {
   putc(c, ofp);
   if (c == '\n')
      putc('\n', ofp);   /* found a newline - duplicate it */
}
```

■ The function getc() is used to read a character from the file
pointed to by ifp and to assign the value to c. If the value of
c is not EOF, then putc() is used to write c into the file pointed
to by ofp. If c is a newline character, another newline character is written into the file as well. This has the effect of double
spacing the output file. This process continues repeatedly until
an EOF is encountered.

14.6 STYLE

A good programming style is to check that fopen() does its work as
expected. In any serious program such checks are essential. Suppose that we want to open *my_file* for reading. A common programming style used to do this is

```
if ((ifp = fopen("my_file", "r")) == NULL) {
   printf("\nCannot open my_file\n\n");
   exit(1);
}
```

If for some reason fopen() is unable to open the named file, the
pointer value NULL is returned. A test for this value is made, and if
it is found, a message is printed and the program is exited.

Another stylistic issue concerns the indiscriminate opening of files
for writing. If fopen() is used to open a file for writing that already
exists, then the contents of that file will be destroyed. Since files
are potentially valuable, the user should be warned if a file already
exists. One way to do this is to first check to see if the file can be
opened for reading. If it can be, then the file exists. In this case,
the user should be warned. See exercise 12.

Most operating systems allow only a limited number of files to be open at one time. When writing a large program, it is essential to keep track of which files are open. A good programming style is to close a file in the same function in which it was opened.

14.7 COMMON PROGRAMMING ERRORS

In making use of printf(), scanf(), and the file and string versions of these functions, a very common programming error is to improperly match the formats in the control string with the remaining arguments. It is the programmer's responsibility to do this properly. A specific example of this type of error is to use the format %f instead of %lf when using scanf() to read in a double.

Many common errors are related to the use of files. An error that beginning programmers often make is to use the file name instead of the file pointer. After a file has been opened, the file pointer is to be used to access the file, not the file name. Constructs such as

```
fprintf(file_name, . . . );   /* wrong */
fclose(file_name);            /* wrong */
```

can cause unexpected run-time errors. Although our compiler does not complain about this type of error, *lint* does. Some other common errors are opening a file that is already open, closing a file that is already closed, writing to a file that is opened for reading, or reading from a file that is opened for writing. What happens in such cases is system dependent. It is the programmer's responsibility to open, use, and close files properly.

When using the functions fprintf(), sprintf(), fscanf(), and sscanf(), a common programming error is to forget to use a pointer to FILE or a string, as the case may be, as the first argument. This is a natural error to make, since the usage of, say fprintf(), is very close to the usage of printf(). On our system *lint* provides a warning for this type of error, but the compiler does not.

Another common programming error involves the use of sprintf() and sscanf(). Input/output with respect to a string is different than with respect to a file. Let us consider the situation with regard to input. The situation with regard to output is similar. Suppose we are using fscanf(ifp, "%c", &c) repeatedly to read in characters from the file pointed to by ifp. With each function call we get the next character in the file. In contrast to this, now suppose that we are using sscanf(s, "%c", &c) repeatedly to read in characters in the string s. With each function call we get the first character in the string. File access is strictly sequential, but string access is not. See exercise 14.

14.8 OPERATING SYSTEM CONSIDERATIONS

It is important to understand that the number of significant digits stored in a float or double is limited. On most machines a float is stored in 4 bytes and a double is stored in 8 bytes. The effect of this is that a float can store approximately 6 significant decimal digits and a double can store approximately 16 significant decimal digits. When a request is made via printf() to print a float with more than 6 significant digits, or a double with more than 16 significant digits, what actually gets printed is system dependent. If a floating value is printed with, say, 20 decimal digits, not all of the digits can be considered meaningful. See exercise 15.

Many operating systems provide for the redirection of stdin and stdout. In some operating systems the standard error file stderr can be redirected along with stdin. The symbols >& are used to do this. See exercise 11.

In many operating systems the output of a command or program that writes to stdout can be "piped" to another command or program that reads stdin. The output of the first command becomes the input of the second command. Let us give an example of this. In UNIX the command *date* writes the current date and time to stdout, and the command *wc*, which is mnemonic for "word count," reads from stdin if no command line arguments are present and writes to stdout. The output of *date* can be piped to the input of *wc* by giving the command

    date | wc

The symbol | represents a pipe. See exercise 18.

Some C systems allow the conversion characters D, O, X, E, F to be used in place of ld, lo, lx, le, lf, respectively, in the control string for scanf().

In most operating systems files are created with associated permissions. The standard permissions are read, write, and execute. Ordinary text files are usually created with read and write permissions. This allows the file to be read from and to be written to. Some files, such as *a.out*, are executable. Typically, an operating system provides a way of explicitly setting the permissions associated with a file. In UNIX the command *chmod* can be used to do this. If UNIX is available to you, you can read about this command in the online manual. Suppose that we use this command to make *my_file* a read-only file. Now, the function call fopen("my_file", "w") cannot open the file for writing, causing the pointer value NULL to be returned.

14.9 SUMMARY

1 The functions printf() and scanf() and the related file and string versions of these functions all make use of conversion specifications in a control string to deal with a list of arguments of variable length.

2 The standard library functions fopen() and fclose() are used to open and close files, respectively. After a file has been opened, the file pointer is used for all references to the file.

3 A file is thought of as a stream of characters that are accessed sequentially. To make use of a file, a programmer can include the header file stdio.h, declare a file pointer, and then use fopen() to open the file. For example,

```
FILE   *fopen(), *my_file_ptr;

my_file_ptr = fopen("my_file", "r");
```

will open the file *my_file* for reading. Similarly, one uses "w" for writing and "a" for appending. A file must be opened before it can be used. After a file has been opened, the file pointer is used in all references to the file.

4 C provides the three standard files stdin, stdout, and stderr. These files are always open. The file stdin is usually connected to the keyboard and used by scanf(). The files stdout and stderr are usually connected to the screen and are used by

printf() and fprintf(stderr, . . .), respectively. The file stderr is also used by the system to write error messages.

5   Files are a scarce resource. Most C systems allow only a few files to be open at one time. In our system only 20 files, including stdin, stdout, and stderr, can be open at one time. It is the programmer's responsibility to keep track of which files are open. On program exit, any open files are closed by the system automatically.

6   The standard library provides a collection of functions that access a file through its file pointer. For example, the function call getc(ifp) reads the next character from the file pointed to by ifp.

14.10 EXERCISES

1   Rewrite the *double_space* program so that it gets the name of the input file as a command line argument and writes to stdout. After this has been done, the command

   double_space infile > outfile

   can be used to double-space whatever is in *infile*, with the output being written into *outfile*. Since the program is intended to be used with redirection, it now makes sense to write the error message to stderr instead of stdout. If the error message is written to stdout, it will be redirected; the user will not see the message on the screen. The symbol > is used to redirect whatever is written to stdout. It does not affect whatever is written to stderr. Try writing the program two ways: with the error message being written first to stderr and then to stdout. Experiment with the two versions of the program so you understand the different effects.

2   Rewrite the *double_space* program so that it uses a command line option of the form $-n$, where n can be 1, 2, or 3. If n is 1, then the output should be single-spaced. That is, two or more contiguous newline characters in the input file should be written as a single newline character in the output file. If n is 2, then the output file should be strictly double-spaced. That is, one or more contiguous newline characters in the input file

should be rewritten as a pair of newline characters in the output file. If *n* is 3, the output file should be strictly triple-spaced.

3   Write getstring() and putstring() functions. The first function should use a file pointer, say ifp, and the system function getc() to read a string from the file pointed to by ifp. The second should use a file pointer, say ofp, and the system function putc() to write a string to the file pointed to by ofp. Write a program that tests your functions.

4   Write a program to number the lines in a file. The input file name should be passed to the program as a command line argument. The program should write to stdout. Each line in the input file should be written to the output file with the line number and a space prepended.

5   Read about the system function unlink(). If available, use the online manual to do this. The following program makes use of this function to remove a file. It is a simple version of the UNIX command *rm*, which is used to remove files. Modify the program to remove one or more files obtained as command line arguments.

```
main(argc, argv)
int     argc;
char    *argv[];
{
   unlink(argv[1]);
}
```

6   After three characters have been read from a file, can ungetc() be used to push three characters back onto the file? Write a program to test this.

7   Write a program that displays a file on the screen 20 lines at a time. The input file should be given as a command line argument. The program should display the next 20 lines after a carriage return has been typed.

8   Modify the program that you wrote in exercise 7 to display one or more files given as command line arguments. Also, allow a command line option of the form −*n* to be used, where *n* is a

positive integer specifying the number of lines that are to be displayed at one time. Most operating systems provide a command that clears the screen. In UNIX the command is *clear*. If such a command is available to you, first try it so you understand its effect, and then use the function call system("clear") in your program just before you write each set of lines to the screen.

9   Write a program called *search* that searches for patterns. If the command

   search hello my_file

   is given, then the string pattern *hello* is searched for in the file *my_file*. Any line that contains the pattern is printed. *Hint:* Use the following code:

```
char    *fgets(), line[MAXLINE];
FILE    *fopen(), *ifp;

if ((ifp = fopen(argv[2], "r")) == NULL) {
   printf("\nCannot open %s\n\n", argv[2]);
   exit(1);
}
while (fgets(line, MAXLINE, ifp) != NULL) {
   . . . . .
```

10 Modify the function you wrote in exercise 9. If the command line option −*n* is present, then the line number should be printed as well.

11 Compile the following program and put the executable code into a file, say *test*. Execute the program so you understand its effects.

```
#include   <stdio.h>

main()
{
    fprintf(stdout, "she sells sea shells\n");
    fprintf(stderr, "by the seashore\n");
}
```

What happens when you redirect the output? Try the command

test > temp

On some systems both stdin and stderr can be redirected. Try the above command using >& instead of > . Make sure you read the file *temp* after you do this. You may be surprised.

12 Write a program called *wrt_random* that creates a file of random numbers. The file name is to be entered interactively. Your program should use three functions. Here is the first function:

```
get_info(file_name, n_ptr)
char   *file_name;
int    *n_ptr;
{
    printf("\n%s\n\n%s",
        "This program creates a file of random numbers.",
        "How many random numbers would you like?  ");
    scanf("%d", n_ptr);
    printf("\nIn what file would you like them?  ");
    scanf("%s", file_name);
}
```

The second function to be used in your program is a "careful" version of fopen(). Its purpose is to warn the user if the output file already exists.

```
#include    <stdio.h>

FILE *c_fopen(file_name, mode)
char    *file_name, *mode;
{
    char    reply[2];
    FILE    *g_fopen(), *fopen(), *fp;

    if (strcmp(mode, "w") == 0
       && (fp = fopen(file_name, "r")) != NULL) {
           fclose(fp);
           printf("\nFile exists.  Overwrite it?  ");
           scanf("%1s", reply);
           if (*reply != 'y' && *reply != 'Y') {
              printf("\nBye!\n\n");
              exit(1);
           }
    }
    fp = g_fopen(file_name, mode);
    return (fp);
}
```

Since this function calls g_fopen(), we must write that too. We think of it as a "graceful" version of fopen().

```
FILE *g_fopen(file_name, mode)
char    *file_name, *mode;
{
    FILE    *fopen(), *fp;

    if ((fp = fopen(file_name, mode)) == NULL) {
       printf("\n\nCannot open %s - bye.\n\n", file_name);
       exit(1);
    }
    return (fp);
}
```

Hint: To write random numbers neatly into the output file, you can use the following code:

```
for (i = 1; i <= n; ++i) {
   fprintf(ofp, "%12d", random());
   if (i % 6 == 0 || i == n)
      fprintf(ofp, "\n");
}
```

Do not forget to declare c_fopen() and g_fopen() as functions that return a pointer to FILE, and random() as a function returning a long.

13 Write a program that reads from stdin and writes to a file that is read in as a command line argument. Each newline character in the input file should be stripped out. Every line in the output file should be exactly 40 characters long. Use the function c_fopen(), which was presented in exercise 12.

14 Accessing a string is not like accessing a file. Write a test program with the following declarations.

```
char   c, s[4], *p = s, *strcpy();
int    i;
FILE   *ofp1, *ofp2;
```

Use strcpy() to copy "abc" into s, and use fopen() to open two files for writing, say *temp1* and *temp2*, with the file pointers returned by fopen() being assigned to ofp1 and ofp2, respectively. Now write

```
for (i = 0; i < 3; ++i) {
   sscanf(s, "%c", &c);
   fprintf(ofp1, "%c", c);
}
for (i = 0; i < 3; ++i) {
   sscanf(p++, "%c", &c);
   fprintf(ofp2, "%c", c);
}
```

What gets written in *temp1* and *temp2*? Explain.

15 In this exercise we want to explain a typical use of sscanf(). Suppose that we are writing a serious interactive program that

asks the user to input a positive integer. To guard against the user making a typing mistake, such as q34 instead of 234, we can pick up the line typed by the user as a string and test each character. You might use code such as this:

```
error = 0;
do {
    fgets(line, MAXLINE, stdin);
    for (p = line; *p != '\0'; ++p)
      if (!isdigit(*p) && !isspace(*p))
        error = 1;
    if (error)
      printf("\nERROR:  Do it again:  ");
} while (error);
sscanf(line, "%d", &n);
```

Rewrite the *wrt_random* program that you wrote in exercise 12, making use of these ideas.

16   Experiment with your system. The following control line gives π correct to 41 significant digits.

```
#define    PI    3.14159265358979323846264338327950288841972
```

Write a test program containing this #define line and the statement

```
printf("pi = %.40f\n", PI);
```

What gets printed?

17   In C code the constants 2 and 2.0 are different; the first is an int and the second a double. Suppose that scanf() is being used to read in a double. What should be in the input stream? Is 2 just as acceptable as 2.0? Explain. *Hint:* Read Section 14.2 carefully.

18   Experiment with your system. Recall that in Section 5.3 of Chapter 5 we wrote the program *capitalize*. It reads from stdin and writes to stdout. Use the *double_space* program that

you wrote in exercise 1 of this chapter together with *capitalize* by giving the command

double_space   infile | capitalize

where *infile* is one of your text files. What gets printed on the screen? Explain.

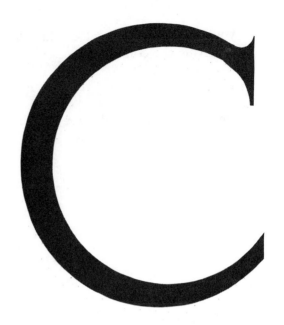

15

SOFTWARE
METHODOLOGY
IN A UNIX
ENVIRONMENT

Effective programming requires discipline and style, along with tools that are to be used with particular languages and systems. In this chapter we will review suggestions made throughout this text, and then synthesize an approach to the programming process that makes use of some UNIX tools.

The UNIX operating system provides tools that are useful for software development in general, as well as particular tools that are specific to C. Because the software tools we discuss in this chapter are often available in other systems as well, even those readers who do not have UNIX available will benefit from reading the chapter.

15.1 LAYOUT AND THE USE OF cb

Throughout our coding examples, we have adopted an easily identified set of layout conventions. Their purpose is to allow the human reader to easily follow the meaning of the program. An example of this is to indent after an if, for, or while, thus making it easy to identify the statements in the body of the construct. Of course, one can violate this rule and still have legal code, but adhering to this convention highlights the flow of control of the program.

The *cb* command, which stands for C beautifier, is provided in UNIX to "pretty print" C code. It reads from the standard input file and writes to the standard output file. If *program.c* contains C code, then the command

    cb < program.c

will "pretty print" it on the screen and the command

    cb < program.c > pgm.c

will "pretty print" it and write it in the file *pgm.c*. The *cb* utility is not very sophisticated. It uses eight spaces (a tab) as an indentation, making no allowance for other user preferences. Some UNIX systems provide *indent*, which allows for many more user options. Both of these "pretty printers" have difficulty with complicated constructs such as long macros with parameters or involved structure definitions. Nonetheless, these tools can be useful. Since style depends in part on individual taste, when one programmer borrows code from another source, the *indent* utility can be used to reformat it. In general, the existence of "pretty printers" does not mean that a programmer should write sloppy code, which finally gets "pretty printed." Constantly making use of a good style reinforces good programming.

15.2 TOP-DOWN CODING

Coding should only begin after the solution to the problem is understood and broken down into a collection of simple pieces. The constant attempt to refine a big problem into smaller subproblems until the subproblems are transparently codable is the heart of the top-down programming process. Ultimately one arrives at a simple subproblem that is easily coded as a short function. Ideally, these functions should perform a single purpose completely. Such functions can be tested in isolation from the other routines without affecting their correctness. A modular style of programming is conducive to building correct larger-scale programs that involve many function calls.

Let us use these ideas to write a program that will examine a file of text, count the number of occurrences of each word, and print the words in lexicographical order, along with their frequencies. A program like this can be used to analyze the works of an author. These techniques are also used in cryptography. The program will need to

1. Extract the words from a file
2. Place them in an array of words
3. Sort them lexicographically
4. Print them along with their frequencies

Each of these tasks can be accomplished by a function. We will write each function definition in a separate file. These files will constitute the modules making up our program. A common header file *word_frequency.h* will be included where needed. In main() we will open the files for reading and writing and then call other functions to carry out specific tasks. Let us first show the header file.

In file word_frequency.h:

```
#include    <stdio.h>
#include    <ctype.h>
#include    <strings.h>

#define    ARRAYSIZE    1000    /* at most 1000 words */
#define    MAXWORD      30      /* at most 29 letters in a word */

struct s_word {
    char            word[MAXWORD];
    struct s_word   *next;
};

typedef    struct s_word    ELEMENT;

char       *get_word(), *malloc();
int        count_linked_list();
FILE       *fopen(), *g_fopen();
ELEMENT    *create_linked_list();
void       bubble_sort(), fill_array(), prn_words();
```

We constructed this header file as we designed the functions that constitute our program. What we see here is the final product. Notice that the structure type struct s_word is declared in the header file. A linked list of these structures will be used to store the words obtained from the input file. Notice that we have chosen the structure tag name as s_word and the member name as word. The letter s in s_word can be thought of as "store" or "structure." For convenience we used the typedef facility to create the type ELEMENT. We have declared all our functions in the header file, even those that return nothing. This helps *lint* to do its work better.

We want to look at main() next, but before we do so, let us explain the intended use of our program. Suppose that the executable code for our program is in the file *word_frequency*. We envision three ways that the program can be used. If we give the command

   word_frequency

then the program will read from the standard input file and write to the standard output file. If we give the command

   word_frequency infile

then the program will read from *infile* and write to the standard output file. Finally, if we give the command

   word_frequency infile outfile

then the program will read from *infile* and write to *outfile*.

```
/* Print words alphabetically, along with frequencies. */

#include   "word_frequency.h"

main(argc, argv)
int    argc;
char   *argv[];
{
   char      *w[ARRAYSIZE];   /* array of words */
   int       n;               /* number of words */
   FILE      *ifp,            /* infile pointer */
             *ofp;            /* outfile pointer */
   ELEMENT   *head_ptr;

   switch (argc) {
   case 1:
      ifp = stdin;
      ofp = stdout;
      break;
   case 2:
      ifp = g_fopen(argv[1], "r");
      ofp = stdout;
      break;
   case 3:
      ifp = g_fopen(argv[1], "r");
      ofp = g_fopen(argv[2], "w");
      break;
   default:
      fprintf(stderr,"ERROR:  Too many command line arguments.\n");
      exit(1);
   }
   head_ptr = create_linked_list(ifp);
   n = count_linked_list(head_ptr);
   fill_array(head_ptr, w);
   bubble_sort(w, n);
   prn_words(ofp, w, n);
}
```

In the switch statement the function g_fopen(), a graceful version of fopen(), is used to open files. A good programming style is to explicitly check that fopen() is able to open the requested file.

```
#include   "word_frequency.h"

FILE *g_fopen(filename, mode)
char    *filename, *mode;
{
    FILE    *fp;

    if ((fp = fopen(filename, mode)) == NULL) {
       fprintf(stderr, "\n\nCannot open %s - bye.\n\n", filename);
       exit(1);
    }
    return (fp);
}
```

If for some reason fopen() is unable to open a file, the value NULL is returned. When this happens, the function g_fopen() prints an appropriate message and exits the program.

After files have been opened, we are ready to read words from the input file. The function create_linked_list() uses get_word() to do this. The words are put into a linked list, and a head pointer to the linked list is returned. We define a word to be a maximal alphabetical string, and we do not distinguish between upper- and lowercase letters.

```
#include    "word_frequency.h"

ELEMENT *create_linked_list(ifp)
FILE    *ifp;
{
   char       s[MAXWORD];
   ELEMENT    *head_ptr = NULL, *p;

   while (get_word(s, ifp) != NULL) {
      p = (ELEMENT *) malloc(sizeof(ELEMENT));
      strcpy(p -> word, s);
      p -> next = head_ptr;
      head_ptr = p;
   }
   return (head_ptr);
}


#include    "word_frequency.h"

char *get_word(s, ifp)
FILE    *ifp;
char    *s;
{
   int   c, cnt = 0;

   while (!isalpha(c = getc(ifp)) && c != EOF)
      ;   /* find a letter, if there is one */
   if (c == EOF)
      return (NULL);
   else {
      *s++ = (isupper(c) ? tolower(c) : c);
      ++cnt;
      while (isalpha(c = getc(ifp)) && c != EOF)
         if (++cnt < MAXWORD)
            *s++ = (isupper(c) ? tolower(c) : c);
      *s = '\0';
      return (s);
   }
}
```

Notice that when a word is found, it is copied into the member word of the structure that is pointed to by p. Words that are too long are truncated silently. An alternate design would be to print a warning to the user.

■ DISSECTION OF THE get_word() FUNCTION

```
#include   "word_frequency.h"
```

■ The header file word_frequency.h provides a central place for information that is to be shared by all the functions. The function get_word() uses symbolic constants and macros that are obtained from this header file.

```
char *get_word(s, ifp)
FILE   *ifp;
char   *s;
{
    int   c, cnt = 0;
```

■ The function is designed to get a word from the file pointed to by ifp and to store the word in s. Notice that the allocation of storage in memory for the word does not take place here. Although we think of c as taking on character values, eventually it will have the value EOF, which is not a character. Therefore c is declared to be an int.

```
while (!isalpha(c = getc(ifp)) && c != EOF)
    ;   /* find a letter, if there is one */
if (c == EOF)
    return (NULL);
```

■ A search is made for the next alphabetic character. If there is none, the pointer value NULL is returned.

```
else {
    *s++ = (isupper(c) ? tolower(c) : c);
    ++cnt;
    while (isalpha(c = getc(ifp)) && c != EOF)
        if (++cnt < MAXWORD)
            *s++ = (isupper(c) ? tolower(c) : c);
    *s = '\0';
    return (s);
}
```

■ Only alphabetic strings will be considered words. All words will be retained as lowercase strings. Notice that the expression *s++ is equivalent to *(s++). It makes use of pointer arithmetic. The macros used here require the definitions in *ctype.h*, which is included in *word_frequency.h*. A count is kept of the number of letters encountered so that the bounds of an array allocated elsewhere will not be overrun.

After a linked list of words has been created, we count the words in the list to make sure that there are not too many of them.

```
#include   "word_frequency.h"

int count_linked_list(p)
ELEMENT   *p;
{
    int   cnt = 0;

    for ( ; p != NULL; p = p -> next)
        ++cnt;
    if (cnt > ARRAYSIZE) {
        fprintf(stderr, "Too many words - bye.\n");
        exit(1);
    }
    return (cnt);
}
```

Next we fill the array w[]. This is an array of pointers to char, which can be thought of as an array of strings.

```
#include   "word_frequency.h"

void fill_array(head_ptr, w)
ELEMENT   *head_ptr;
char      *w[];
{
    int      i = 0;
    ELEMENT  *p;

    for (p = head_ptr; p != NULL; p = p -> next)
       w[i++] = p -> word;
}
```

Next we must sort the words and print them in lexicographical order, along with their frequencies. For simplicity, we use a bubble sort. Once the words are sorted, it is easy to count their frequencies. Multiple occurrences of a word will now be found in consecutive array positions.

```
#include   "word_frequency.h"

void bubble_sort(w, n)
char   *w[];
int    n;        /* n is the size of w[] */
{
    char   *temp;
    int    i, j;

    for (i = 0; i < n - 1; ++i)
       for (j = n - 1; j > i; --j)
          if (strcmp(w[i], w[j]) > 0) {
             temp = w[i];
             w[i] = w[j];
             w[j] = temp;
          }
}
```

```
#include   "word_frequency.h"

void prn_words(ofp, w, n)
FILE    *ofp;
char    *w[];
int     n;        /* n is the size of w[] */
{
    int   cnt, i;

    for (i = 0; i < n; ++i) {
        cnt = 1;
        while (i + 1 < n && strcmp(w[i + 1], w[i]) == 0) {
            ++cnt;
            ++i;
        }
        fprintf(ofp, "%7d  %s\n", cnt, w[i]);
    }
}
```

When a program is written in more than one file, *lint* can be used to check all the files simultaneously. If this is done, *lint* will check on syntactic consistency across files. To check the *word_frequency* program, we can give the command

> *lint main.c g_fopen.c create_linked_list.c get_word.c *
> *count_linked_list.c fill_array.c bubble_sort.c prn_words.c*

Notice that we used a backslash \\ to continue the command to another line. The files can be given to *lint* in any order. If we suppose that the program has been written in its own directory, and that the only *.c* files in the directory are those used to create the program, then we can give the command

> *lint *.c*

Used in this context, the * is a "magic" character. The effect is as if all the file names in the directory ending in *.c* had been typed.

Finally, we want to compile the *word_frequency* program. Since each function is written in a separate file, we give the command

> *cc −o word_frequency *.c*

This causes corresponding *.o* files to be created, with the executable code for the program placed in the file *word_frequency*. If we want to modify one of the functions, say get_word(), then we edit the file *get_word.c* and recompile the program by giving the command

  *cc − o word_frequency get_word.c *.o*

The effect of the * in this command is as if all the file names ending in *.o* had been typed. The use of *.o* files speeds the work of the compiler.

15.3 THE USE OF *make*

For both the programmer and the machine, it is inefficient and costly to keep a moderate or large size program entirely in one file and to recompile it repeatedly. Most C compilers allow for the separate compilation of functions. The purpose of the UNIX utility *make* is to keep track of all the files connected with a program. The use of *make* greatly facilitates both the construction and the maintenance of programs.

To use the *make* utility to develop or maintain a program, a file whose default name is *makefile* or *Makefile* is created. This file contains the dependencies of the various modules of the program, along with appropriate actions to be taken. In particular, it contains the instructions for compiling the program. Such a file is called a "makefile."

For simplicity, let us imagine that we have a program contained in three files, say *main.c*, *prn_info.c*, and *sum.c*, and that there is a header file, say *sum.h*, that is included with each of the *.c* files. We want the executable code for this program to be in the file *sum*. Here is the contents of a simple makefile that could be used for program development and maintenance:

  In file makefile:

```
sum: main.o prn_info.o sum.o
        cc −o sum  main.o  prn_info.o  sum.o

main.o prn_info.o sum.o: sum.h
```

The first line indicates that the file *sum* depends on the three object files *main.o*, *prn_info.o*, and *sum.o*. The second line indicates how the program is to be compiled if one or more *.c* files, corresponding to the *.o* files, have been changed. The *make* program automatically knows that each *.o* file depends on a corresponding *.c* file. Therefore, this information does not have to be included in a makefile. The second line in the file is the hardest one to get correct. *It must begin with a tab.* What looks like eight blanks preceding the cc in the second line is actually a single tab character. The last line in the makefile indicates that the *.o* files depend on the header file *sum.h*. After this makefile has been created, the programmer can compile or recompile the program *sum* by giving the command

   make

The *make* command will read the file *makefile* and take whatever action is necessary.

A makefile can be thought of as a list of dependencies followed by appropriate actions to be taken, if any. The first line of the above makefile is a dependency line; the second line is the action to be taken. The third line is a dependency line. For this line no action needs to be specified. If the *.h* file is changed, then all the *.c* files will be recompiled when the command *make* is given.

A makefile consists of a series of entries that specify dependencies and actions. An entry begins with a series of blank-separated target files, followed by a colon, followed by a blank-separated series of prerequisite files. All the lines beginning with a tab that follow this are the actions, such as compilation, to be taken by the system to update the target files. The target files are dependent in some way on the prerequisite files and must be updated when the prerequisite files are modified.

As another example of a makefile, let us show what we used to develop the *word_frequency* program. It contains a few new ideas.

In file makefile:

```
# The makefile for the word_frequency program.

OBJS = main.o                    \
       bubble_sort.o             \
       count_linked_list.o       \
       create_linked_list.o      \
       fill_array.o              \
       g_fopen.o                 \
       get_word.o                \
       prn_words.o

EFILE = word_frequency

${EFILE}:  ${OBJS}
        cc  -o ${EFILE}  ${OBJS}

${OBJS}:  word_frequency.h
```

■ DISSECTION OF THE MAKEFILE FOR THE
word_frequency PROGRAM

```
# Makefile for the word_frequency program.
```

■ Comments can be put in a makefile. A comment begins with a # and ends with a newline character. That is, a comment begins with a # and extends to the end of the line.

```
OBJS = main.o                    \
       bubble_sort.o             \
          .  .  .  .  .
```

■ This is a macro definition. The identifier OBJS can be thought of as a symbolic constant for the list of *.o* files, or object files, that occur on the right side of the equal sign. A backslash \ is used to continue to a new line. The general form of a macro definition is given by *string1 = string2*

where *string2* consists of all the words to the right of the equal sign on that line. The line is continued if it ends with a backslash. A construct of the form $\{string1\}$ can be used to replace the construct by the contents of *string2*.

```
EFILE = word_frequency
```

■ We are using the name EFILE to stand for "executable file." It is convenient to have just one place where this file is specified.

```
${EFILE}:  ${OBJS}
       cc  -o ${EFILE}  ${OBJS}
```

■ The first line is a dependency line. The second line specifies the action to be taken. Note carefully that the second line begins with a tab. The construct ${EFILE} is replaced by word_frequency. The construct ${OBJS} is replaced by the list of *.o* files.

```
${OBJS}:  word_frequency.h
```

■ This is a dependency line. The construct ${OBJS} is replaced by the list of *.o* files. The effect of this line is to cause the *make* command to recompile all the *.c* files if a change has been made to the header file.

15.4 THE USE OF *lint*

The programmer's task is to go from a problem specification to efficient and maintainable code. The first steps are to reduce the problem in a top-down manner to a series of easily codable functions. These should be individually hand simulated for small cases to test that the program logic is correct. The code is then checked for syntactic correctness. While this can be done with *cc*, where available it is best done with C verifier *lint*.

The command *lint* takes one or more files containing C code and issues a variety of messages aimed at improving program correctness, efficiency, and portability. For example, *lint* indicates if data or functions are declared but unused. It will also detect whether code is inadvertently unreachable. Generally speaking, one should always use *lint* before proceeding to actual compilation. Suppose that the file *example.c* contains the following code:

```c
#include   <stdio.h>

main()
{
    char    c, x = '1', y;
    int     z = '?';
    float   dbl();

    goto L1;
    while (1 != 0) {
L1:    z += (long) x;
        while ((c = getchar()) != EOF)
            printf("Absolute nonsense: %c %d\n", c, z);
    }
    return (x);
}
```

The command

lint − hxa example.c

gives the following suggestions:

```
example.c(10): warning: constant in conditional context
example.c(10): warning: loop not entered at top
example.c(11): warning: long assignment may lose accuracy
example.c(12): warning: nonportable character comparison
example.c(15): warning: statement not reached
example.c(5): warning: y unused in function main
dbl defined( ???(7) ), but never used
```

The reader should consult a UNIX manual to find the meaning of the options −*hxa*. There are other options as well.

15.5 THE USE OF *prof*

The resident UNIX C compiler is invoked by the *cc* command. This command has a number of useful options, some of which are listed in the table that follows. In this section we want to describe the use of the −*p* option, along with the use of the *prof* command. This is very useful for developing efficient code.

Some useful options to the cc command

−O   attempt code optimization

−E   generate C code with the macros expanded and print on stdout

−S   generate a *.s* file containing assembly language

−D*name* = *def*
    place #define *name def* into the C code

−U*name*
    remove any #define *name* from the C code

−c   produce a *.o* file, but not *a.out*

−p   add code to allow an execution profile post mortem

The −*p* option produces an executable program, and when that program is invoked, the file *mon.out* is produced. This file is then used by the *prof* command to generate an execution profile of the program. Let us illustrate how this is done with the *word_frequency* program. First, we compile the program with the −*p* option.

    cc −o word_frequency −p main.c g_fopen.c . . . prn_words.c

Next, we create a text file, say *temp*, and execute the program.

    word_frequency temp

After this command has executed, we see that a new file named *mon.out* has been created. This file will be used by the *prof* command. Finally, we give the command *prof word_frequency*

This command causes the following to be printed on the screen:

%time	cumsecs	#call	ms/call	name
43.8	4.08	83435	0.05	_strcmp
29.1	6.80	1	2717.50	_bubble_sort
20.2	8.69			mcount
1.6	8.84			_monstartup
1.3	8.95	97	1.20	__doprnt
1.1	9.05	1	100.03	_create_linked_list
1.1	9.15	408	0.25	_malloc
0.5	9.20	409	0.12	_get_word
0.4	9.24	408	0.08	_strcpy
0.2	9.25	1	16.67	_fill_array
0.2	9.27	97	0.17	_fprintf
0.2	9.29	2	8.34	_fstat
0.2	9.30	1	16.67	_prn_words
0.2	9.32	4	4.17	_read
0.2	9.34			_write
0.0	9.34	4	0.00	__filbuf
0.0	9.34	1	0.00	__flsbuf
0.0	9.34	1	0.00	_count_linked_list
0.0	9.34	1	0.00	_gtty
0.0	9.34	1	0.00	_ioctl
0.0	9.34	1	0.00	_isatty
0.0	9.34	1	0.00	_main
0.0	9.34	1	0.00	_profil
0.0	9.34	27	0.00	_sbrk

Not all of the named functions are user defined; some, such as
_read, are system routines. Such a profile can be very useful when
working to improve execution time efficiency. It is easy to see that
the bulk of the time is spent in strcmp() and bubble_sort(). One
way to improve the efficiency of this program is to use a more
efficient sorting routine; see exercise 2.

15.6 STYLE

An efficient programming style is to make use of the sophisticated tools that are available to the programmer. As an example, consider the editor that you use to write code. If the editor has options designed explicitly to help with the programming task, you should learn how to use those options. See exercise 16 in Chapter 1.

Another example of a sophisticated tool designed to help the programmer is *make*. For the development of all but the smallest programs, *make* is extremely useful. Of course, there is some effort involved in learning to use this utility, but the payback is large. You can begin to learn how to use *make* by following the example presented in Section 15.3 very closely. Later, you can read a manual to learn more about the use of *make*.

Another good programming style is to make frequent use of *lint*. This utility can be used to check a single file, and it can be used to check multiple files that constitute all or part of a program. It is important to realize that a command such as

> *lint file1.c file2.c*

may cause *lint* to complain, even though each file passes *lint* individually.

15.7 COMMON PROGRAMMING ERRORS

A common programming error from a design standpoint is to write functions that are large and unwieldy. When this happens, the code should be redesigned and split into multiple functions so that it is more readable and maintainable. Modularity is a key idea in software methodology.

Certain programming errors, such as an unwanted null statement following a for statement or an else that attaches to the wrong if, can be very difficult to spot. These are not syntax errors, so *lint* is of no help. However, *cb* can be used to help uncover such errors. The use of *cb* will display indented code, and an indentation different from what is expected indicates a logical error or a typing error.

Programming errors are easily made when passing arguments to functions. It is easy to pass arguments of the wrong type, or to pass the wrong number of arguments. If all the files are given simultaneously to *lint*, then these kinds of errors will be caught. Of course, *lint* cannot catch an error caused by the interchange of two arguments of the same type. When using functions in the standard mathematics library, *lint* commands of the form

> *lint file1.c file2.c . . . -lm*

should be given. This allows *lint* to make use of the mathematics library to cross check mathematical function calls in user defined functions.

As a final programming error of a procedural nature, let us discuss the problem of trying to increase the efficiency of a program. If there is no analysis of the program, efforts to improve efficiency may result in little or no improvement. Let us give an example. It is not too difficult to rewrite the *word_frequency* program so that strcpy() is not used. Without an analysis of the program, we may think that this will improve the execution efficiency of the program. However, the output from the profiler *prof* given in Section 15.5 shows that the use of strcpy() accounts for less than one-half of 1% of the running time of the program. To try to improve on this small percentage does not seem worthwhile.

15.8 OPERATING SYSTEM CONSIDERATIONS

In this chapter we have discussed the use of the UNIX tools *cb*, *make*, *lint*, and *prof*. Other operating systems may provide the same, or similar, facilities. Here we want to mention *grep*, another tool that is very useful for program development. The name *grep* stands for "get regular expression." It can be used to search for string patterns in files. Here is an example of its use. In exercise 3 at the end of this chapter we suggest a modification to the *word_frequency* program that results in the removal of the symbolic constant ARRAYSIZE from the program. Which functions make use of ARRAYSIZE? To find the answer to this question, we can give the command

> *grep ARRAY *.c*

This causes the string *ARRAY* to be searched for in all the *.c* files. Any line containing the string will be printed with the name of the file prepended. This allows us to easily identify those functions that need to be modified in the exercise.

Graceful versions of some of the functions in the standard library are often used in serious programs. An example is the function g_fopen() given in Section 15.2. In exercise 5 at the end of this chapter we suggest that a graceful version of malloc() be written. This function is particularly useful on small systems, where memory is a limited resource. If malloc() is unable to allocate the space requested, the user should be notified and the program should exit immediately.

15.9 SUMMARY

1   Given a large programming problem, reduce the problem to small subproblems.

2   Code in a nicely laid out and documented style.

3   If a program consists of more than one module (file), then common information to be shared by the modules can be placed in header files. Header files typically contain #include's of system header files, #include's of other user-defined header files, symbolic constants, useful macros, debugging tests, declarations of functions, declarations of structures, and typedef's.

4   When developing or maintaining a large program, use the utility program *make* to keep track of the state of the code.

5   Use *lint* to check on the syntactic correctness, portability, and other static features of the code.

6   Use the profiler *prof* to investigate the efficiency of the code.

15.10 EXERCISES

1   The following function is poorly written code. State each good programming practice that it violates, with the offending piece of code cited. Recode the function to eliminate goto's, a primitive control structure, replacing them with appropriate flow of control statements. Change identifiers and layout to a more readable style. Make the function as general and portable as possible.

```
q(q1) int q1[];
{int q2, q3= -10000000;
q2 = 0; F:
if (10 - q2==0)
goto E;
if (q3<q1[q2]) q3=   q1[q2];++q2;
goto F; E:return(q3);}
```

2   You already know how to write a bubble sort routine. Learn
     how to write quicksort; see *A Book on C* by Al Kelley and Ira
     Pohl (Menlo Park, California: Benjamin/Cummings, 1984).
     Investigate the efficiency of each of these sorting routines. First
     write a program that creates a file of, say 1000, randomly dis-
     tributed integers. Then write two versions of a program that
     will sort a file of integers, one program making use of your
     bubble sort routine and the other making use of your quicksort
     routine. Make use of the *prof* utility to compare the efficiency
     of your two programs. In addition to a file of 1000 randomly
     distributed integers, try files with 100 and 10000 randomly dis-
     tributed integers. You should find that the difference in
     efficiency is not very significant on a small file, but as the file
     gets larger, the difference becomes more and more noticeable.

3   Write a version of the *word_frequency* program that uses the
     function calloc() to create storage dynamically for the array w.
     This will make the use of the symbolic constant ARRAYSIZE
     unnecessary. Modify the header file and the functions so that
     ARRAYSIZE is not used.

4   The bubble_sort() function used in the *word_frequency* program
     is very slow. Pick some other sort routine that you know, such
     as shellsort or quicksort, to write another version of the
     word_frequency program. Use the profiler *prof* to compare the
     efficiency of the two sorting routines.

5   If *make* is available to you, do this exercise in conjunction with
     exercise 6. Just as g_fopen() is a graceful version of fopen(), so
     g_malloc() should be a graceful version of malloc(). Write such
     a graceful version and incorporate it into the *word_frequency*
     program. *Hint:* Recall that if malloc() is unable to allocate the
     space requested, then NULL is returned.

6   Use the *make* utility to create the version of the
     word_frequency program suggested in exercise 5. *Hint:* Mod-
     ify the makefile given in Section 15.3 by adding *g_malloc.o* to
     the list of *.o* files. Do not forget that there must be a tab char-
     acter preceding the cc in the makefile.

7   Read Section 15.5 carefully. Notice that the number of func-
     tion calls is listed in the output of the profiler *prof*. How
     many words were in the file *temp*? For one of the functions,
     the number of function calls is quite large. Can you explain
     why?

8   (Advanced) Modify the version of *word_frequency* that you
     wrote in exercise 3. The template for the structure
     struct s_word is given in the header file *word_frequency.h* as

```
struct s_word {
   char           word[MAXWORD];
   struct s_word  *next;
};
```

Change this to

```
struct s_word {
   char           *word;
   struct s_word  *next;
};
```

Now the library function calloc() can be used to create space
as needed to store each word. As each word is obtained from
the input file, it can be stored in the string s in
create_linked_list() just as before. If the string length of s is
n, then calloc() should be used to create space in memory for
a string of size *n* + 1. This will provide space to store the
word, including an end-of-string sentinel \0. After the pointer
value returned by calloc() has been assigned to the structure
member word, use strcpy() to copy s into word. If available to
you, use *make* during program development, and use the
profiler *prof* to compare the efficiency of the new program to
that of the original. The chief advantage of the new program
is that, usually, a lot less memory is used to store the linked

list of words. This is because the length of most words is much less than MAXWORD.

Appendix:

ASCII Character Codes

Left/Right Digits	ASCII American Standard Code for Information Interchange									
	0	1	2	3	4	5	6	7	8	9
0	nul	soh	stx	etx	eot	enq	ack	bel	bs	ht
1	nl	vt	np	cr	so	si	dle	dc1	dc2	dc3
2	dc4	nak	syn	etb	can	em	sub	esc	fs	gs
3	rs	us	sp	!	"	#	$	%	&	'
4	(	)	*	+	,	−	.	/	0	1
5	2	3	4	5	6	7	8	9	:	;
6	<	=	>	?	@	A	B	C	D	E
7	F	G	H	I	J	K	L	M	N	O
8	P	Q	R	S	T	U	V	W	X	Y
9	Z	[	\	]	^	_	`	a	b	c
10	d	e	f	g	h	i	j	k	l	m
11	n	o	p	q	r	s	t	u	v	w
12	x	y	z	{	|	}	~	del		

Some observations

1. Character codes 0–31 and 127 are nonprinting.
2. Character code 32 prints a single space.
3. Character codes for digits 0 through 9 are contiguous.
4. Character codes for letters A through Z are contiguous.
5. Character codes for letters a through z are contiguous.
6. The difference between a capital letter and the corresponding lowercase letter is 32.

The meaning of some of the abbreviations

nul	null	nl	new line
ht	horizontal tab	esc	escape
cr	carriage return	bs	back space
bel	bell	vt	vertical tab

Index

A

B

C

As Benjamin/Cummings accelerates its exciting publishing venture in the Computer Science and Information Systems, we'd like to offer you the opportunity to learn about our new titles in advance. **If you'd like to be placed on our mailing list** to receive pre-publication notices about our expanding Computer Science and Information Systems list, just fill out this card **completely** and return it to us, postage paid. Thank you.

NAME_____ _____

STREET ADDRESS_____

CITY_____STATE_____ZIP_____

BUSINESS_____

ASSOCIATION AFFILIATION:_____

_____

TELEPHONE (_____) _____

AREAS OF INTEREST:

41 ☐ Operating Systems (Please specify)_____

_____

42 ☐ Programming Languages (Please specify)_____

_____

43 ☐ Systems Languages (Please specify)_____

_____

44 ☐ Artificial Intelligence
45 ☐ Computer Graphics
46 ☐ Software Documentation
47 ☐ Systems Analysis and Design
48 ☐ Systems Architecture
49 ☐ Data Communications
50 ☐ Software Engineering
51 ☐ Microcomputer Literacy

52 ☐ Other (Please specify)_____

_____

☐ I am writing.
   Area:_____

KyP